SAFE, SECURE AND STREETWISE

READER'S DIGEST

SAFE, SECURE AND STREETWISE

THE ESSENTIAL GUIDE TO PROTECTING YOURSELF, YOUR HOME AND YOUR FAMILY FROM CRIME

THE READER'S DIGEST ASSOCIATION SOUTH AFRICA (PTY) LIMITED, CAPE TOWN

EDITOR:
Sandy Shepherd

ART EDITOR:
Gusti Prohn

RESEARCH EDITOR:
Frances le Roux

WRITER:
Brian Johnson Barker

ILLUSTRATOR:
Grant Schreiber

PROJECT MANAGER:
Carol Adams

PROJECT COORDINATOR:
Grant Moore

INDEXER:
Sarah Maddox

First edition © 1997
The Reader's Digest Association South Africa (Pty) Limited,
130 Strand Street, Cape Town 8001

ISBN 1-874912-85-8

Safe, Secure and Streetwise was edited and designed at The
Reader's Digest Association South Africa (Pty) Limited.

The publishers cannot accept responsibility for any damage or
injury that may arise as a result of consulting this book.

CONTENTS

DON'T BE A VICTIM

You have the right to live your life free of crime and to expect that you can go about your day-to-day business without threat of attack. However, it is an inescapable fact that crime is part of our society. Even so, you need not become a victim or another crime statistic – if you take the necessary precautions.

The key word is avoidance. If you apply the advice given in this book, you should be able to train yourself to avoid or prevent most situations in which you or your family are likely to become the victims of violence, or in which your home or possessions become a target for burglary or theft.

South Africa vs the rest of the world

Not all countries produce reliable data on their respective crime rates. Despite this, it seems certain that South Africa is one of the most violent countries in the world, in that its murder and rape rates are among the highest (see the UN Survey of Crime Trends, pp12-13). Sociologists have found that crime flourishes where countries and their departments of state, such as the police, are in uneasy transition and this is undoubtedly one of the reasons for the high crime rate in South Africa.

Most of the crime statistics for South Africa in this book come from the Crime Information Management Centre (CIMC), and reflect reported crimes across the country. But they don't tell the whole story, which is that most crime takes place in townships and informal settlements. The horrific crime rates in South Africa are not experienced generally and to the same degree by everyone. The likelihood of becoming a victim is far less if you don't live in a high-risk area. Even so, you still have to be alert, and take the necessary measures to prevent yourself from becoming a victim, whoever you are and wherever you live.

Working together

In South Africa, as in many other countries, the rights of the individual have become paramount. But this has also meant the decline of community rights and of community responsibilities. In many high-risk areas, law-abiding people live as the near-hostages of criminals. Yet in communities that have decided to work together to monitor crime in their areas and involve the police, crime rates are going down. This is clearly an important way to beat crime.

While keeping a low profile, appeal to the police for more frequent patrols and for assistance in starting a system of Neighbourhood Watch. You could also offer your own assistance as a police reservist.

As an individual, don't do anything to mark yourself as a major organiser and don't reveal your activities and intentions to anyone you don't trust fully. Write letters signed by your community to your newspaper, local ministers of religion and school headmasters, and the councillor of your local authority.

Draw up a petition stating your complaints, and get as many residents as possible to sign it. Present copies of the petition to your Member of Parliament as well as to the ministers of Housing and Safety and Security on the provincial council. Petition the President if you must – governments exist to protect the people of the country.

Tell the police

Results published in mid-1997 of a study conducted by the financial institution Nedcor showed that more than 50 per cent of the people interviewed expected to be victims of crime within the next 12 months. Those who felt most threatened were residents of Gauteng and of KwaZulu-Natal. The same survey also showed that only 58 per cent of crime victims actually bothered to report the crimes to the police.

There are many reasons for people not reporting crimes. For example, the victim may fear that a police investigation will reveal information that he or she would prefer to conceal. A man is beaten and robbed while in a brothel, perhaps, and doesn't want his wife to know that he associates with prostitutes. Undoubtedly, however, some crimes are not reported simply because the victims have lost faith in the will or ability of the police to solve them. In complete contrast, though, the public response to police-sponsored TV programmes that appeal for information on crimes and criminals is enormous.

The series *Police File*, which ran for almost 10 years until 1990, achieved the remarkable success rate of 267 per cent in its last year. This apparently impossible figure is explained by the fact that, for each case publicised, police were able to solve almost three more cases as viewers came forward to offer additional information on the suspects. In 1997, the programme that followed *Police File* – *Crime Stop* – was receiving an average of 10 000 telephone calls per 24 hours, or nearly 417 calls per hour. This response alone shows that ordinary South Africans do care about the quality of life in our communities, and that they are prepared to do something to gain a crime-free society.

Crime Stop tells viewers that 'we want their names, not yours'. Callers to the national toll-free number 0800-111213 (oh eight hundred, eleven, twelve, thirteen), keep their anonymity but are assigned a code number to identify them and the case they called about. *Crime Stop* pays its informers, anything from a few hundred rand for a casual tip-off that might lead to a stolen car, to around R250 000.

Information supplied by *Crime Stop* informers has enabled police to infiltrate drug and theft syndicates, often resulting in further rewards. Once a case has been solved, the informer whose information 'cracked' it phones to claim the reward, quoting the number assigned previously.

Security works only if you use it

Mrs Norling and her adult son, Albert, lived alone in a house in one of Cape Town's southern suburbs. It appears that, just a minute after Albert had left for work one morning, Mrs Norling thought she heard him back at the front door, having forgotten his keys, perhaps – and she opened the door. Albert found his mother's battered and naked body in their home when he returned from work late that afternoon. Mrs Norling must have been so sure she was opening the door to her son that she didn't bother to engage the chain limiter that was fitted, or look through the peephole. The point of this story is that if any apparatus has been installed for your security, or if any safety procedure has been devised, it is essential that you use it.

Many people say that locks, bars and alarms have no place in the home, but they are preferable to allowing burglars and murderers in. And since criminals are cowards and prefer to attack when you're on your own or unable to summon help, you need to make doubly sure in these situations that you have taken all possible precautions for your safety.

As with all security equipment, examine the latest available and read any catalogues or magazines you can find that can give you comparisons or consumer advice. Your local newsagent or library should be able to help you obtain copies of such magazines published in South Africa. Locks and bars will not solve the problem of widespread violent crime, but – correctly installed and properly used – they will help to keep your home safe.

Advice in action

Having taken all the measures to protect your home, you may still feel the need to carry a weapon of some kind. Any lawful measures you take to defend yourself and prevent yourself from becoming a victim of crime have the support of the country's legal guardians. Note 'lawful' measures – what you do must not be against the law, such as shooting someone who merely comes onto your property.

Depending on the level of security around your home, a stranger who finds his or her way onto your property may not, in fact, be a trespasser with criminal intent. The stranger may have a lawful reason to be there even without your permission or consent, and is not necessarily a criminal. You are not entitled to attack the trespasser on the grounds that you suspect him or her to be a criminal. He or she may be a meter-reader, for example, or a postman or someone seeking directions. To be safe, however, make sure of your own immediate security first, by staying indoors, and asking the stranger what he or she wants.

However you intend to protect yourself – by carrying a firearm, by learning unarmed combat or by clasping a can of pepper spray – you must be prepared to use your chosen method of defence at the shortest notice. You should also be as practised at using it as you can make yourself. We advise you to attend self-defence classes or target practice regularly.

If you are attacked, only you, on the spot, can be the judge of whether you should resist at all. It is usually safest to submit and do as your assailant asks. You should try to remember as many details of the incident and your attacker as possible, and report them to the police. But if you are in grave danger, or if there is clearly an opportunity for escape, try to get away. Even a person who is heavier and stronger than you are may be temporarily disabled by a hard blow to the groin or a jab in the eyes. If an assailant threatens you with a weapon such as a firearm or knife, however, presume that he really will use it, and plan your reaction accordingly.

About this book

This book is for everyone – a house-owner or a flat-dweller, a resident in a retirement village, or a resident in gangland. It tells you about making your home virtually impregnable … about security in your car or while using public transport … about walking safely on the street … about keeping con men out of your life … about your security at your workplace … about keeping the members of your family safe … and about defending yourself.

The UN Fifth Survey of Crime Trends on the following two pages lists those countries who supplied crime statistics from 1990-94. They reflect reported crimes only, but place South African crime (CIMC figures) in a global context, as a comparison.

Check lists and warning boxes draw your attention to things you should remember, or interesting statistics. They serve as ready reminders for your safety.

Quizzes place your levels of security in context and help you assess whether you need to improve your security or not.

Throughout the book, the stories of real crime victims are retold, with names changed to protect those involved. These real-life dramas are accompanied by a police comment that highlights what the victim should or should not have done in the situation.

Profiles of various types of criminals, created by police psychologists, provide an insight into their psychological make-up to give you some understanding of their actions – but without condoning them.

Lists of telephone numbers and addresses at the end of the book provide ready contact with sources of help or further information, for you and your family.

Unless your luck is completely out, having read this book you should not be caught unawares, and even if you are, you will be prepared enough to survive.

COUNTRY	TOTAL CRIMES	HOMICIDES	MAJOR ASSAULTS	TOTAL ASSAULTS	RAPES
AUSTRALIA		875			14027
AUSTRIA	504568	283	189	33667	553
AZERBAIJAN	18553	667		418	77
BAHAMAS	21260	227	335		215
BELARUS	120254	1029	1784	3221	672
BELGIUM	577902	343		33329	899
BOLIVIA	57081	1687			2261
BULGARIA	199318	948		1079	903
CANADA	2919557	596	225616	225616	31690
CHILE	1229300	626		45383	961
COLOMBIA	212017	27130	28697	28748	1930
COSTA RICA	45662	298	855	2052	294
CROATIA	64051	367	1111	1168	94
CYPRUS	4330	12	115	976	7
DENMARK	546928	263	1070	9881	481
ECUADOR	58414	2073	2898	2958	935
EGYPT	20957	871	211	108	9
ESTONIA	35739	385	248	411	2981
FINLAND	389287	533	2038	19836	387
FRANCE	3919008		63435		6526
GEORGIA	17643	788	307	573	49
GREECE	303311	298		7566	258
HUNGARY	389451	477	8464	11077	828
INDIA	5512245	72543			13208
INDONESIA	153401			10062	1678
ISRAEL	75789	389	1657	15351	550
ITALY	2173448	3040		20873	869
JAMAICA	52771	743	1065	13855	1070
JAPAN	1863390	1746	17920	24032	1616
JORDAN	36753	298	945	14946	36
KAZAKHSTAN	201796	2664	4223	6088	1862
KUWAIT	18969	940	754	1523	9
KYRGYZSTAN	41155	564	690	1790	400
LATVIA	40983	412	714	1059	129
LITHUANIA	58634	560	353	956	165
MACEDONIA	23438	80	177	527	38
MADAGASCAR	10752	63	97	1158	50
MALAYSIA	75976		2846	2846	965
MALTA	7696	11	37	83	10
MARSHALL ISLANDS	1761	2	19	19	2
MAURITIUS	38346	36	25	12862	34
MOLDOVA	37317	414	583	1291	267
MOROCCO	227296	472	2228	2396	932
NICARAGUA	47173	1128		8991	1323
PANAMA		323		2763	290
PHILIPPINES	93300	6338	17883		2494
QATAR	4597	12	26	222	14
ROMANIA	237004	1732	1063	6733	1391
RUSSIAN FEDERATION	2632708	34302			13956
ST VINCENT & THE GRENADINES	7994	16	1163		123
SAO TOME & PRINCIPE	1256		414	414	
SINGAPORE	50807	51	143	601	81
SLOVAKIA	138068	205			213
SLOVENIA	43635	111	407	1816	240
SOUTH AFRICA[1]	2034589	26832	210250[2]	404014	42429[3]
SOUTH KOREA	1309326	4514	5495		6173
SPAIN	692915		12129	12129	1211
SUDAN	529696	1002	17836		610
SWEDEN	1112505	1050	4290	53665	1812
SWITZERLAND	357794		3612	3612	275
SYRIAN ARAB REP	2282	174		72	100
TURKEY	220445	1794		32245	503
UKRAINE	572147	5008	17091		1715
UNITED KINGDOM					
(ENGLAND & WALES)	5249478	726	11015	210311	5067
(NORTHERN IRELAND)	67886	341	499	3633	208
(SCOTLAND)	527064	113		5917	569
(BERMUDA)	6109	8	376	612	19
UNITED STATES OF AMERICA	13989500	23330		1113180	102220
URUGUAY	74156			6981	
WESTERN SAMOA	1215	10	237	242	9
ZAMBIA	71622	1456	22056		337
ZIMBABWE	693567	1779	25622	67598	3091

ROBBERIES	MAJOR THEFTS	TOTAL THEFTS	BURGLARIES	DRUG OFFENCES	POPULATION
14370					17931000
2442	3454	127076	90162	11963	8031000
295		4859	1183	2234	7472000
544	5846		442	747	274000
7013		72372	20525	1441	10355000
1448	4133	275484	154659	14959	10080000
11543	14592	28396		118	7237000
6597		161811			8443000
28888	1003322	1003322	387877	60594	29248000
72058		17576		8799	13994000
28486	50103	80519	8533	13812	34520000
16067	3733	15995	12704	423	3071000
389	26978	31081	18232	857	4504000
14	972	990	1291	135	734000
4880	35602	206278	106338	15661	5205000
21814	4133	26882	7917	16112	11221000
375		1760	5772	88022	57851000
		24719		33	1499000
2122	4630	115234	98656	5926	5095000
73310	1378926	2573074	484901	53892	57747000
328		5988		1113	5458000
812	2536	57343	37123	2531	10426000
2570	47062	135620	78877	259	10261000
23933		303564	121536	20304	918570000
6777			41905	701	192217000
450	40	9815	2953	8807	5383000
29981		1333089		38290	57193000
5461	5257	12992	1461	5895	2496000
2684	268887	1310077	247661	23059	124793000
500	2143	6567	1622		5198000
11919	2091	100727	155	9584	17027000
162	0	171	1552	2109	1620000
1987		10956	9342	2546	4596000
1142		27211		278	2548000
806	27936	38580	7355	334	3721000
132	6034	6733	9531	116	2142000
31	67	3396	1289	321	14303000
6072	44122	51159	21553	10350	19489000
33	2814	4095	1909	246	364000
1	0	3	18	25	54000
767	704	11111	960	1882	111300
2288		14531	8632	289	4350000
	897	1829		14811	26590000
13325		7655	117	986	4401000
3662	12308	16270		2978	2583000
9169	12240				67038000
		590	295	17	540000
4161		104033	30386	267	22736000
148546		1314788		74798	147997000
44	2564		1215		111000
	15	15	6		125000
812	11158	26943	2459	1844	2930000
1244		58807	43069	88	5347000
294	1690	15763	10422	407	1942000
117323		801529[4]	317079	47323	404360000[5]
4580	60255		1031	1725	44453000
55678	72313	72313	140723		39143000
846	398		78025	1751	28947000
5331		506642	141278	30785	8780000
1954		195409	66466	40144	6995000
18	85	202	1624	2692	13844000
1542		75054		2339	61183000
32553	311845			28410	51910000
59765	1645688	2501778	1257916		51439203
1567	28723	33233	16902	1286	1631822
5297		238233	88394	19281	5132400
93	279	1566	1134	414	63000
618950		9419100	2712800		260651000
3072	46455	49527		1435	3167000
2	348	359	40	116	164000
3287	22660		13046	340	9196000
12378	1144	164724	57943	10487	11150000

The Fifth UN Survey of Crime Trends (1990-94)

This chart is an extract from the full survey. It gives the crime statistics for reported crimes around the world, in selected crime categories, for the year 1994 (the latest date available). It includes only those countries that supplied their statistics to the UN survey.

The following notes explain the numbered entries for South Africa.

1. South Africa did not supply statistics for this chart – the figures given here were gathered by the CIMC and inserted later.

2. These figures are for 'assault with grievous bodily harm'.

3. These rape figures do not include statutory rape.

4. Theft includes stock theft, shoplifting and pilfering.

5. This population figure is projected from the 1991 census.

13

INTRODUCTION

SAFE AS HOUSES?

Housebreakers are just as likely to burgle a shanty as a mansion. And their handiwork – anything from petty theft to trashing your home – will leave you not only poorer, but suffering an enormous amount of stress and anxiety. You may be injured or even murdered, so do your utmost to keep intruders out of your home and off your property.

Vital safeguards

The most important safeguard is physical security – locks and bolts, bars, fences, doors, windows and shutters. Then comes electronic security – alarm systems, monitoring systems such as closed-circuit television, and electronic control (often remote) of exits and entrances. However, no security system will work efficiently unless you plan carefully, are disciplined, and take common-sense precautions. It is more often than not a good idea to involve your neighbours.

Getting together . . .

Surveys of burglaries have shown that up to 70 per cent of the entry points in burgled houses are visible from at least one neighbouring house. This suggests an obvious advantage to neighbourly cooperation. Like you, your neighbours are concerned about the safety of their families and their property. If you include neighbours in your security arrangements, you may strengthen your fight against crime.

Approach your neighbours and start with a general discussion of local security. Suggest what you might be able to do for them, and try to assess your neighbours' reliability from their response. At this stage, keep the details of your own home security to yourself – you're merely recruiting volunteers to keep an eye on suspicious characters in your neighbourhood.

The degree of cooperation is up to you, but establish clearly what is expected of one another. Will you just 'keep an eye open' or undertake to telephone one another or the police if anything suspicious occurs? Whatever you decide, keep the arrangements simple – they'll be less likely to go wrong. Under no circumstances expect neighbours to put themselves at risk, whether by confronting suspected criminals or in any other way. Avoid taking the law into your own hands, especially where this involves firearms.

A house in the average street is likely to have neighbouring properties on both sides, at the back, and on the other side of the road. So, excluding yourself, at least four neighbours are required in a 'cell' of a cooperative home-protection scheme. More such cells, or others organised on a different basis, make up a Neighbourhood Watch or the closely related Crime Watch and Business Watch (see You and Your Neighbourhood, pp16-17). For information on a community-based home security scheme, pay a visit to your local police station. And while you're there, check the notice board (usually in the charge office) for useful ideas, information, names and addresses.

. . . Or going it alone

If your home has many people coming and going, a neighbour can't be expected to know who should and should not be there. Conversely, neighbours who strike you as unreliable, or careless about what they leave lying about, or unconcerned about the security of their homes, or whose property has a frequently changing population, may not be ideal partners in security. You will have to tighten both internal and external security. If you share the property with tenants, for instance, see that your section is well locked, barred and alarmed, so that other occupants do not have access from inside. Burglarproofing, including alarms, should eliminate most risks from outside. For the rest of the property, use bars and, in addition, restrict the limit of window openings by blocking the channels of sliding windows at the set height, or by fitting short roller stays, together with lockable sliding rods, to casement windows.

Burdens shared

In some circumstances, where you live in a sectional title property, for instance, you may be legally obliged to contribute – usually indirectly through the levy – to your own security and that of other residents. And it is expected, although it may not be legally enforceable, that no resident will put anyone else at risk – by forgetting to lock the entrance, for example.

If you own a freestanding property, you may be able to share some of the security costs with your neighbours. A service lane running between your property and your neighbour's, for example, may be jointly owned by both of you (check with your local building department). In this case, it would make sense for you and your neighbour to split the cost of installing a security gate with razor wire on the top at the entrance to the lane, to which both you and your neighbour would hold the key.

Once you've got to know your neighbours, choose one whom you're prepared to trust with most, if not all, of the workings of your security measures. If your house is fitted with a monitored security system, and if you've asked a neighbour to do anything that might trigger the alarm, it's only fair to give him or her the code number to be used when the security company makes its response check by telephone. You might also have to show your neighbour how to shut off and reset the alarm. Of course, if there is no neighbour to whom you'd like to entrust information, you might have to select a friend or relative who lives reasonably close by. The inconvenience of distance is offset by the assurance that your security secrets are safe.

YOU AND YOUR NEIGHBOURHOOD

Learn to recognise the people who live around you and those who pass your property. Once you can recognise your neighbours quickly, you'll be quicker to spot would-be criminals.

Building your awareness

Even if you don't know your neighbours' names, try to memorise where they live, at what time you usually see them, and how they travel. Where do your neighbours park their cars when they're at home? If a neighbour's car passed you on the road, would you recognise it, and would you notice if it was being driven by strangers?

Getting to know your neighbourhood

Is your home close to a gathering-place such as a shopping centre, liquor store, railway station, sports ground or taxi rank? If so, it may become an attractive target. It's easy for a criminal to lose himself in the crowd, or to pass on stolen goods so that, even if you found the goods, you'd never be able to trace them back to him.

Are there green belts, or undeveloped or overgrown properties nearby? These also make convenient refuges or escape routes. Popular short cuts on foot are usually indicated by broken fences, worn trails on the grass, erosion and, very often, a trail of litter. If you live near a gathering-place or empty plot you must take greater precautions, and become even more aware of strange faces and suspicious behaviour.

Learn the names of the roads in your area, so that you can report and pinpoint a crime accurately. Become familiar with how access to these streets is controlled, whether by traffic lights, stop or yield signs, or one-way streets, so that you become attuned to someone blatantly disregarding the road signs (criminals in a hurry are likely to do so).

In an emergency, you might need key people such as doctors, firemen or the police. Make a list of contact numbers so that you will know where to find help and be able to plan your security much better.

Neighbourhood Watch

In the areas where community-based organisations such as Neighbourhood Watch have been introduced, they have significantly reduced the level of crime. To set up a Neighbourhood Watch, contact your local police station. A police liaison officer usually explains at an inaugural meeting what a Neighbourhood Watch is – and what it is not.

A Neighbourhood Watch area usually has one or more 'safe houses', where someone is home all or most of the day, and where, for instance, children can receive help and temporary shelter if they feel threatened on the street. Members of the watch display warning notices on their homes.

Every street, street block or block of flats has a coordinator, who is often an energetic retired person or the person with the most time to devote to the watch. The coordinator is in regular contact with the watch's members and, when necessary, with the police. In an emergency, any member of a watch can contact the police direct.

Members of a Neighbourhood Watch supply additional eyes and ears for the police, but are not a substitute for the police. Passive observation is the chief technique, rather than vigilante action or unwarranted 'snooping'. Where neighbourhood patrols are organised, they should be to observe and record only, leaving the 'action' to the police.

Neighbourhood Watch has revived community spirit. Neighbours meet as friends with a common objective, ensure that children are safer on the street, make contact with people living alone, and experience some relief from the fear of becoming victims of crime. Related police-assisted organisations include Crime Watch, Business Watch and the latest development, Teen Watch.

CHECK LIST

MAKING IT SAFER, TOGETHER

1. Do spot checks of members' homes from the pavement to look for security lapses.

2. Ensure that all homes are clearly marked with their numbers.

3. Know the basic layout of neighbours' premises and what their security measures are.

4. Improve security in likely target areas.

5. Keep a list of your neighbours' work addresses, telephone numbers and car registration numbers.

6. Be aware of regular or routine movements so that you'll spot deviations quickly.

7. See that communication – such as an exchange of timetables – flows between participants of the watch.

8. Reach reciprocal agreements on how to react to burglar alarms.

9. Record descriptions of suspicious strangers or vehicles.

10. While showing concern for neighbours' safety, always respect their privacy.

YOUR HOME, YOUR CASTLE

Your security is only as good as the weakest padlock you've used, or as your thinnest, unprotected external door. Don't compromise your safety by buying cheap fittings just because they're cheaper than others – install the best defences you can. Most housebreakers like to get in and out easily – make it difficult and they'll go somewhere else.

The barrier system

There are three lines at which you can establish physical protection: the perimeter, which is your garden boundary; the exterior of your house, including doors and windows; and the interior, consisting mainly of doors, with special installations such as a safe, a safe section and a strongroom. Locks may be electronic, number-coded or key-operated. And the operation of gates may be manual or electronic.

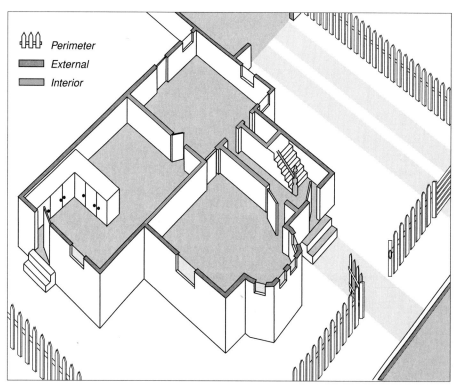

Perimeter
External
Interior

Your home should have three lines of barriers between you and the outside world – the perimeter wall or fence, the exterior windows and doors, and interior doors or entrances. The same three lines apply whether you live in a house or a flat.

The best defence works only if you combine it with the proper precautions: restrict opportunities for outsiders to look in through doors or windows, and move specially attractive or valuable items out of their sight; keep keys safely out of reach of doors and windows, and keep a strict check on the whereabouts of duplicates.

Monitor your security system constantly. Most burglaries are committed by opportunists – someone walking by who sees an open door, looks in, picks up an expensive radio, some silverware or some jewellery, and walks out again.

Alarm systems

In addition to physical barriers, you may have an alarm system. An alarm may be triggered in several ways, such as the movement of a door or window, the movement of air or a change in temperature produced by a person's presence, or the activation of a switch either on a fixed panel or on a hand-held transmitter. Informal alarms, such as a squeaky garden gate or a crunchy gravel path, are also useful.

Alarms may be silent or audible on site, and linked to a security company. On its own, an alarm won't keep intruders out, but it will let you (or a remote monitoring station) know that they're trying to get in. Burglars know – better than most of us – that almost nobody pays any attention to an antitheft alarm. In most areas, even the police no longer investigate triggered alarms, because of the pressure of their other obligations, and because well over 90 per cent of call-outs are false alarms (see The Alarmed House, pp50-3). Burglars probably also know how many minutes they have in which to enter, gather up the most easily transported valuables, and get away before the security patrol arrives.

Which system to use?

The ideal security arrangement is a combination of barrier and alarm systems, and, depending on how much money you have available, might even include a closed-circuit TV or video camera. An audible alarm may send an inexperienced housebreaker running away, but will not fluster an experienced burglar. If you're caught in the house with an intruder, a noisy alarm may make him aggressive; a silent alarm linked to a security service may be preferable.

Case your own joint

Once your system is installed, look at it from the criminal's point of view. Walk round your property and try to work out how he'd get in. A screw with a half-slotted head that can't be unscrewed can probably be smashed. Bars screwed to wooden window frames can be kicked loose. Non-opening panes can be removed from the window frame. Remember that criminals are not bound by the niceties that restrict law-abiding people.

The rising rate of domestic break-ins

The following figures, supplied by the Crime Information Monitoring Centre (CIMC), show reported incidents only of residential house-breaking.

1994	228,021
1995	244,063
1996	246,438

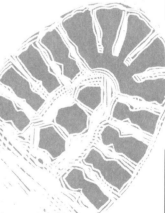

How good is your security rating?

So you think your home is secure – burglars can't get in and you're safe inside? Here are just a few questions to test that cosy assumption. Answer each question honestly, by ticking the appropriate column next to each one. Then check your final score and what it reveals.

YOUR HOME	NO	YES	USUALLY	SOMETIMES
1 Are all external doors fitted with deadlocks?				
2 Is your patio door fitted with locks at the top and the bottom?				
3 Are all windows fitted with security locks?				
4 Do you lock the doors and close and lock all windows before you go out?				
5 Do you keep external doors locked when you are in the garden or garage?				
6 Is your perimeter alarm on all the time?				
7 Do you always use the door chain or limiter when opening the door?				
8 Do you either own an alert dog or have a burglar alarm system fitted to your home?				
9 Would you know if the identity document presented by an alleged policeman or council worker was false?				
10 Do you belong to the local Neighbourhood Watch?				
11 Are your windows screened so that people on the street cannot see into your rooms?				
12 Can you reach a panic button from anywhere in your home within a few seconds?				
13 Are any of your lights connected to a time switch?				
14 Do you tell the police, a neighbour or a friend when you go away on holiday?				
15 Do you keep firearms in a secret hiding place, where an intruder can't find them?				
16 Have you put secret identifying marks on your movable property?				
17 Do you have a list of the serial numbers of your appliances such as TV sets and VCRs?				
18 Have you installed security lights outside your house?				

YOUR HOME	NO	YES	USUALLY	SOMETIMES
19 Do you ever leave a radio or tape-recorder playing when you go out?				
20 If you don't have an answering service, do you lower the volume of your telephone when you go out?				
21 Do you leave lights on when you go out at night?				
22 Do you leave lights on when you go to bed at night?				
23 Is it difficult for intruders to reach the back or the side of your house?				
24 Are the street lights outside your house adequate, and are they in working order?				
25 Do you keep the number of your local police station next to your telephone?				
26 Did you notice that question 15 is a trick question? Given enough time, an intruder will find your firearm, no matter where you hide it. Use a safe. NO earns you 6 points.				

Here's how to add up your score.

For every time you answered YES, multiply by 6.	YES x 6 =	
For every time you answered USUALLY, multiply by 4	USUALLY x 4 =	
For every time you answered SOMETIMES, multiply by 2	SOMETIMES x 2 =	
For every time you answered NO, multiply by 0	NO x 0 =	
	TOTAL SCORE	

Now check your real security.

117 - 156 You've put a lot of effort into securing your home. The challenge now is to stay vigilant.

75 - 116 You've thought about security, but there's room for putting more intentions into practical form.

37 - 74 If you haven't been burgled yet, you're lucky. There's lots of room for improvement – in action and in attitude.

0 - 36 It can happen to you and it almost certainly will, unless you improve your security now.

Remember – security doesn't end with installations. Your constant vigilance is a vital component.

THE BURGLARPROOF HOUSE

There is actually no such thing as a burglarproof home. Given enough time and incentive, really sophisticated burglars can probably break in almost anywhere. As a general rule, though, even the slickest burglar prefers easy pickings in a poorly protected home. Apply the same high levels of security throughout your home – don't be tempted to install a cheap or inadequate system at the back door, for instance, just because you believe that a burglar won't try to get in that way.

Alarm sensors on all windows

Light to illuminate window area

Light to illuminate door area

Patio door secured with vertical-bolt locks

Expanding safety gate (inside patio door)

Security gate at front door

Peephole in front door

Child's peephole in front door

Alarm warning sign

Locked front gate with electronic release

Audio/video intercom

Locked automatic gate

Light to illuminate gate area

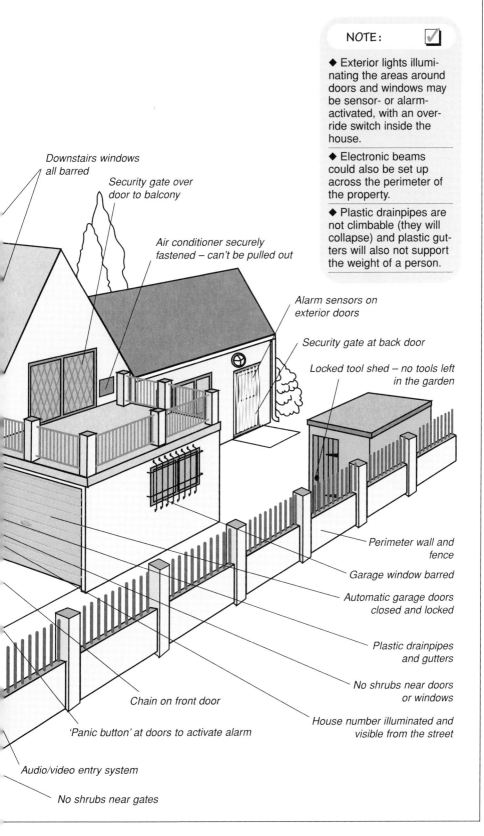

NOTE: ☑

◆ Exterior lights illuminating the areas around doors and windows may be sensor- or alarm-activated, with an override switch inside the house.

◆ Electronic beams could also be set up across the perimeter of the property.

◆ Plastic drainpipes are not climbable (they will collapse) and plastic gutters will also not support the weight of a person.

Downstairs windows all barred

Security gate over door to balcony

Air conditioner securely fastened – can't be pulled out

Alarm sensors on exterior doors

Security gate at back door

Locked tool shed – no tools left in the garden

Perimeter wall and fence

Garage window barred

Automatic garage doors closed and locked

Plastic drainpipes and gutters

No shrubs near doors or windows

House number illuminated and visible from the street

Chain on front door

'Panic button' at doors to activate alarm

Audio/video entry system

No shrubs near gates

THE FRONT LINE

The perimeter of your property is probably the first aspect of your home to be noticed by a passer-by – including burglars on the lookout for an easy target. Criminals know that a well-maintained wall, fence or hedge on the boundary means that this surrounds the home of someone who cares about his or her property, and about security – and that breaking in is not likely to be easy.

Local and legal

Walls and fences, especially those on the street, are subject to local bylaws and other regulations, to make sure they don't pose a danger to the public or that they are not a public nuisance. Check with the building section of your local authority before you start putting up a wall or fence. You may have to provide a plan and working drawings, but this will be cheaper than having to take down a half-completed or even finished structure.

Different regulations may apply to a party wall, or a wall on a boundary between properties. Your neighbour is not obliged to contribute to the cost of a party wall that you build, even if his or her property is improved or made more secure by that wall.

Find out whether your home-owner's insurance policy covers damage to a perimeter wall, and whether this includes public liability – that is, damage or injury caused to other people.

Walls

The traditional solid wall is built of bricks or cement blocks. A plastered and painted wall may be slightly less expensive to build than a face-brick one, but requires more maintenance.

Precast walls (often referred to as 'vibracrete', an early trade name) consist of specially hardened

DRAMA IN REAL LIFE

Those that trespass

A former army boxing champion, Willie Smit, was the conscientious security manager for a large business in Mossel Bay. Alerted by his staff to signs of an attempted break-in one night, he approached the site quietly from outside, having reasoned that the burglar would still be trying to cut through the bars. Sure enough, there was a dark silhouette at the window and Mr Smit heard the sound of sawing. The burglar, later identified as Koos April, spun round as Mr Smit reached him, but was unable to escape. The burglar was severely beaten up. Six years later and, since that night

permanently brain-damaged, partly spastic and unable to walk without support, Mr April was awarded damages of R675 000 against Mr Smit and Mr Smit's employers.

Police comment: The right to defend self and property does not include the use of excessive force or assaulting a trespasser, even where it is clear that the trespasser does, in fact, have criminal intent. Mr Smit should have called the police first and then apprehended the burglar, restraining him with the aid of some of his employees until the police arrived.

cement 'planks' slotted into precast posts. This type of wall can be put up very quickly, is available in many decorative finishes and should require almost no maintenance. Both solid and precast walls can be topped with spikes.

Low walls can be topped with a tall metal or wooden fence, which provides security but also allows you to see into the garden from the outside, or out into the street from the inside.

Wire fences

Post-and-wire fences are made of wire mesh fastened to horizontal straining wires strung between galvanised, tubular steel posts. They are a cheap form of fencing but are relatively easy to breach – by cutting the mesh, climbing over, or even by untying the mesh from the straining wires. However, these fences can be made more difficult to get through by planting a dense or thorny hedge on the inside.

Use plastic-coated wire at the coast or in damp conditions; galvanised wire is adequate elsewhere. And use the same type of wire – either plastic-coated or galvanised – throughout for mesh, straining wire and binding wire, to reduce corrosion. Wire fences may form a useful secondary enclosure – for watchdogs, for example.

Barbed wire or looped razor wire can be combined with walls or fences, placed at the top to prevent people from climbing over, or used at strategic points, such as around drainpipes or on the roof.

Rigid fences

Cast or wrought metal railings between metal posts or brick piers make an attractive and secure barrier, and allow you to see through them. The rods used must be thick enough to resist bending, should be difficult to cut, and should be placed close enough to one another to prevent a child passing between them. Railings may be used to increase the height (to the legal maximum only) of a brick wall and are available in non-rusting metal that

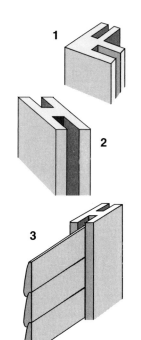

Precast cement corner posts (1) and several middle posts (2) can be used in many configurations with slotted cement planks (3) to make a highly adaptable, low-cost 'front line'.

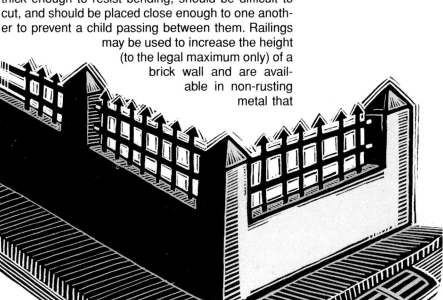

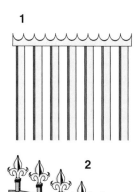

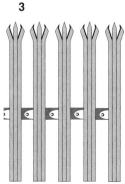

The prime object of a fence is to create a barrier against criminals, but it's possible to combine aesthetics with security. A saw-toothed edge (1) makes a neat, unobtrusive barrier. Fleur-de-lis spikes (2) provide a decorative yet effective deterrent. And steel palisade fencing with a triple splayed point (3) looks attractive, but discouragingly destructive.

requires little maintenance. Wooden fences are a cheaper option but they provide little protection and require a lot of maintenance. Like wire fences, however, they may be used to build a secondary enclosure.

Electrified fences

Although more commonly associated with game and cattle control, electrified fences are also used to deter human trespassers, on farms and on city properties. However, their use is strictly regulated, and failure to comply with the regulations may result in prosecution. Consult your local authority's building survey department. The disadvantage of these fences is that electric storms and nearby plants can set off a false alarm, as can intruders deliberately short-circuiting the fence until you switch off the system thinking it is faulty. They also require continuous maintenance.

Fences with teeth

Spikes and pointed uprights are made in a vast array of configurations, chiefly to prevent anyone climbing over a wall or fence. Often, they are also used at lower levels to stop would-be trespassers getting a foothold, but check with your local authority before placing them here. There may be a bylaw forbidding the installation of spikes and similar features below a minimum height – typically, around 1,8 metres.

Hedges

Natural vegetation barriers can be used instead of, or together with, walls or fences. Kei apple can be grown into a hedge that is almost impenetrable, fearsomely thorny and resistant to damage. Similarly, roses, such as the Macartney rose (*Rosa bracteata*), provide a dense and thorny but attractive barrier. Sisal hedgerows, too, are an effective deterrent.

The ideal barrier

Before building to the maximum permissible height (usually around two metres), or growing a high hedge, remember that it may be more useful to have a lower wall, so that neighbours – or you when you arrive home – can observe any suspicious activity in your garden. This applies especially if you don't have sensors to detect anyone who has scaled the wall or gone through the hedge. A good combination is a brick or block wall about 750 millimetres high, topped with a rigid, spiked fence, giving an overall height of about two metres. Make sure that the tops of the brick piers are also protected.

Avoid decorative features such as projecting shelves and alcoves that provide grips or footholds. Do not join perimeter walls to the house or any outbuildings, because they give easy access to the roof. And preferably taper the wall to the thickness of one brick at the top, or 75-100 millimetres, to allow room for one row of spikes or fencing.

THE WAY IN

Your gates are the only legitimate physical and direct connection between your property and the road outside. So they are perhaps the most important single feature in home security. But proper control of the gates is probably the most neglected aspect. Remember, an open gate is simply another hole in the fence.

Getting gated

It's worth spending some time assessing what gates you need and whether, for instance, you should change the position of existing gateways. Avoid having recessed gateways and gateways close to corners – they offer hiding places for criminals. Your gates should be at least as high as the surrounding walls or fences, and have minimum clearance at the bottom. Consider also a remote release.

It is essential that any gate should allow you to enter quickly, with the gate shutting immediately behind you. If you have to put parcels down outside the gate to open it, you have overloaded yourself and are leaving yourself vulnerable to attack.

Once you've installed the right gates, in the right places, get into the habit of following a safe routine in operating them. It's the installation that costs money. Proper control, which is just as important, costs nothing. An electrical alarm or advisory system that tells you the gates are open or closed can be rigged up fairly inexpensively. The best check, though, is for you to look for yourself.

No introductions

Whether you live in a detached house or in a flat, remove your name from the gate, letter box or any other place where a passer-by might read it. Your name and home address make a useful tool for a burglar or con man. Knowing your name, he looks up your telephone number, phones from a nearby kiosk or cellphone and, if there's no reply, presumes you are not at home and that your home is a fair target. Swindlers or con men use your name to pretend they know you or legitimately know something about you.

To enable deliveries to reach you, you need only display the number of your house or flat. Make sure that it can be read from outside the gate. Position your letter box so that mail, once put in, can be removed only from within your property. A padlock on a letter box will discourage casual snooping.

Passing through

Organise a disciplined system for using the gates. For instance, make it a condition that the person who opens or unlocks the gate must watch the gateway while it's open, and then be responsible for closing and locking it again. An exception is motorists leaving home. They should get out and away into the traffic as briskly as possible, and ideally the responsibility for watching or locking the gate should rest with another member of the household, who must be on hand.

Before opening a gate from the outside, check that there are no suspicious people or vehicles close by. And before you open the gate from inside, make sure you know who or what is on the other side. Keep hedges and other plants trimmed so that they don't obstruct your view, and make sure the entire gateway area is well lit at night.

When arriving home, it is advisable, if at all possible, to have a trusted household member watching for your arrival, and in contact with you by cellphone.

Remote control or manual

Good-quality remote-control gates usually offer greater safety than manual gates, because you don't have to leave your vehicle to open or close them. In the case of a manually operated gate, every responsible member of your household must know where the key is kept and how to use it. The person who uses the key must also return it – as soon as the gate has been locked – to the place in which it is normally kept, which should be out of sight and reach of small children. Also keep remote controls, whether fixed or hand-held, out of reach of children. And don't make it easy for a burglar to find gate keys and remote-control units. If he can't open a gate (without a great deal of attention-getting noise and bother), he probably won't be able to make off with large or heavy objects from your home.

The manual system

Check that all fittings are in good condition and securely fastened and attached. Where bolts and padlocks are accessible from outside, make sure that they cannot be unscrewed or levered off. Check the gateposts for strength and, in the case of wooden posts, for soundness of the wood at ground level and below.

The fittings on many wooden gates are easy to loosen or dislodge completely with an unobtrusive bump from a (probably stolen) motor vehicle. Fit bolts that pass through steel brace plates on both sides of the gate to strengthen the construction.

Simple, foot-operated catches may be installed to hold the two parts of the gate open and out of the way of the vehicle passing through. When you remove a

Control in the wrong hands

Frans Meyer's luxury German saloon car suggested he was doing well, and his address in an exclusive suburb confirmed it. But he and his wife, Vera, were taking no chances and were fully protected by high walls, alarms, electronic gates and an efficient security service. Arriving home one day, Frans noticed that the electronic gate across the driveway was partly open, and then he saw a stranger come out and quickly walk away. Frans hurried inside, to find that all was in order and Vera unaware that anything might have been wrong. She had asked the gardener – a fairly new employee – to cut the lawn outside the front wall, and she had given him one of the hand-held control units so that he could operate the gate himself. It's unclear whether or not he pressed the wrong button, but it's certain that nobody was watching that driveway entrance while the gate was open. And so it stayed open. They never found out who the stranger was. Like the gardener, he might have made an innocent mistake, but he might also have been an opportunist thief or worse.

Police comment: Frans and Vera threw away their investment in security by the way they operated their system. The more people who have access to the workings of your security system, the greater are the chances that something will go wrong. Vera should have made sure that, while Frans was out, only she had access to the control unit.

padlock, place it back on the staple once you've lifted the hasp. Lock the gate again as soon as it's closed. This way you won't mislay the padlock.

A gate that sags causes loosened joints. Prevent this by supporting the gate underneath with a caster running on an arc of metal or a smooth masonry track. Closing devices such as springs and counterweights may be used, but the person who opens the gate should always wait to make sure the gate has been locked again, before leaving it.

Electronic gates

The great advantage of electronic gates, which are usually of the single sliding or twin side-hung type, is that they should require no physical effort to operate (except in the event of a power failure).

The better types of electronic gate are fitted with an obstacle-detection beam that is activated when the gate encounters an obstacle and halts the gate, or with auto-reverse sensitivity which causes it to reverse direction, so as not to damage a car or injure a person caught between a gatepost and the gate. However, it also means that electronic gates can be easily jammed, forcing you to get out of your car. Keep a set of manual release keys at hand in case of failure.

These gates can be activated by an intercom connection, so that you don't have to leave the house to open them. The remote control can be programmed to make the gates open wide enough to allow a pedestrian through and to allow the gates to stay open for a predetermined time.

Activate the gates to open only when they, and the area around them, are in sight and clear of anything suspicious. Don't ever leave the remote control for the gate in your car, even when you're at home. After all, it's the key to your front line of defence against crime.

PERIMETER ALARM SYSTEMS

As crime has flourished, so householders have moved their first line of defence outwards. Formerly, this line was the exterior of the home itself, but now it has shifted to the borders of the property. This makes good sense – the farther away you keep a potential burglar, the less likely he is to be able to hurt you. Also, the sooner you know that someone is trying to get into your home, the more time you have to summon aid or oppose the intruder.

The first line of defence

Unfenced gardens are an invitation to all sorts of people to enter. If challenged, they can always claim to be looking for water, employment, bus fare, or the address of a person you've never heard of and who may not even exist. But they may, in fact, be checking out the state of your security. These visitors are not always the burglars themselves, but their scouts, and it's important to discourage them. Unfortunately, walls and fences keep out friends as well as a proportion of foes, so you need to know when there is someone outside whom you do want to see.

The ordinary alert

Door bells, whether you place one at the front door or next to the front gate, offer the easiest way for a legitimate caller to attract your attention. Consider placing the switch or bell push in a concealed position known only to family and friends, or fitting a bell with a switch that is pressed in a particular sequence in order to be activated. These bells prevent disturbance by unwanted or unscheduled callers, and you can always make arrangements for legitimate calls or deliveries.

The wiring from the door-bell switch next to the front door – and the switch itself – can be readily extended to the front gate, although this may mean exposing wires to the weather. Most door bells operate off a low voltage (and many are battery-operated), but you might still be held liable for damage or injury caused by faulty wiring. The wiring must conform to the standards laid down by your local authority.

Apart from the weather, your outside installation must be able to resist thieves and, especially, vandals. Select a fitting that has no fixing screws visible from the front and that has a touch-sensitive switch, rather than a switch that has to be physically moved.

The dumb bell

Fit a simple switch to inactivate the door-bell circuit, in an easy-to-reach place near the door that you normally use when going out. You can then switch off your door bell when you go away. If a criminal ringing the bell doesn't hear it, and if nobody comes to the door, he can't be sure that you haven't heard the bell inside, peeped at him and simply decided to ignore him. In fact, he can't even be sure that the bell is working. If he can hear the door bell, he knows he has only to keep his finger on it to bring an irate householder to the door. If no-one appears, he knows there's nobody at home. This deception of the disconnected door bell doesn't work if the front door is within his reach – your 'caller' knows that incessant knocking will produce the same result as persistently ringing the bell, if there is anyone at home.

Using an intercom

An intercom enables you to speak from inside your home to someone at the gate, and is often linked to a remote control for opening the gate. Some people – members of the same household – routinely use code words when identifying themselves by intercom. If you use code words at all, keep them simple, short and unambiguous. Ideally, though, code words should be kept for emergencies. Emergencies include being held up by muggers looking for an easy way in, just as you're about to operate the intercom, or trying to warn a friend or family member about an intruder inside.

Alarms and warnings

Gates can be wired so that an alarm will sound (or a light will come on) if an attempt is made to force them open. Circuitry can be arranged to switch on a visible or audible signal even when the gate is opened legitimately – by remote control or other method. Useful though these refinements are, they can go wrong and should not become a substitute for physically checking the gate itself – by looking out of a window, for instance.

Among alarms that may be used on the wall or fence itself, the most useful detect a person's movement through a specific area (as infrared detectors do), or vibrations set up in the structure (such as the wall) on which a detector is mounted. However, the seismic type of detector, which picks up vibrations, may not be suitable for a wall close to a busy street or in an area where there are high winds. In these situations, a combination of detectors is best.

Some infrared detectors are sold with a closed-circuit TV (CCTV) camera, which monitors

a person's approach to a gate, wall or fence and can be linked to a video recorder. Whether you have such a detector or not, CCTV focused on a gate with an intercom, as well as all other entry points, is a good idea. A video intercom is inexpensive and generally can use old door-bell wiring. Put steel mesh over the outdoor unit to prevent vandalism.

Light on the matter

Any perimeter alarm system must be combined with lighting – ideally, both sides of the wall or fence should be illuminated. Some of the lighting, sufficient to light the protected area without disturbing the neighbours or passing traffic, should be left on at all times, to discourage burglars from even making an attempt, while some of the lighting should switch on only when an alarm is tripped.

Fit a master switch indoors, so that you can switch on the lights at will, independently of the alarm system. You could also install an alarm that advises you when any part of the lighting circuit is broken or has stopped working.

In the event of a power failure it is possible to keep most of the system 'live' for short periods through the use of photoelectric cells and storage batteries, or even a stand-by generator.

Breakthrough?

Have a plan of action ready for when your perimeter alarm is triggered. It may be a false alarm, but you can't count on it. Your priorities now are double-checking that your next line of security – doors and windows – is intact, getting help, and keeping yourself and your family safe. Depending on the nature of your perimeter protection, you may need to have a telephone and remote-control unit handy until help arrives.

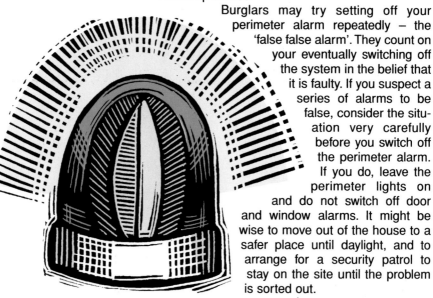

Burglars may try setting off your perimeter alarm repeatedly – the 'false false alarm'. They count on your eventually switching off the system in the belief that it is faulty. If you suspect a series of alarms to be false, consider the situation very carefully before you switch off the perimeter alarm. If you do, leave the perimeter lights on and do not switch off door and window alarms. It might be wise to move out of the house to a safer place until daylight, and to arrange for a security patrol to stay on the site until the problem is sorted out.

LIVING ALARMS

Your dog may be the most dependable link in the chain of your domestic safety. A dog is often alerted to danger even before an alarm has been triggered, and may be your first line of defence. Train it and treat it well and it will be your loyal guardian. Untrained and neglected, it could be a menace not only to intruders, but also to you and your family.

Guard dogs

Not every dog, or every breed of dog, makes a suitable pet or a successful guard dog. Decide, before you get a dog, exactly what you want it for.

A guard dog is one you keep solely or primarily to protect your property. If you're serious about having a guard dog – the favourites are the German Shepherd (Alsatian), Rottweiler and Doberman – first consult a professional dog trainer or a dog-obedience school. You will be able to obtain names and addresses from the telephone directory, listed under the type of dog you want or already have, such as the German Shepherd Training Association.

It is important that your dog be trained under professional supervision as a guard dog rather than as an attack dog. As a guard dog it will protect your family and your property. Depending on its nature and training, it will begin warning off potential trespassers by barking and with a display of hostility. If this doesn't succeed, it will almost certainly attack, but will still respond to orders from its leader (you). The training of an attack dog, on the other hand, may produce an animal more inclined to aggression and pursuit than to the defence of territory, in which case trespassers – or unannounced visitors – may be killed.

A good relationship between you the handler and your guard dog, as well as between the dog and members of your family and staff, is vital. Don't get a large and potentially lethal guard dog unless you're sure that you can devote to it the training, time and patience it deserves.

The dog as pet

A pet is kept for play and pleasure. The chances are that a pet dog will bark vigorously at strangers, and will be aware of intruders before you are. But you can't expect it to put up a heroic defence of your property or your person. Any dog, including a lapdog, will be more dependable if it receives a degree of obedience training. When handled correctly it will naturally protect what it considers to be its pack – your family.

Training your dog

All dogs are amenable to training and in fact benefit from it, because training establishes a hierarchy that exists in a pack, a grade of relationships that a dog

Good dog, bad dog

Some breeds are more excitable than others, and dangerous to your children as well as to intruders.

◆ Rottweilers may be viciously territorial and easily become excited by noise and quick movement.

◆ Doberman Pinschers are often highly strung and aggressive.

◆ Spaniels (and Corgis) are sensitive dogs that may resent the attention that is so often diverted to children, and tend to snap.

◆ Collies and Border Collies are working breeds and are likely to nip when excited.

◆ Staffordshire Bull Terriers are relatively safe with children if excitement is avoided. Some Staffies, as well as English Bull Terriers, are raised as fighting dogs – these should be avoided.

◆ German Shepherds (Alsatians) are quick to respond to perceived aggression with aggression but don't deserve the bad press they often receive.

◆ Labradors and large retrievers are physically impressive, and therefore intimidating, but are usually very patient with children.

actively seeks. You are the leader, and you dictate the rules, and as long as the dog always knows what those rules are you can trust one another. Don't try to mix a dog's roles, though. Being treated sometimes as a pet and sometimes as a guard dog will almost certainly confuse the animal, leaving you with neither one nor the other.

Teach your dog from puppyhood, if possible, so that you can establish yourself as the leader of the pack. Repeat an exercise with it five or six times a day for several days, and show your approval often, rewarding it now and then, so that its response to an order from you becomes a conditioned reflex. Use simple words, no more than two at a time, and limit the vocabulary of your orders to 50 words. Treat your dog with authority but with fairness and gentleness. Be patient, and punish little but firmly so that the dog is discouraged from disobeying you.

Basic obedience exercises include training your dog to sit, lie down, sit and stay or lie down and stay, and to walk at your side without pulling against the leash or without a leash at all (to heel). These exercises can be done without professional help.

Guard dogs are further taught to guard objects and to protect their owner, by means of growling, barking, and defensive snapping and nipping. They are also taught controlled attacking skills – to attack only on order, after an assault has been attempted or an object stolen, to bite the clothing, leg or forearm only and to loosen their grip only on an order to do so. Guard and attack exercises are best taught together by a professional trainer.

Securing your dog

The sight of a large and aggressive dog roaming your garden (the 'yard dog') will discourage most intruders. The disadvantages are that, unless a dog has been well trained, it is vulnerable to poisoning, being set loose, distraction or mutilation. (Oven-cleaning aerosol may be sprayed at the eyes of dogs that are lured to a perimeter fence. It usually contains caustic soda and causes excruciating pain and blindness.) It is a good idea to build a secondary enclosure, which should include your house, which your dog can patrol freely. A tethered dog is of little use as a protector.

Consider keeping a smaller dog inside the house as well – it will be more useful against a criminal who has broken into your home.

Responsibilities – to your dog

Your main obligation is to provide your dog with a home, suitable and sufficient food and water, and the amount of regular exercise it needs. A brisk daily walk is essential – the larger the dog, the longer the walk needed. If there is an open field or beach where it can run safely, so much the better, but this is only for dogs that come when called.

A dog that receives insufficient attention and exercise is going to be bored and stressed, which it usually shows by barking incessantly and apparently aimlessly. (This often means that there's nobody at home.) Other signs include wild chasing about, usually along a fence, and digging or damaging your property (such as washing hung out to dry). A stressed or anxious dog may appear sulky or withdrawn, and is liable to bite the people in its own household. A dog that receives too little food, attention or exercise will eventually accept these things from a stranger, who thus has a head start in burgling your home.

Staffordshire Bull Terrier

Responsibilities – to the public

Any dog may eventually be provoked into biting, some more readily than others, so you are legally obliged to protect the public against it. The larger your dog, the more serious the consequences of an attack are likely to be. The victim of an attack may sue you in court for a very large sum of money as compensation. Make sure that the dog cannot get off your property – see that walls and fences are in good condition. Gates should have efficient self-closing mechanisms, and the dog should be under strict control (not locked away) during the period that any gate leading to the street is open.

Place prominent warning signs, either worded or showing a graphic depiction of an open-jawed dog, along the perimeter of your property and on every gate that leads onto the property. Additional warning notices, stating that people enter at their own risk, may be fixed to the gates. However, not everybody who comes onto your property uninvited is a trespasser with criminal intent. Anyone, including a child or an illiterate person, may open your gate and enter with good reason. If they were attacked, you might be held liable for damages, although it would be in your favour if you had placed warning notices. If you think that your dog is vicious or likely to bite with little or no provocation, keep all perimeter gates locked – you're more secure with locked gates, anyway.

Doberman Pinscher

Collie

Other animals

Geese, which have a strong territorial sense, make noisy and intimidating 'watchdogs'. Other birds claimed as reliable alarms include turkeys, cockatiels and parrots. Goats – especially males – are also known to be aggressive guardians. Don't, however, keep them in the same enclosure as valued plants. Local bylaws and ordinances are likely to restrict the type of domesticated animal you may keep on an urban property, while permits are needed for keeping any wild animal. Check with your local authority.

The keeping of indigenous snakes, spiders and scorpions is subject to regulations and requires a permit, but even the rumoured presence of these creatures is likely to be discouraging.

Rottweiler

Golden Labrador

LIGHTING YOUR HOUSE

Given enough time and incentive, such as exceptionally valuable pickings, criminals will eventually break into any home. But adequate lighting tells them you're on the alert and, seeing it, most prowlers will move on.

Eliminating the shadows

Most night-time housebreaking attempts are made during the weekend, when residents are expected to be out. And where there is no lighting, or inadequate illumination, burglars can work at breaking into your home knowing that they are unobserved, and that they therefore have time.

Lighting for security must illuminate all standard points of entry into your grounds, as well as those into your home, garage and any outbuildings. It must also light up all potential entry points, such as the space beneath the stoep or veranda, an air-conditioning duct, even a chimney.

Use lighting to eliminate any shadows where muggers or intruders can hide, along the perimeter, within the garden or against the house. In remote or lonely areas, however, be careful not to overdramatise doors and windows with lighting. The sharp contrast between darkness and light may, in fact, draw attention to your home. It may be better to arrange lighting so that some light spills onto the walls and ground near the doors and windows.

Light sources

An important light source in towns is the street lighting provided by your local authority. Advise the electricity department if lights in your neighbourhood are faulty or inadequate. Apart from street lights, many other types of security light are available, such as floodlights, which emit a wide, spreading beam, or spotlights, which cast a relatively narrow beam. Some security lights have compact halogen tubes which produce an intensely bright light. Alternatively, you may prefer to adapt fittings that use ordinary domestic light bulbs or fluorescent tubes.

Fluorescent tubes are the cheapest to run, followed by conventional bulbs, with halogen tubes consuming the most electricity. For this reason, many people fit fluorescent tubes or conventional bulbs to lights that are permanently on at night, and fit halogen tubes to lights that switch on in response to an intruder.

To see the effect of general lighting, start with a light source of at least 200 watts (200W) at each corner of the house, building up the light intensity if necessary. (If the light has a cover, though, check the wording on it to see that the wattage shouldn't be lower. The bulb may overheat and burst, or damage the cover.)

Next to each external door, position a light at a height of between 1,6 and 2 metres. Adjust the light to shine full on anyone standing outside the door, without too much spillage of light onto the person inside. A light placed higher than this will tend to create dark shadows on a caller's face and may mask his or her identity. Look through the peephole or door viewer while somebody stands outside, to make sure that the light is adequate.

Get a friend to move about the garden while you check from the street and from the edge of your property, for shadows dark and large enough for him or her to hide in – especially those that are close to doors or windows. Make sure also that the street number of your house is visible, and that your garage or parking area is well lit.

Then go inside your house and check whether you can see your 'intruder' from the windows. Increase the wattage if necessary, and change the position of the lights to light up the shadowy areas. Remember, though, to shade or deflect bright lights so that they won't keep you or your neighbours awake. Once you've lit the entry points and removed the darker shadows, most prowlers will think twice before attempting to break in.

Timers, sensors and alarms

If you usually arrive home after dark, install a light switch activated by a timer or a light-sensitive cell that you can set to come on as daylight fades and to switch off at sunrise. This should switch on at least the lights at the entrance you use, those along the path you take to the door, and those at the door itself. (The same lights should be adequate to light the way for visitors.) The most certain giveaway of your absence is to allow outside lights to burn throughout the day.

Although you may decide to have some lights burning all night, it is convenient to have others that switch on in response to a particular stimulus – usually the presence of a person. These detecting devices, or sensors, are operated by a control unit that regulates the time for which the light will remain on. You can adjust sensors for sensitivity, and adjust control units to operate a particular pattern of lighting, and keep the lights on for any period from a few seconds to indefinitely. Some sensors include timers, which you can set to turn on and off at up to four times during the day or night. In a windy area, or where tree branches may move within a sensor's range, lights operated by a timer only may be more suitable.

Several types of movement sensor are available, the most widely used being the passive infrared (PIR)

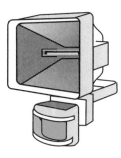

A security floodlight fitted with a halogen tube and a motion sensor is ideal for lighting up the garden or driveway.

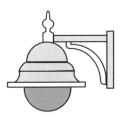

Fit a wall-mounted down-light above a door or entrance to illuminate steps and any visitors.

A wall-mounted half-light casts a beam with a 180° range and is suitable for lighting shadowy areas against house and perimeter walls.

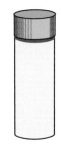

Install a freestanding light with a 360° range along pathways or in garden beds to light up potential hiding places.

detector (see The Alarmed House, pp50-3). Other types that react to movement coming within their field are those that emit radio or ultrasonic waves.

Although these sensors switch on a series of lights, which may deter an intruder who has been detected, it's usually also advisable to have an audible alarm, activated with the lights, to alert you to the situation. You need to know as early as possible that someone is trying to get into your home.

According to your overall security arrangements – and individual factors, such as the acuteness of your hearing – you can arrange for the alarm to sound in just one room of your home, at the monitoring station of your security patrol company, or outside your home – where it will also alert neighbours and the intruder himself.

Putting it together

Do-it-yourself lighting systems, with detailed plans and diagrams, are available from electrical suppliers, supermarkets and hardware stores. However, electricity is dangerous, and electrical accidents – caused by ignorance or carelessness – may be fatal. Also, a quick 'home fix' may not be acceptable for the Electrical Certificate of Compliance you need when you sell your home, and you may then be forced to have your work redone professionally. If you are not confident of being able to modify your lighting system yourself, consult a registered electrician.

External wiring and fittings must be suited to outside conditions. They should be waterproof, for instance, and the wiring should be able to withstand long exposure to sunlight without disintegrating. The most vandal-resistant lights have polycarbonate bulkhead fittings and are screwed flat against the wall. Some lighting control units may be connected to several indoor or outdoor sensors and can be simply plugged into a 15-amp (15A) wall socket. Always check the manufacturer's instructions and recommendations again before finalising the wiring and switching the system on.

Lights and shades

The illuminated window is the exception to the lighting rule – it attracts rather than discourages potential housebreakers. When you switch on an inside light, you're illuminating the room not only for its occupants, but for everyone – including a criminal – who cares to look in. This is when your prized possessions show up most clearly. So, as far as possible, remove the incentive to break in.

◆ Don't place desirable or readily saleable items where they can be seen through windows. Alternatively, during the daytime, obscure the view into your home with blinds or muslin or net curtains, which allow light to filter through but also make it difficult for anyone to see in.

◆ At night, always draw curtains or lower a blind before switching lights on. Keep your curtains closed tightly and your blinds completely down whenever the light is on, whether you're home or not.

Leaving the lights on

When you go out at night, leave enough lights on to make it look as though there really is somebody at home. Leaving on only one light, such as the stoep light, is a giveaway to anyone who has been watching your property and knows that you don't usually leave that light on. Vary the lights, so that no pattern is identifiable as the one you use when you leave the house.

A typical 'we are out' pattern uses stoep or front door, living room and passage lights, and burglars know this. Add a light or two elsewhere to suggest activity throughout the house, and it becomes more convincing. Lights that are turned on and off randomly by timers will raise even more doubt about your absence. Ensure that a prospective intruder, no matter from which direction he comes, will see at least one light burning in your home.

Going to bed

Housebreakers are no heroes, and if they are going to enter while you're home, they would prefer you to be asleep. Switching off the lights when you retire tells anyone who's watching that you'll soon be asleep. So leave a light on every night, but a different one.

Whenever you get up at night, switch on lights and, unless you'll disturb another sleeper, move about fairly noisily. If you do have an intruder, the chances are he'll run for it as soon as he realises that you're awake (see Unwanted Guests, pp78-9).

Install switches so that you can control any exterior lighting and lights in other parts of the house from your bedroom or from the room in which you spend most time in the evening. These master switches should override automatic circuits, such as sensors.

DOORS – A LINE OF DEFENCE

A door offers the simplest way to enter and exit a home, and is the most convenient route to use when removing property. Open doors are irresistibly inviting, so keep your outside doors not just closed, but locked as well – especially if you don't have the additional protection of a security gate.

Door construction and doorways

Many modern doors offer almost no security. Typically, they consist of two layers of plywood separated by a layer of papier-mâché egg-trays. This 'hollow core' pattern may be adequate for internal doors, but won't withstand even a half-hearted assault. Under impact the frame, or the door, can split at the height of the lock, and within a few seconds a burglar can gain access to your home. Thin, decorative panels and glass panes are also weak points.

An ideal outside door should be made of solid wood at least 45 millimetres thick and with a stile or border 120 millimetres wide, or more, to enable you to fit a good-quality mortise lock into the side. The door should fit snugly in its frame, with a gap of no more than 3 millimetres – too small for the tip of a crowbar.

The frame itself, if not of metal and mortared into the wall, should be of sound wood – not warped or rotting – and securely attached to the wall. Many frames are held to the wall merely by nails or wooden pegs. These fixtures should be replaced or reinforced with screws and expanding plugs. If you have a timber-frame house, the door frame should be bolted or screwed to the main structure.

Your security should not stop at your front door – examine all outside doors leading into your home and fix or reinforce them if they are not sound.

Single doors

An external door should swing on three strong hinges, with each leaf of each hinge secured by the number of screws for which it has been designed. A door that opens outwards is a security risk because it is relatively easy for criminals to knock the pins from the protruding hinges and lift the door from its frame. However, you can make it difficult to lift out the door, by fitting hinge-bolts midway between the hinges.

Split doors

Also known as stable doors, these consist of a door with a horizontal division, and are useful for keeping small stock or pets out (or toddlers in) without closing the entire door. Each leaf of the door should be fitted with a suitable lock (only the top leaf is usually lockable) and two bolts should be fitted to hold the leaves together so that, when desired, the door can be used as a conventional single door. (The door forms a more

Key points about keys!

◆ Pay cash for new keys – your credit card or chequebook could give away your address to someone who also knows which keys you've bought.

◆ When you're out of the house, keep keys securely on your person – in a pocket or a special compartment in a hem, or on a cord under your clothes.

◆ Don't keep keys in a handbag and never mark keys with your name or address. If your handbag is stolen, your address may easily be identified from the handbag's contents.

◆ Keep a front door key near the door, for emergency use, in a secure hiding place that's easily accessible.

secure barrier when the leaves are bolted together.) Outward-opening split doors should be fitted with hinge-bolts.

Double doors

These have a vertical division, and cover an opening slightly less than double that of a single door. They are usually panelled or fitted with glass panes which, together with the weakness inherent in their design (they are attached to each other only in the middle), makes them attractive to intruders. Each door should have three hinges and, when closed, be capable of being bolted securely to both the bottom and the top of the door frame.

The doors should be locked together by a mortise lock with a square-faced bolt having a 'throw' of at least 25 millimetres (see Keeping it Locked, pp44-5). This can be backed up by two sliding bolts placed one third of the height from top and bottom respectively. A stout wooden or metal bar placed across both leaves and anchored to each is the most secure closure.

Sliding doors

Also known as patio doors, these doors fitted with large sheets of glass are usually secured by locks of doubtful value. Many sliding doors are made in such a way that they can simply be lifted out of the bottom track and laid aside.

To secure sliding doors, fit at least two vertical bolts along the lower edge so that, when closed, the bolts pass at least 30 millimetres into the floor. The same arrangement should be secured at the top, although you may have to fit brackets to the rail to receive the bolts when closed.

To prevent the door from sliding, fit lockable bolts to pass from the sliding section into the fixed section. Temporary measures, such as a broom handle in the sliding channel, are also effective. A hasp, bolted to the wall, and a staple, bolted to the door with a pad-lock, is a good alternative to the standard lock. The best way to burglarproof a sliding door, however, is to cover it with a safety gate.

Reinforcing a door

A rigid L-shaped section, or angle iron, of steel can be screwed to the frame of an inward-opening door to cover a gap between the door and frame, and prevent a bar from being inserted into the gap. Where the door opens outwards, attach a flat steel strip to the outside surface of the door, or screw an L-section of steel to the edge of the door, to cover the gap between the door and frame.

When you attach any form of reinforcement to an external door, use flat-head bolts or non-retractable screws. The bolts are secured by a nut turned tight up against a metal washer, and so are not easily pulled out. An ordinary screw can simply be turned out with

Inward-opening door

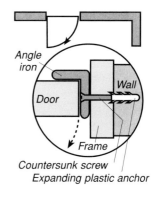

Countersunk screw
Expanding plastic anchor

Outward-opening door (a)

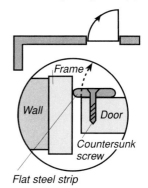

Flat steel strip

Outward-opening door (b)

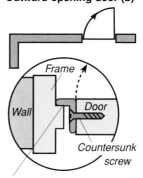

Angle iron

Foil a housebreaker armed with a crowbar by covering the gap between the edge of a door and its frame with angle iron or a flat strip of steel. Attach the steel with bolts or countersunk screws (as shown) that can't be turned out.

a screwdriver (or even a coin) and, especially where wood has been allowed to become excessively dry, is likely to pull out under pressure.

Consider replacing glass panes and thin, recessed panels with solid wood or panels of glass-reinforced plastic (GRP), which must be firmly secured. Bond GRP to the existing door or, where glass has been removed, to the new wooden insert, using the adhesive recommended by the manufacturer. Alternatively, protect glass and panels with bars or rigid mesh.

Windows next to the door frame may allow a criminal to reach in to the lock. Prevent this by installing laminated or toughened glass in the window frame, or by applying an adhesive plastic film to the inside of the existing glass. The plastic film makes it difficult to break out the glass. To add extra strength, fit bars or rigid mesh.

If your door is fitted with a mail flap, someone could reach inside the flap to unlock the door – with a length of wire, for instance. To prevent this, screw an open box of metal plate 2 millimetres thick (or planed wood 10 millimetres thick) to the inside of the door around the end of the flap nearest to the lock. The top of the box should extend along the width of the mail flap, and should protrude from the door about 100 millimetres. If the flap is no longer used for postal deliveries, close it by mounting a wooden block in the slot behind it.

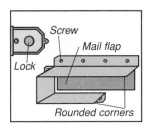

Attach an open metal or plywood box to the inside of a mail flap to prevent anyone from putting their arm through the flap and opening the lock.

Seeing through it

If you have to open your front door (or any other door) to see who's calling, you're throwing away its security value. A 'peephole' or door viewer is a simple solution that requires you only to drill a hole in the door and fit in the peephole. Try a few before making your choice. One about 50 millimetres in diameter is adequate.

Wide-angle viewers give a large field of vision, but at the cost of making callers appear so small and distant that you may not be able to recognise them. Select one that combines clarity with the width of field that you require. Where children are likely to answer the door, fit another viewer at a suitable height.

Use viewers in combination with a stoep light (see Lighting Your House, pp36-9). If you can't see through the viewer, or if the image is indistinct or foggy, don't open the door – the caller may be deliberately blocking or distorting your view.

Chains and limiters (see Keeping it Locked, pp44-5) allow a door to be opened through only a small arc, to let you see outside. These devices must be strong and of good quality, and must be attached by screws no shorter than 35 millimetres.

Safety gates

Safety gates are burglar bars for your external doors. They are usually hinged on the same side as the door and, ideally, are fitted with a double-throw deadlock. They can be rigid or expanding. Expanding gates are

suitable for large areas, such as sliding doors, although they may also be used in standard doorways. Keep a security gate locked at all times.

If you're having a security gate made, it is advisable not to have a spring-loaded latch or any other device that holds it in the closed position, since this could lull you into believing it is locked. It is not, unless a key has been turned in the lock or it has some sort of electric door release. Attach the gate, and the section to which it locks, to a masonry wall and not to woodwork.

If the layout of your front or back doorway allows it, position the safety gate at least one metre in front of the door to provide a safety lobby. This means that when you are entering or leaving your home, there will always be a locked barrier between the inside and outside. On coming home from shopping, for instance, unlock the gate, put your shopping in the security lobby, lock the gate and only then unlock the door.

A security gate, apart from being another obstacle for the criminal to tackle, means that you can leave the door it protects open for ventilation. It may be useful to order a gate with the bars on the lower half placed close together (50 millimetres apart instead of 100 millimetres) to prevent pets from passing through.

Door discipline

Make it a rule that the front and back doors are always locked, unless members of the family are actually on the stoep or within close range of the door. The last one off the stoep, whether going indoors or elsewhere, must lock the door and put the keys in their correct place. Similar rules can apply to other doors. Too often, doors are left unlocked while the householder 'pops next door for two minutes'. It takes much less than two minutes for someone to walk into your home, pick up something valuable, and walk out again. See that every member of the family practises the security that doors demand.

KEEPING IT LOCKED

Whenever you move into a new home, replace the locks, or the relevant parts of the locks. You can never be too sure of the honesty of the former occupants or people who had access to their keys.

Rims and mortises

The locks found on most doors are either surface-mounted (rim locks) or fitted into the door from the edge (mortise locks). Most are key-operated, but others are controlled mechanically by a digital code, or electronically by digital code or by remote control. There are also lockable bolts made for a wide range of applications, such as securing sash or casement windows and sliding doors.

Rim cylinder latch

Also known as a night latch or 'Yale', the advantage of this type of lock is that it can be locked by merely closing the door. However, these locks can often be opened with a credit card or steel rule inserted between door and frame. Newer versions block this technique, but some may still be forced open with a flat-bladed screwdriver. Also, where a would-be intruder can break a pane of glass and pass his hand through to reach the latch, he will be able to open the latch from the inside. Many versions of these locks are additionally vulnerable in that the face plate can be prised off and the locking mechanism removed to open the door. Key-in-knob locks generally suffer from the same deficiencies as the rim cylinder latch.

A deadlocking cylinder night latch has a bolt that cannot be forced back and is the most secure.

Mortise locks

Many new houses are routinely fitted with three-lever mortise deadlocks, which can only be locked with a key. But these locks have a limited (and numbered) range of key patterns, all of which can be bought over the counter in a hardware store, so they are inadequate as security for external doors, although lockable inserts can be fitted to block the entry of a key.

A five-lever lock is of better quality and offers much greater security. If the home you move into has a five-lever lock, you can take the lock to a locksmith and simply change the levers inside it rather than replace the whole lock. Alternatively, since the traditional lock pattern is gradually being replaced by the high-security cylinder type, replace your lock with this type. Do not, however,

fit any mortise lock to a door with a thickness of less than 40 millimetres – there may be insufficient wood on either side to resist severe pressure.

Deadbolts

Deadbolts come in both rim-fitting and mortise forms. The locking mechanism is a bolt – preferably square-faced and of hardened steel – that can be moved only by turning the key, usually through two complete turns. This 'double throw' should cause the bolt to protrude at least 25 millimetres beyond the face plate into the door frame. Many have hardened steel side plates (to prevent a would-be intruder from drilling through the lock) and concealed fixing screws (visible only when the door is opened). Reinforcing kits that protect the lock area with high-tensile steel plates can be bought ready-made or made up to order.

Master keying

Identical cylinders can be inserted into almost any form of lock, including padlocks, deadlocks and locks for specialised applications. This means that only one key is then needed to open all the locks, rather than a large bunch of keys. Master-keyed locks, too, are a group (or 'suite') of locks that can be operated by a single master key. Unlike keyed-alike locks, however, each lock also has its individual key that will not fit any of the other locks.

Digital locks

Mechanical and electronic digital locks are opened by entering a sequence of numbers (usually four or five) onto a keypad. The keypad of a mechanical digital lock is mounted as part of the lock, whereas an electronic keypad may be mounted almost any distance away, or be completely portable. A radio transmitter and receiver can also activate an electronic lock.

Some electronic locks, which usually work from a 12 volt electrical current, can handle sophisticated programs, including delayed locking and unlocking, and jamming in response to repeated faulty signals. It is sometimes possible to adapt existing locks to an electronic system by replacing the strike – the section into which the bolt slides when the lock is engaged.

Chain locks and limiters

When in use, chains and limiters advertise that someone is home, but neither gives a high degree of protection – a vigorous kick on the door may pull out the retaining screws. However, chains can be upgraded by securing them with longer (and thicker) screws or, preferably, with bolts.

A limiter is a rigid metal arm attached to the door frame, and sometimes to the strike. Like the chain, the arm of the limiter prevents the door being opened beyond a set width. Chains and limiters provide greater security when used with a doorstop wedge.

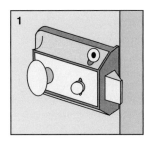

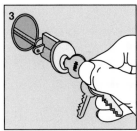

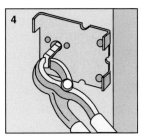

A cylinder lock can be effectively changed by replacing just the cylinder. (1) Unscrew the old lock from the back of the door. (2) Unscrew the plate that holds the cylinder in place, and from the front of the door, remove the old cylinder. (3) Fit a new cylinder through the front of the door. (4) Screw the back plate onto the back of the door. Using pliers, snap off the tail of the cylinder so that it protrudes by about 15 millimetres. Screw the lock back on. The advantage of a cylinder lock, such as a night latch, is that it is not as easy to pick as a mortise lock.

WINDOWS, BARS AND SHUTTERS

Windows are among the burglar's favourite entry points because they offer one of the easiest ways to get in, often without breaking the glass. In fact, burglars prefer not to break the glass, because of the noise and the risk of injury to themselves.

Open invitation

Too often, windows are left unlocked or inadequately locked. Non-opening windows are left unprotected and can be simply lifted clear of the frame after the putty (usually dried and crumbling) has been removed. Look at your windows – from the outside and inside – before a criminal does. Regard all windows as being within his reach – even the one you think is too small for anyone to get through. If you don't protect it well, someone will get in.

Wooden frames and windows

No matter how strong the locks or bars at your windows might be, if you attach them to excessively dried or rotten wood, they will offer almost no protection at all – they can simply be pulled or kicked off.

Check the soundness of your wooden frames and windows and, if necessary, reinforce, repair or replace them. If putty is cracked, dried, and easy to remove, replace that too, remembering to seal and paint the new putty after about a week.

Metal frames and windows

Check carefully for rust on older installations, especially near locks, handles and hinges. Repairs to steel frames may involve welding, drilling or sawing and the removal of the panes. In coastal areas it may be more economical and convenient to replace rather than attempt to repair, especially if having the windows regalvanised means that you will be without them for a few days. Replace the putty where necessary.

The security of aluminium-framed windows can be improved by adding surface-mounted locks, but make sure that all additions, including screws, are suitable for use with aluminium, and that their attachment will not weaken the frame.

Window locks and keys

Many commercially available window locks are operated by a short, metal rod with a hexagonal, star-shaped or square cross section. Although the ready availability of the key means that these locks are of relatively low security, their use is still a deterrent – burglars like to get in quickly and quietly.

Where any window is a metre or more in length, it's advisable to fit two locks on the window, rather than just one. Do not place screws too close to the glass – it may crack.

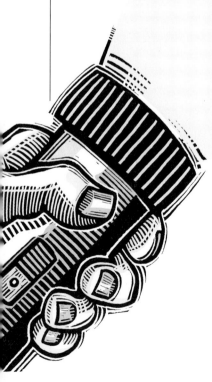

Try to place locks where they are easy for you to get at in order to close them and make the windows secure. A lock that is difficult to reach is more likely to be left open, which reduces your security.

Sash windows

Usually wood-framed, and also known as double-hung windows, these slide up and down. The standard lock for these windows is fairly easily opened from the outside. But locking bolts are available, which allow the window to be locked when fully closed or slightly open. A length of wood wedged into the sliding channel is an economical way of blocking the lower sash.

A large-paned wooden window, such as a sash window, is more likely to warp than a smaller one, and, without separate bars, it is possible for intruders to get in by breaking a single pane.

Casement windows

These are hinged at the top or at the side, and are usually secured to the frame by a drop-handle lever, also known as a cockspur. Lockable versions are available, including some that lock automatically whenever the window is fully closed. You can make a simple lock for this type of window by screwing an L-shaped bracket to the standing frame so that, when the window is closed, the bracket is covered by a pivot attached to the shutting stile. Another option is to fit cranked barrel bolts to the top and bottom of the window, to slide into recesses drilled in the frame.

Louvre windows

The glass slats of these windows are usually easy to remove, so even if the frame is fitted with a secure lock, this should be backed up with bars. Even so, it is a good idea to replace the louvre section with a more solid construction.

Self-barred windows

Windows with the glass divided by glazing bars into small panes are probably proof against the average housebreaker, who may be reluctant to risk the noise involved in virtually destroying the window to get inside. Glazing bars at close intervals make for a stronger frame, but the windows themselves are really effective only if fitted with secure locks.

Small-paned windows can be reinforced by bars attached to the standing window frame, which are overlapped by the glazing bars when the window is closed and form a permanent barrier when the window is open or closed.

Glazing

Windows in most homes are fitted with annealed or float glass that is three or four millimetres thick. On breaking, this glass is liable to produce long, jagged shards. But there are several types of glass that offer

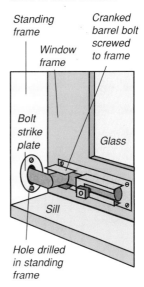

Cranked barrel bolt fitted to the frame of a casement or sash window

Standing frame
Cranked barrel bolt screwed to frame
Window frame
Bolt strike plate
Glass
Sill
Hole drilled in standing frame

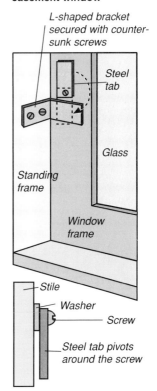

L-shaped bracket fitted to the standing frame of a casement window

L-shaped bracket secured with countersunk screws
Steel tab
Glass
Standing frame
Window frame
Stile
Washer
Screw
Steel tab pivots around the screw

greater security. Wired glass is ordinary annealed glass in which thin, steel mesh has been embedded. The glass breaks on impact but usually holds together until the mesh is broken. Toughened or tempered glass requires much greater force to break, and disintegrates into tiny pieces, less likely to cause injury than the splinters of annealed glass. Laminated or safety glass is made of alternating, bonded layers of annealed glass and a special plastic film. The effort (and time) needed to break through laminated glass depends on its thickness – usually 6,5 millimetres in home installations.

Adhesive film

Plastic film fitted to the inside of windowpanes decreases the amount of ultraviolet radiation that filters through the glass, and also reduces the tendency of glass to shatter on impact. Some types of film provide a one-way mirror effect – in daylight, people outside are unable to see in – but this reverses at night when interior lights are switched on.

Adhesive film is available in various thicknesses, up to bomb-blast resistant. The average DIY enthusiast should be able to apply plastic film to areas up to approximately 600 millimetres square with no special equipment. After removing the backing from the adhesive side of the film, you slide the film onto the clean, wet glass and then press the film from one side to the other and from top to bottom, to remove air bubbles.

Bars

Whether you have them fitted inside or outside is a matter of preference, but well-made, well-installed bars will discourage almost any would-be burglar.

Like locks, bars are only as effective as their attachment, and bars fastened in crumbling mortar or rotting wood offer almost no security at all. The bars themselves should be made of mild steel, a widely used combination being horizontal rods of 12 millimetres diameter with vertical rods of 10 millimetres diameter. Square-section steel bars can also be used, in the same combination.

Secure internal bars to the wall with galvanised or stainless-steel screws and plastic split anchors, or with metal sleeve anchors, driven into the wall at least 50 millimetres from the window aperture and no further than 200 millimetres apart. External bars should protrude no more than 150 millimetres from the wall, and the bars at top, bottom and both sides should be 75 millimetres from the wall. Vertical bars should be no more than 100 millimetres apart. The whole structure should be secured with nonbreakable security bolts.

All vertical bars, internal and external, must be 'tied' together by a horizontal member or some other fixing to prevent them from being bent aside. In coastal areas, bars can be galvanised (the hot-dip method is

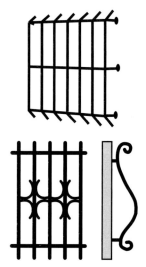

Burglar bars over the outside of a window should be fitted with nonbreakable security bolts to be really effective.

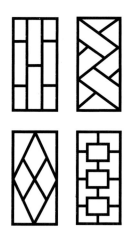

Burglar bars on the inside of a window are most secure when fitted into the standing frame of the window.

the most effective), plastic coated or both galvanised and plastic coated against corrosion.

Most ready-made window bars sold in hardware stores and supermarkets have insufficient attachment points, so examine them carefully before you buy them. Some are also made of inadequate materials, which criminals recognise.

Shutters

Most shutters are designed and installed for their decorative appearance rather than their security potential. Nevertheless, they may discourage the opportunist burglar, simply because they give the impression of solidity. Lock both shutters to the windowsill, preferably with cranked barrel bolts, and to one another.

Wooden shutters require full maintenance at least once a year. This includes tightening the structure with glue or screws as needed, scraping, and repainting or oiling. Remove the hinges so that you can also treat the section normally covered by the hinge leaf.

Wooden shutters on their own are probably not adequate as protection. Much more substantial are steel shutters, which may be of the sliding type, which can be secured inside with multiple locks. Roller shutters are made of steel, aluminium or hardened plastic and require a storage box at the head of the window. Operated by hand or by motor installed inside, they are suited to most windows except those with curved frames. The motors can be linked to a new or existing alarm circuit.

Emergency exits

Bars work both ways, and the more effectively they keep out intruders, the more surely they will keep you in. Install fire sensors, and devise an emergency escape route to be used in the event of a serious fire breaking out in the home. The usual solution is to have a section of bars on a particular window adapted so that it can be opened from inside. Keep the bars securely locked and store the keys in a secure but secret place. Check frequently that the keys are where they should be and that the escape section of the bars moves freely when unlocked.

The safer section

Many people use bars and a security gate to divide their homes into day and night sections. Typically, the night section, also referred to as the safer section, consists of bedrooms and a bathroom. It is equipped with a telephone or radio, backup batteries (where used) and a fire extinguisher, and is the control centre for the home alarm system. Ideally, it should adjoin the home of a neighbour who can be alerted – by shouting, if necessary – in the event of trouble. Your own safer section could consist of just one room – your bedroom, for instance – that has a securely lockable door, well-protected windows, and a phone.

THE ALARMED HOUSE

Alarms cannot prevent a burglar from breaking in, but they do warn you or your security service that urgent measures need to be taken. By detecting burglars at an early stage of their attempted intrusion, and by calling for a response, alarms take away one of the criminal's greatest assets – time.

Crying wolf

The sound of an electronic alarm – issuing from a neighbouring home or a parked vehicle – has become so common that it attracts little general attention. Those who hear it assume that it's probably a false alarm and, in almost 98 per cent of cases, that's just what it is. Not even the remaining two per cent represents criminal activity. About one quarter of these – or less than a half per cent of the total – are caused by 'unforeseen technical problems' such as changes in the weather. The rest, less than one and a half per cent of all triggered alarms, signals criminal activity.

A newly installed system is expected to give a few false alarms, but repeated false alarms may lead to your address being regarded as merely troublesome rather than actually under threat. The diversion of security staff by false alarms also draws their attention away from genuine alarms.

To do it yourself or not

Kit assemblies or individual alarm system components make it possible for most DIY enthusiasts to install their own alarm systems. However, it is unlikely that a security company will undertake to accept signals from anything but their own installations. Remember, too, that an alarm system that is not linked to the monitor of a security service will probably attract little attention unless you have made some prior arrangement with a neighbour. Most security companies operate an alarm installation service, with options to suit your purse and the type of protection you need.

The alarm

The basic elements of an alarm system are: the detectors; the alarm signal, which may be audible on site or transmitted to a security service; a battery to supply power in the event of a break in mains electricity; keys – usually keypads – for setting or arming the system; a control panel; and personal assault (panic) buttons.

An alarm is triggered when detectors in the circuit respond to predetermined circumstances, such as the movement of a door or window, or the presence of a person in a particular area. Usually, a siren is activated on the premises, as much to disconcert intruders as to alert neighbours.

The siren may be mounted outside – under the eaves, for instance – or inside the home, but should not be in a position where a burglar could cut the wires. It must conform to the sound regulations laid down by your local authority. Alarms can be set to sound for, say, between four and eight minutes and then reset themselves to respond to any further break-in attempt.

Whether the sound of an alarm ringing in his ears will make a burglar abandon his plans depends on the burglar's nerve and experience. An experienced burglar knows how long, on average, it takes for the security patrol to respond, and would probably be aware of having triggered an alarm, even a silent one. With an audible alarm, however, he is faced with the unpredictable factor of neighbourhood response, and might just decide to quit.

Wired and wireless

The wired or hard-wired alarm system, in which wires radiate from a central control box, usually via the ceiling, is a more-or-less permanent fixture and may add slightly to the value of your property. A radio-operated system can be installed more quickly and can be taken with you if you change address. Both systems contain the same range of detectors and other components, including remote control and panic buttons.

Magnetic switches

The magnetic contact, also known as a reed switch, is one of the most widely used to detect movement of doors or windows. The switch is attached to the fixed or standing frame, and is held closed by a magnet attached to the moving part. When the door or window is opened, the magnetic force is removed from the switch which then interrupts the current and – if the system is armed – sets off the alarm.

Shock sensors

Also known as seismic sensors, their various forms may detect force resulting in vibration, and even a particular range of sounds. They are sometimes used on windows to detect breaking glass.

Shock sensors are adjustable for sensitivity, but even so, if installed near airports, railways or busy roads they may result in many false alarms.

Broken-glass sensors

These sensors include audio detectors, which are tuned to respond to the frequency of the sound of breaking glass, and thin strips of foil or other

A control panel with touch keys controls all aspects of an alarm system.

An audio detector responds to the sound of breaking glass and triggers an alarm.

A panic button should bring immediate help from the security company.

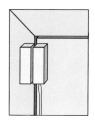

A magnetic contact on doors and windows sets off the alarm when the door or window is opened.

electroconductive tape applied to panes at least 300 millimetres from the edge of the glass.

When the electroconductive type of system is armed, a low-voltage current passes through the strips. When the glass is broken, the strips shear, breaking the current and setting off an alarm.

PIR detectors

Passive infrared (PIR) detectors respond to changes in infrared energy, especially the body heat that radiates from animals, including humans. They are the most widely used detectors. Modern PIR detectors respond only when the source of heat moves across their range and changes the surrounding temperature by about 5 per cent. These detectors are not affected by static sources of heat.

PIR detectors are available in a variety of configurations, to detect movement across a wide angle or at a long range (up to about 40 metres). They are useful for covering corridors, rooms, lofts and also outside areas (where their installation should be waterproof). A PIR in the space between the ceiling and the roof should detect intruders entering that way. Proximity to swimming pools, draughts, sunlight and vehicle headlights may cause a PIR to trigger a false alarm. Don't cover sensors with curtains or furniture.

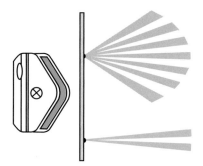

A PIR detector (viewed from above) with a wide or long range is suitable for a room, loft, corridor or garden.

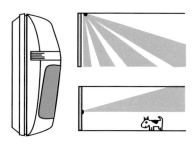

A PIR detector (viewed from the side) with a multi-level range is ideal for a window or door. A detector can be set to create a 'pet alley' for homes with pets.

Smoke detectors

As well as a break-in alarm, you should install smoke detectors in case of fire. They can be mains- or battery-powered. The battery-powered versions are available from a hardware store and can be installed easily. Fit an alarm on each floor of your home, between the living and sleeping areas, and not in a kitchen, bathroom or garage, where fumes or condensation could set it off or prevent it from working.

Panic buttons

The purpose of these is to summon immediate assistance in the event of assault or serious accident. Place panic buttons on every external door, as well as

on a remote control. As the buttons should be within two to three seconds reach, ideally there should be one in each room. The response to a panic-button alarm is usually immediate, and the preliminary telephone call from the security service (see below) is dispensed with.

Panic buttons, which typically operate up to 50 metres or more from the mains installation, can be set to perform a variety of functions in addition to triggering the alarm. They can operate locks, especially those of external doors, and dial several telephone numbers (such as doctor, ambulance, fire station or police). Where an audible, on-site alarm is activated by a panic button, it should ring until switched off – that is, it should not switch off automatically.

Response to an alarm

When the alarm is given in the security company's monitoring room, the first response is to telephone the householder to determine whether the alarm is genuine. In reply to this telephone call, the householder quotes a secret code that tells the security company all is well and that the alarm was a false one. If the telephone is not answered or if the correct code is not given, the local police or nearest security patrol are directed to that address.

Testing the system

If the alarm system fails when you need it, your investment will have been wasted, and you may find yourself in serious danger. Test the system according to the supplier's instructions and, in addition, be alert for loose or damaged contacts and switches. In coastal areas, particularly, be aware of corrosion of the wires as this leads to false alarms. It may show itself by a slight swelling of the wire's insulation.

Alarming statistics

A recent study in the United States showed that:

◆ A residential home without an alarm system is 2,2 times more likely to be burgled than one with an alarm system.

◆ Commercial businesses without an alarm system are 4,5 times more likely to be broken into than those with one.

*The Security Officers'
Board, or SOB (logo
above), is the only officially
recognised regulatory body
for the contract security
industry in South Africa. All
legally registered security
guards and companies are
registered with them and
monitored by them. Before
you appoint a security service to protect your home,
check its credentials with
the SOB.*

SECURITY SERVICES

The prime function of security services is to prevent or limit damage, loss or injury to a client or a client's property.

Insurance and security systems

If you're investing in an alarm system to keep out intruders, it's likely that the contents of your home are insured through a householder's or other policy. Your insurer will give you a list of approved installers of alarm systems and 'armed response companies'. In many cases the response company will also be the installer of the system. If you want to use a security company not on this list, check your insurer's require- ments before negotiating with a security company.

To a large extent, your insurer's selection of alarm systems and security companies is made in your own interest. If you have householder's insurance but do not have a contract with a security service, and your home is burgled, your insurer will require you to bring your domestic security precautions up to a required standard before reinsuring you (see Insuring Possessions, pp92-3.)

Choosing your security service

The companies recommended by your insurer have been investigated and may be presumed to be reliable and to offer comparable service. Even so, find out from friends whether they use any of these compa- nies, and evaluate all praise or complaints that you hear. Then ask your neighbours – those whom you know well – which companies they employ, and listen to their recommendations.

As a general rule, it's better to employ a security service not already represented in the neighbour- hood. As part of their contract, security patrols visit your area to check on the houses they service. And if you and your neighbours all contract with a single company, there need be only one visit to the area. But if three or four companies are contracted, that means three or four visits by security patrols, which helps to maintain the impression of high local security.

It is possible to change from one security company to another when a contract expires, without financial loss, because the monitoring equipment used by these companies is usually compatible with various alarm systems.

What the service does for you

Usually, once you've signed the contract, your securi- ty service company starts by installing an alarm sys- tem and showing you how to operate it. The company undertakes to patrol your property regularly, monitor your alarm at all times and to respond appropriately whenever the alarm is triggered.

When your alarm goes off, the first response from your security service is to telephone your home immediately. If the person answering the telephone gives the security officer the correct secret code, the alarm is presumed to have been a false one, requiring no further action. Where a panic button is triggered, however, a security patrol is dispatched immediately.

Some personnel are trained in first aid or paramedical services, and some organisations also employ officers who have had fire-fighting and rescue training. Most companies work closely with private clinics and other groups owning ambulances and even helicopters. Security company personnel have no special legal powers in addition to those of an ordinary citizen, although their training may include basic law and criminal procedure.

Other services

Monitoring and patrolling are continuous. But you can ask for irregular, unannounced visits, which are more effective than following a timetable. Additional services – if appropriate arrangements are made in advance – include escorting you onto your property, removal of trespassers, mail collection, additional patrols during holidays, and making good any damage (caused by an attempted break-in, for instance) during your absence.

The cost

When you pay for the installation of an alarm system, including parts and labour, the system becomes your property. Since it will have been designed for your particular premises, there may be little point in taking it with you when you move. But you can, reasonably, add its replacement cost to the price of your home. Prices of systems depend on their type, quality and size – the number of sensors, for example – so consider these factors when compiling a short list of systems. If you plan on having your system monitored, talk to a few of the companies' clients to see what standard of service they get. Typically, no additional charge is made for routine patrols or for a response to an alarm. Use of ambulances and special materials is subject to a schedule of tariffs.

A PLACE OF YOUR OWN

Its restricted points of access make a flat look more secure than, say, a freestanding house, but there are some problems that go with it. For one thing, you're dependent for much of your security upon people you don't know – your fellow residents.

Before you buy or rent

If the apartment block and, specifically, your prospective unit, is not as secure as you'd like it to be, find out the policy on improving security. Every residential scheme has a set of regulations. There is bound to be a clause that requires you to obtain permission before doing any alterations, even driving a nail into a wall. The strictest regulations usually apply to rented premises.

Take every opportunity to visit similar apartments in the block, to see what other people have done to add to their security. You may pick up some good ideas, and it will help you to get to know your prospective neighbours. Then explain to the letting agent or the chairman of the body corporate what you'd like to do. You may, for instance, want to install burglar bars at all windows, a different pattern of bars on the balcony, and a security gate at the front door. But will you be able to remove them when you leave, or is there a guarantee that you will be paid their replacement or similar value? In law, improvements that you make to the premises as a tenant – the addition of a security gate, for instance – do not become the property of the landlord. You are at liberty to remove them when you end your tenancy. If you are the owner of the dwelling-unit, any additions or improvements that you make should automatically be your own property and add to the value of the unit.

Finding out a few details

Check the neighbourhood. Bus or railway stations, taxi ranks and a busy local nightlife may mean that you can expect late-night loiterers who may be merely noisy or actually dangerous.

Choosing a flat several floors above ground level is not necessarily a safe option. You'd have farther to go if ever you had to evacuate the block in a hurry, and determined burglars and, especially, rapists, have been known to risk serious injury or death to get into chosen premises several storeys above ground.

The view that makes you vulnerable

The lounge window that so perfectly framed the view of Table Mountain was the factor that persuaded Helen, a 26-year-old accountant, to buy her flat on the fringe of central Cape Town. The apartment was on the third (top) storey of the small, flat-roofed block. The front door and balcony door had strong security gates, and the balcony windows were fitted with bars. The picture window in the lounge had no bars, but was not within reach of drainpipes or balconies. Nobody could get in there, her friends assured her, and it would have been a pity to spoil the view. A few months after moving in, Helen was attacked and raped in her bedroom in the early hours of the morning. Her assailant had climbed up a drainpipe to the roof and then swung from the parapet straight through the open lounge window.

Police comment: Never underestimate the determination of the criminal. In this case, he risked death or severe bodily injury to commit what was clearly a well-planned crime. It is never advisable to leave any window open at night that a person could climb through.

If there is no on-site parking area, find out how safe it would be to leave your car in the street. Ask the owner of a car parked nearby whether cars are regularly broken into or stolen from there.

A trick trespass

Without breaking in or running the risk of being assaulted as a criminal, see if you can get into your prospective apartment block without authority. Use the intercom to call up any number until you find one that doesn't answer – say, number 33. Then call another number and say that you've arrived to see the occupant of number 33, but the intercom seems to be broken. Full-time criminals are probably far more plausible and inventive than you are, so if you manage to get in, they certainly will. And if you do get inside the property, report and try to correct the fault that made it possible.

Your front door

On moving into your new apartment (or other dwelling), your first pro-safety action should be to replace the locks on your entrance door. It's likely to be a costly time, as all sorts of petty expenses crop up when you move home, but the relatively small amount needed for your safety is by far the most important.

So-called 'builders' locks', of the two- or three-lever mortise type with numbered keys, are fitted to many front doors. You should really replace these with a mortise deadlock. Where a rim cylinder latch is fitted, you may be able to replace only the cylinder, but there are several disadvantages to this type, such as being able to be forced open with a credit card (see Keeping it Locked, pp44-5). Consider having a deadlocking night latch installed.

A strong chain or limiter, securely attached, is essential, no matter how good the overall security may be, and it must be engaged whenever you're in, whether the door is locked or not. A viewer should be fitted to solid doors and those with opaque glass. Because the design of an apartment block often restricts the penetration of daylight, many units have front doors with glass panels to admit whatever light is available. Glass panels in or adjacent to an external door are a security risk, but replacing the door may be undesirable or not permitted. So fit a security gate outside the door, making sure that it is attached to the masonry and not the wooden framework of the door. Keep it closed and locked at all times – this will not only prevent it from obstructing the corridor, but will also advertise your seriousness about your security.

The windows

All windows, even non-opening ones, should be protected with bars, including those that are above the ground floor level. Doors and windows that open onto balconies should also be barred and, where there is no satisfactory perimeter protection for the property as a whole, the balconies themselves should be enclosed. Balconies provide convenient hiding places, which makes apartment blocks so attractive to burglars. Remember to close your curtains before switching on lights at night – it's easy to overlook this precaution, especially when you're high above the street. Also, since bars pose a fire risk, install smoke detectors.

Communicating

Stay in touch with your neighbours and try to remember as many names and faces as you can – especially of those who are on your floor. If you know your immediate neighbours well enough, suggest that you link your homes with a simply rigged battery-operated bell, to be operated when help is needed.

If your neighbour rings the bell, telephone him or her to check that he or she is safe. Agree on a simple code to indicate trouble – such as the number of the flat, in reverse. If there's no reply, call the police and explain that, although there is someone in the flat, nobody answers the telephone, despite your arrangement. It's important to agree on a response and to stick to the agreement – a misunderstanding could be embarrassing or even fatal.

If a stranger arrives at your main door, it is safest not to walk to the door to inspect the caller but rather to talk to him or her at the end of the intercom. Don't admit anybody you don't know.

Who is allowed in?

In addition to certain officials of local authorities and the state (see A Stranger at the Door, pp80-1), landlords and their agents have the right to enter and inspect their property, and this is usually a condition of the lease. However, the law expects this right to be exercised at 'reasonable' times – that is, during the daytime – and only after notice has been given to the tenant. On the other hand, it may be an offence for a tenant to persistently refuse to allow a landlord to enter the apartment.

Where repairs need to be carried out, the landlord and appropriate workers must be admitted – again, after giving reasonable notice. Your landlord does not have an automatic right to possess a key to gain entry to your flat, but it is not unreasonable for him or her to have one, or to ask for one if you change the lock. He or she would almost certainly be justified in entering without notice in an emergency, such as fire or flood. In ownership schemes, such as those under sectional title, rights similar to those of the landlord are vested in the management committee or body corporate.

A room to retire to

Many senior citizens live in retirement homes in which they have only a single room – sometimes shared with other residents – to call their own space. Even this space is regularly 'invaded' by domestic and nursing staff, family and friends. There is no hiding place in any room that the staff doesn't know about. This doesn't necessarily mean that they are dishonest, but they've probably had to search for valuable keepsakes that nervous residents hid somewhere in their rooms – and then forgot where they had put the items.

Even a lockable cupboard supplied in a room may not be secure enough for valuables such as jewellery or large amounts of money. The locks on most of these cupboards are of low security and, anyway, there are probably several duplicate keys in circulation in the home.

Most retirement homes have a safe – usually in the superintendent's office – in which residents may deposit small valuables, cash or a few documents, but it may be preferable for prospective residents to place their valuables and important documents with trusted relatives or friends, their attorney or a bank.

Keep just enough cash on hand to pay for newspapers, perhaps, or occasional gratuities, and keep it in a pocket or, when going to bed, placed with medicines or dentures. (Valuables placed under the pillow are inevitably going to be forgotten there one morning.)

Whether the room door is locked or not may depend on the institution's policy, but it's a good idea to ensure that, if ever help is needed in the room, people can get in without delay. The management will usually have considered this aspect and made suitable arrangements. Retirement homes generally have basic security measures installed, such as security gates and window bars. Whether you will be allowed to modify these depends on local policy, so check with the management before making any change.

SECURING THE BLOCK

It's rare to find all the desirable features of a well-secured apartment block, mostly because to introduce them would raise rentals or levies to an unacceptable level. You may have to compromise, but don't allow your safety measures to fall below what you regard as a reasonable standard, and try to get your fellow residents on board with your ideas.

Three levels of security

The security measures of any residential scheme, whether it's an apartment block or a retirement village, have three aspects. There's the scheme as a whole, including the common property and perimeter. There is the security that affects the individual residential units. And the third and most important aspect is the cooperation of other tenants or owners in ensuring the safety of all in your common home.

Residents' associations

Try to interest fellow residents in forming a safety committee, in addition to the association prescribed by law – such as a body corporate for a sectional title property. The powers of such a committee would depend on your own circumstances, but where decisions would involve residents in expense or inconvenience, it would be wise to seek the approval of the body corporate before trying to implement them.

The most satisfactory security arrangements are usually the simplest, such as getting to know the other residents in the block, or telling a neighbour when you're going out. An alarm linking adjacent flats provides a useful way to call for help when you need it, and can be rigged easily with a battery-powered bell (see A Place of Your Own, pp56-9).

If necessary, you and the other residents could club together to employ a guard or night watchman. The costs could be paid directly for this purpose or met through increased rentals or levies.

Outside looking in

Walls, fences and gates should be realistically secure, especially where on-site parking is provided, because of the vulnerability of drivers as they enter and leave (see The Way In, pp27-9 and The Front Line, pp24-6). If the main pedestrian exit opens more or less directly onto the pavement, a high perimeter wall close to the building may be unacceptable. The driveway, however, should still be properly secured. In the event of a power failure that interferes with the operation of an electric gate, residents should know where to find a manual override key.

Check the rest of the perimeter – that is, where the edge of the property is bounded by neighbouring properties. Every window that can be seen from outside should be barred (see A Place of Your Own, pp56-9). Window and door openings on most blocks are standardised, and you might be able to secure a discount for volume if all or most of the occupants agree to order bars at the same time.

The main entrance should have an intercom connected to each unit, or a security guard posted at the entrance with access to a telephone. Clearly numbered postboxes should be attached nearby so that the postman can reach them without having to open the gate. Residents should be able to retrieve their mail from within the security wall or gate.

Lightweight plastic downpipes will discourage attempts to climb them, and may be greased or wrapped with barbed wire or razor wire as an extra precaution. You could also coat pipes with anti-climb paint, starting about two metres above ground level to avoid accidental contact with passers-by. Anti-climb paint is a substance that retains its 'sticky' qualities, making the pipe difficult to climb, and marking anyone who comes into contact with it.

Public places

Lifts, stairs, undercover parking areas and laundries are places where you need to pay extra attention to security. You're safer in these places if you go with a companion, but this isn't always possible. Well-placed mirrors on stairs and in corridors will show you whether there's anyone around the next corner before you get to it. Mirrors are also useful for checking the inside of lifts, and seeing that there's nobody lurking on a landing.

If there's anyone in a lift whom you don't know or don't trust, or if the lift is going the wrong way for you, don't get in. Similarly, in the parking or laundry area, keep moving or turn around and leave if you feel threatened by someone there – you don't owe apologies or explanations, and it's better to lose your car or your washing than your life.

Through the safety committee, try to ensure that lights in all public places – the common property – are left on at night. If the parking area, especially, is separate from the residences, ask that it and the route from it to the residents' apartment doors be adequately lit all night.

Key versus card

Since it is harder for a housebreaker to duplicate a key card than a metal key, consider plastic key cards and electronic locks for external doors. Identical to credit cards, key cards are magnetically encoded to operate electronically controlled locks and are light and convenient to carry. The locks themselves are just as secure as mechanical locks. If you lose a key card, it is relatively easy and inexpensive to change the code of the lock and to issue new cards, whereas replacing a mechanical lock is prohibitively expensive.

CHECK LIST FOR A SECURE BLOCK

1. Main door with electronic door control and closed-circuit TV or intercom.

2. All other external doors key-operated and fitted with automatic locking devices.

3. Electronic door control to covered or underground parking areas.

4. The front door of every apartment or unit fitted with a peephole or door viewer and a good-quality chain or limiter.

5. Adequate and tamper-proof lighting switched on throughout the night in all parts of the common property.

6. Lifts with one or more mirrors placed to give a complete view of their interior, and to give alighting lift passengers a complete view of the landing.

7. Exterior lighting linked to a detector that switches on if anyone approaches the building other than by the path.

8. Adequate anti-fire precautions, including a secure escape route.

9. Postboxes on the outside of the external doors.

10. Specific people delegated to control these security measures.

TRESPASSERS WILL BE PROSECUTED

BEYOND THE LIGHTS

Living outside a built-up area – on a farm or in a seasonal resort, for instance – requires both self-reliance and dependence on neighbours. A highly efficient communication and response system is also essential, as is a sound relationship with the local police.

Getting together

Start by speaking to your immediate neighbours, several of the nearest permanent residents, and members of the local ratepayers' association. Once you have agreed on the sort of system you want to establish (see You and Your Neighbourhood, pp16-17), explain your intentions to your local police station commander.

The basic scheme

The emphasis of a watch scheme is on improved security and awareness of people's movements in your area. In the countryside, you should include firespotting. The area itself may be determined by existing local authority boundaries, police patrol zones or existing units, such as an agricultural settlement.

When members of the scheme believe themselves or their property to be in danger, they contact a controller who alerts and dispatches a reaction team of perhaps two or three members of the scheme and informs the police. Depending on the size of the area and its situation, first contact might be with the police.

The reaction team makes sure the caller is safe and, if necessary, requests support. These messages, too, are relayed to the police.

Staying in touch

Set up a communications network involving all the members, with a base station that is manned at all times. Citizen band (CB) radios are useful and are available as both base sets and portable sets. You can apply through a post office for a frequency.

In areas with good reception, cellular phones can be used. Many models can be preset to dial an emergency number at the touch of a single key. Limit use of the network – overfamiliarity may lead to failure to recognise an emergency call – but also make regular checks to ensure each user's safety. Check signal strengths to as many sites as possible, to work out where signals can be neither transmitted nor received satisfactorily, and make a note of these 'dead' areas. Keep spare batteries for CB radios and cellphones.

Securing your home

Apply the same basic security measures to your home as those used in towns, including bars, safety gates and alarms. Enclose your home and garage with an electrified fence or a high-security fence wired to an alarm. Fit a pedestrian gate and a vehicle gate, and do not distribute keys among your staff. Rig an intercom at the gate and closed-circuit TV between the gate and your house. Floodlighting is essential, illuminating the buildings and the fence, and should be kept on all night. If crops, trees or hedges provide hiding places close to the enclosed area, prune them or cut them down. Rows of cactus, kei apple or sisal, however, can make an efficient additional barrier. Guard dogs, inside and outside the house, are essential in remote areas. But be aware too of night sounds, such as the cry of a disturbed plover, which are often a reliable warning.

Strangers

Put up signs throughout your area, prohibiting trespassing, and encourage the staff on your property to report all strangers. As soon as you can, locate the strangers, but do not confront them on your own. Offer whatever reasonable help they need to get them on their way, and tell them that their presence has been reported by several people. Knowing that they have been observed, most strangers with bad intent will almost certainly move on.

Establish a time for dealing with legitimate callers. Let it be known, for instance, that you don't sell livestock, or 'talk business' after certain hours, and adhere strictly to this rule.

Staff security

Explain the principles of sharing the responsibilities for security to your staff. If it is feasible and if most of your staff want it, enclose their homes with a security fence and gate. Make sure you know who lives on your property and who visits your staff regularly. If there appears to be trouble in the staff quarters, get other members of the Neighbourhood Watch scheme to go with you – don't investigate on your own.

DRAMA IN REAL LIFE

Slaughter of the innocents

The Western Cape is famous for its flowers that, every spring, draw thousands of people to view this colourful abundance. Among the visitors were a tourist, Ms Smith, and her daughter, who were staying with widowed Mrs Olivier in her rural guesthouse. A male friend of Mrs Olivier joined them for a late supper. But they were destined not to finish it. Five men suddenly burst into the house and violently assaulted the occupants, leaving Mrs Olivier, Ms Smith and her child stabbed to death, and the friend seriously injured, but feigning death. When the gang had left, taking money and valuables, firearms and a motor vehicle, the friend was able to telephone the police and raise the alarm.

Police comment: This incident seemed all the more shocking for having taken place in a rural area. But because of the relatively low level of security in many country districts, this is exactly where it was most likely to happen. In this case, a window had been left open through which the assailants entered. Barred windows, security gates or securely locked outside doors, and an alert dog in the house should be seriously considered for any rural dwelling, including holiday homes.

HIGH-RISK LIVING

Some of the items you should have ready to hand

◆ Fire-extinguishers (dry powder type suitable for general inflammable materials, oil fires, electrical fires).
◆ Fire-smothering blanket (not the old type that is made of asbestos fibre).
◆ Two-way radio with a link to neighbours or another selected source of assistance, or a cellphone (fully charged and with a list of call signs or numbers).
◆ Powerful torch with fresh spare batteries.
◆ First-aid kit.

The general principles of home security apply in high-risk areas too, since criminals have no respect for rank, rights or property. But communities of ordinary people fighting crime together have had some success in reducing the crime rate in these areas.

If you live in a high-risk area, you could be doing yourself a favour by getting together with neighbours and the police to reduce crime.

Favourite targets

While the activities of criminals threaten almost the entire population, the favourite targets are at opposite ends of the spectrum of earnings and privilege. The possessions of the wealthy – especially their jewellery and motor vehicles – have a high cash value but are usually well protected. On the other hand, although profits from crime in the townships may be relatively small, the turnover is great, and there are fewer risks involved. Where motor vehicles are concerned, you're often on your own when criminals strike, but you can lessen the risk (see On the Road, pp94-121).

High-risk areas

Crime tends to thrive in the presence of almost any form of social or economic instability. High-risk areas for crime include areas of ethnic unrest and violence; areas of gang activity; industrial areas, where unsuccessful job-seekers and others may be tempted into opportunistic crime; economically depressed areas, where incomes are marginal and unemployment is high; remote or isolated areas (see Beyond the Lights, pp62-3); areas of political unrest and intolerance.

Developed urban areas

If you live in a well-established suburb, see that your home is fitted with the basic protection of security gates and bars, and a perimeter wall or fence. Fit shutters to windows on the street frontage at least, and, in addition, fit plastic safety film to the window-panes (see Windows, Bars and Shutters, pp46-9). The plastic film will make the panes opaque during the day while letting in the light, but remember to draw the curtains before switching on any lights because interior lights make the film transparent, allowing a view in.

You may need to improve perimeter lighting, unless there is sufficient spill from lighting at doors and windows. Check the intensity of lighting around the whole house, not just on the main road frontage. Consider keeping at least one large dog.

Comings and goings

The strictest gate control is required, which may mean installing gates that can be opened only by remote control or by physically unlocking them with a key. You may need to fit an intercom or a bell at the gate. Ideally, gates should not be unlocked or opened unless you're sure that all doors to the house are locked. Whenever the gate is opened, a responsible member of the household should watch it until it is closed again, to ensure that criminals do not seize this opportunity to slip onto the property.

Keep clear

Keep your garden as uncluttered as you can, with no ready-made hiding places behind trees or shrubs. If adjoining or nearby plots are overgrown and likely to attract illicit occupation, appeal to the owners or tenants to keep them clear. If this fails, contact your local authority who may be able to exert pressure.

Informal settlements

If you move into an informal settlement, unless there are obvious disadvantages, try to select a site as far upwind as possible (to reduce the fire hazard), and at least a block or two away from vehicle routes. If you arrive in the settlement with friends, settle as a group, so that you already have the nucleus of a community of people who will be prepared to help one another. Don't travel alone, but walk to shops, stations and taxi ranks with people you know. Don't keep more money than you need on yourself or in your home. Open a bank account and ask your employer to pay your salary directly into it.

Intimidation

In areas dominated by gangs, residents frequently receive demands of money for 'protection'. In practice you do not receive protection, but the gang then undertakes not to demand more money until a certain date, or may agree not to molest your family or burn down your house if you pay regularly. It is virtually impossible for law-abiding people to successfully confront a gang of established, armed criminals, on their own. Instead, try to mobilise your community, the police and all levels of government to act against gangs.

Intimidation leaves individuals feeling a great deal of pent-up resentment and rage towards the gangsters, against whom they are helpless. This also leads to feelings of guilt, inadequacy, despair and depression, and withdrawal from the social round, even within the family. Talk to your friends about your own experiences, even the negative ones, and encourage them to talk about theirs. As you help one another to recover, you can plan a strategy for the future.

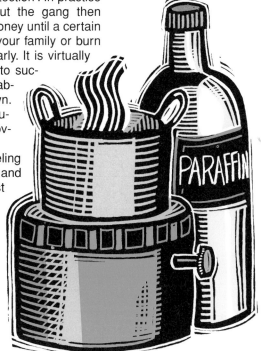

KEEPING IT SAFE

Before you buy a safe to keep in your home, consider several things – apart from the purchase price. First, can you get the safe into your home without attracting too much attention? Do you have a suitable place in which to keep it? Where are you going to keep the keys to the safe? If an armed burglar got into your home and demanded that you open the safe, what would you do?

Do you need a safe?

The law requires that if you own a firearm (see Firearms, pp258-65) it must be kept in a safe place or carried with you. The law does not insist that a firearm be kept in a safe itself, but the responsibility of owning a lethal weapon requires that a gun safe should be seriously considered.

Safes specifically designed for storing firearms – from a dozen or so rifles to a single pocket pistol – are widely available, and generally have a shelf or other space suitable for small valuable items, such as jewellery. Many collectors, who like to keep their collections close by or whose collections require regular maintenance, purchase safes or even separate strongroom doors to be built into specially constructed rooms. What you want to store will dictate the size of your safe. The intended contents may also determine whether you need a fireproof safe (for documents or stamps, for instance), an attack-resistant safe, or one that combines both properties.

Sooner or later the fact that you have a safe is going to be noticed, word will get around and eventually reach the ears of someone who will be interested to see (and perhaps be determined to take) what your safe contains. Firearms apart, if your valuables can be stored safely in some other manner, you probably don't need a safe. Check with your insurance company. It may prefer that you keep your valuables in some other safe place, such as a bank vault.

New or second-hand?

Old safes look impressively robust, but the materials many are built from will not stand up to a determined assault by a modern burglar. The locks on second-hand safes – especially on those made before the 1940s – are of relatively low security and may lack the protective, reinforced steel plates of some later models. However, a qualified locksmith may be able to upgrade the cabinet and replace the lock to provide adequate security for a relatively modest price. At the very least, a seven-lever lock (or a combination lock) should be fitted.

Where to put it

'Out of sight' is a good tip to remember. Consider your roof space, or a reinforced cupboard under the stairs, or the cellar or attic, if you have one. Some safes are designed for installation in other, equally well-concealed hiding places, such as under the floor or within an inside wall.

Because most freestanding safes are extremely heavy, they should be stood only on a firm, sound floor – preferably concrete. They can be concealed by being placed in built-in cupboards, disguised as items of furniture or even as air-conditioning units, in the belief that a burglar is unlikely to want to look inside an air conditioner.

Any safe that is not actually purpose-built into its surroundings should be securely bolted down. Many tall gun safes need to be mounted within a specially built, close-fitting alcove, and bolted to the rear wall and floor. This type has an armoured door and a cabinet of ordinary heavy-gauge steel.

Underfloor safes

For storage of smallish items, an underfloor safe embedded in concrete and covered with a carpet and an item of furniture is probably the most secure. Unless you have a large amount of goods to be hidden away, consider a four-brick wall safe placed in the floor, rather than an underfloor safe. The floor cavity needed for the wall safe is shallower than for a proper underfloor safe and is less of an undertaking to chisel out. If you have a wooden floor, the safe can be placed beneath it on a prepared platform, with reinforced concrete built up around the safe.

The main disadvantage of an underfloor safe is that it is relatively inconvenient to use, since you have to move everything away from it before you can open it.

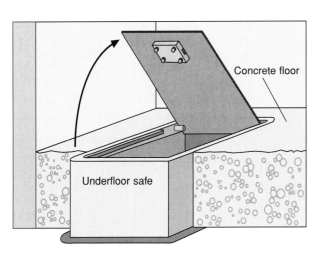

Concrete floor

Underfloor safe

To fit a wall safe as an underfloor safe into a concrete floor, chisel a cavity into the floor 25 millimetres wider and deeper than the safe itself. Lay concrete at the base of the cavity and place the safe on top of it. Then pack concrete around the sides of the safe. No part of the safe should project above the floor level. When the concrete is dry, cover with a carpet and a piece of furniture.

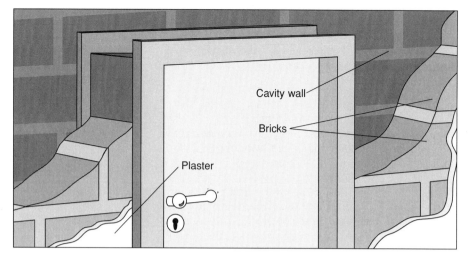

Cavity wall

Bricks

Plaster

To fit a wall safe into a cavity wall, make a space 25 millimetres larger on all sides than the safe itself. Remove the plaster and the bricks. Mix up some concrete and place a layer on the bottom of the cavity. Place the safe onto the wet concrete. Cement the sides of the safe in place (first protecting the hinges with masking tape). When dry, neaten the edges with plaster or smooth cement. Cover with curtains or a picture.

Wall safes

Wall safes are ideal for storing handguns and, depending on the size of the safe, items such as jewellery and documents. In deciding where to place the safe, make sure that no electrical conduits or waterpipes are embedded in the wall. In most homes, the only suitable walls to fit a safe into are outside walls or internal support walls, with a thickness of at least 230 millimetres (for a solid, double-skin wall), or at least 280 millimetres for a cavity wall. Wall safes can be concealed behind curtains or pictures.

Do not place a wall safe closer than one brick-length or 250 millimetres to a window opening because it may then be easy for a burglar to dig out. It may also not be possible to anchor a safe securely in a wall that is built of cement blocks.

Safe disguises

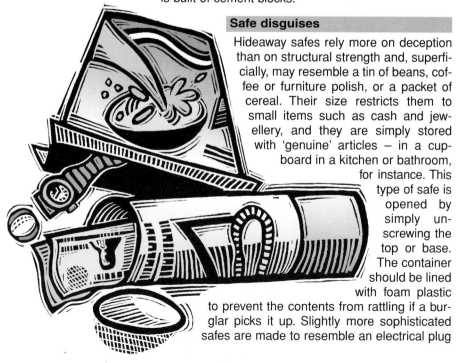

Hideaway safes rely more on deception than on structural strength and, superficially, may resemble a tin of beans, coffee or furniture polish, or a packet of cereal. Their size restricts them to small items such as cash and jewellery, and they are simply stored with 'genuine' articles – in a cupboard in a kitchen or bathroom, for instance. This type of safe is opened by simply unscrewing the top or base. The container should be lined with foam plastic to prevent the contents from rattling if a burglar picks it up. Slightly more sophisticated safes are made to resemble an electrical plug socket or power point and are recessed into a wall where they are well disguised. This type is usually fitted with an adequate lock.

Mark your valuables

Marking your property is easily and inexpensively done. The advantages of doing this are that your property will be more difficult to dispose of, so a burglar may be reluctant to take it, and if it is recovered, the police will be able to trace you and return it. Permanent marking pens, engraving pens, electric engraving tools, die stamps and invisible ink (which shows up under ultraviolet light) are some of the materials that can be used. As a minimum, use your dialling code and telephone number as your identifying mark. If your phone number changes, place an 'X' in front of it and mark the item with the new number.

Before marking insured items, check with your insurance company, in case they have a preferred system, and never mark antiques or valuable collectables without first consulting an expert in the relevant field. Keep a written list of these and other items, such as TV sets or VCRs, recording the manufacturer's serial number as well. Colour photographs of valuables may also play an important part in reclaiming stolen goods that are later recovered.

Hiding the key

Place the key to your safe in an inventive hiding place. Unless you keep a firearm in the safe, it shouldn't matter how long it takes you to unlock it, so your hiding place can be really devious. You could hide the key in a book from a bookshelf (being careful not to use a prominent volume, such as the only hard-bound book in a row of paperbacks). Glue half the pages together and, with a sharp knife, cut out a section in which to lay the key. Return the book to your shelf.

A combination number is most likely to go undetected if you write it in your book of telephone numbers. If the safe contains a stamp collection, for example, you could enter the combination under P for Phil, after a dialling code to ensure a realistic number of digits.

If a burglar finds the safe he will certainly demand the key. The safest course is to give it to him. However, if you think it might be worth the chance, or if you need to play for time, say that the key is at the bank, or with your brother (or father, or son, depending on your age), who will arrive soon. Offer him something else instead, perhaps something he hasn't yet noticed, and persuade him that the things inside the safe are not readily saleable. If he still demands the key, don't try your luck any further.

FOOLING SOME OF THE PEOPLE

Housebreakers prefer homes they can enter and leave quickly, preferably when no-one is there. Make them believe that there may be several people at home when in fact there are none at all, and they'll probably move on.

Helping hands

Electronic switches and circuitry linked to timers, especially to control lighting, radios or the TV, can realistically suggest someone is at home when there is not. But a truly convincing deception needs human assistance. Get the help of a trusted friend or neighbour, or engage the services of a house-sitter or a security patrol. Before employing professional caretakers, however, try to obtain a recommendation from someone whose opinion you value.

As you were

Avoid establishing patterns that let people know you aren't home. Your absence becomes particularly obvious when the stoep light is left on all day, curtains stay drawn and the gate is never unlocked.

An inexpensive time switch or a daylight-activated switch can be wired to control a normal pattern of lights indoors and out. Two timer circuits are even more convincing. But try hard to make them believable – don't leave a 10-minute gap between one light switching off and another turning on when it takes you only three minutes to walk from one to the other. Rather make one light switch on a few minutes before the other switches off.

If it follows your usual pattern, ask your neighbour to unlock your gate in the morning and lock it again before nightfall, at the same time that he or she opens or closes the curtains, and empties your letter box.

Keeping up appearances

Most of us go on holiday during summer, the season when gardens grow most vigorously and require most attention. Organise – at least – the cutting of the lawn. If someone can be persuaded (or hired) to water the garden regularly, their presence will reinforce the impression that your home is occupied. However, the arrival of a vehicle advertising 'garden services' or a team of uniformed workers may be a giveaway, so, once again, your friend or neighbour is the ideal temporary gardener. A few flowerpots placed in the garden and occasionally moved about, and a bag of garden refuse outside your house on collection day, will suggest that someone is home.

Beware of which dog?

A sign warning of dogs on the premises will almost always cause a burglar to think twice about entering.

ABSENCE CHECK LIST

1. Advise your neighbour or a close friend when you will be away.

2. If necessary, engage the service of a recommended house-sitter or security patrol, and a garden service.

3. Notify the police and your alarm company that you will be away, and for how long. Give them contact numbers.

4. Make sure that someone will clear the letter box, open and close the curtains, and lock and unlock the gate daily.

5. If you and your neighbour take the same newspaper, get him to suspend his – he can read yours.

6. If animals can't be cared for at home, book them into a pets' home, giving a friend's or neighbour's address instead of your own.

7. See that windows, doors, and their locks are in good condition.

8. Check that time switches and other automatic or electronic apparatus are correctly connected and set.

9. Soundproof the telephone.

10. Don't discuss your holiday until it's over.

However, if he rings the door bell or knocks incessantly and doesn't hear some sound from the dog, he'll know there is no dog. Consider buying an alarm that is triggered by ringing the bell or tampering with a window, for instance, which sets off prerecorded sounds of a large dog barking. The sequence of sounds available, and the volumes, are quite realistic.

You could also try recording your own or a neighbour's dog, and connect the resultant tape, through the alarm or door-bell switch, to an amplifying system. If you have a real dog, and it can be properly looked after on your property while you're away, let it stay home as a deterrent.

Advertising your departure

Notices in newspaper columns frequently ask for companions to share driving or fuel expenses between major cities on a particular date. Anyone responding to such an advertisement can easily discover the advertiser's name and address and already knows exactly when the home is likely to be unoccupied. If you advertise, give the address of a friend you know will not be going away, and interview responders there.

Telephone time

Before leaving your home, turn down the volume of your telephone – the ringing may attract attention and any criminals hearing it will know that you're not home. Then pack your telephone into a box (a shoe box is usually suitable), tape the handset to the base, put the lid on and cover the box with cushions. This should deaden the ring completely.

If you disconnect your telephone, it might be reported as being out of order. This may result in Telkom officials calling and leaving notes on your door or gate, which will inform passers-by that you are away. If you're using an answering machine, don't ask callers to give the date on which they call – just let them hear your usual message that you'll contact them later.

Pack up and go

If you're leaving on a motoring holiday, pack the car just before you leave, out of sight of passers-by to attract as little attention as possible (see Before You Leave, pp124-5). While you're doing last-minute checks in the the house, your partner (and children) can go for a walk. Drive away, but return after five or ten minutes to take a supermarket bag into the house. (It doesn't matter what's in the bag, but curious people should think it might be groceries.)

Disconnect the door bell, to confuse a criminal who might ring to check whether somebody is at home. Hearing nothing at all, he may conclude that the bell is not working, and so won't know whether you're in or not. Now lock up and leave, without the bag. Pick up the rest of your family and set off on your holiday.

woof woof

PEOPLE AT WORK

Many burglars are skilled and conscientious operators – they need to be, because their careers, income,
freedom and, sometimes, their lives depend on it.
They usually do their job well, and their job is to steal
your property. They are callous and cowardly criminals, and are not to be admired. Most of them are
capable of appalling violence – against your person
and your property.

Matters of economics

As a general rule, the housebreaker who is prepared
to force doors and windows, twist bars and maim dogs
so that he can get inside your home is a career professional. The opportunist or solo operator who makes
a quick grab and slips out again, perhaps within much
less than a minute, may have some other job, probably informal, and almost certainly very poorly paid.
The professional, too, is often poorly paid, and may
work for a syndicate. The team, usually of three men,
that steals a TV set, for instance, may receive as little
as R30 to share, while the TV set is sold for as much
as R200. When they take the TV set, however, they
probably also take a video recorder, a microwave
oven, a music centre, a camera and accessories, and
leather jackets. In addition, they may remove some
goods for their own account – alcohol, food, clothing,
and expensive luggage in which to carry their loot.
Their profits – and your losses – soon mount up.

Making the choice

Professional housebreakers keep their eyes open for
anything that suggests a house may be empty. A
funeral notice, for example, may tell a burglar exactly
when the occupants of the house the deceased lived
in will be out. A simple act of deception and an innocent question to a neighbour will help the burglar identify the house.

A professional housebreaker may keep a home under observation for several days or longer. He will note
the security precautions – if any – and get to know the
residents' movements. His observations soon tell him
exactly when will be the best time to strike.

An opportunist, on the other hand, will simply go up
to the front door and knock or ring the bell. If the door
is answered, he has his story ready. But if nobody
answers and no dog barks, he sets off to explore the
property for an easy way in. He may be a self-
employed opportunist, or he may be scouting for a
professional.

Timing

The time to break in is when there's nobody at home.
Most break-ins take place on a weekday during daylight hours, when people are at work, out shopping or

at school, and their leaving and returning movements tend to be routine and repetitive. Break-ins during the weekend take place mainly at night. The holiday season, when families are away from home, is also a busy time for housebreakers. On New Year's Eve, for instance, any house that's empty at 10.30 at night is almost certain to be empty until at least 15 minutes past midnight. Weather plays a role, too, in burglaries – fewer burglars are out during rainy weather than when it is fine.

In and out

Housebreakers want to know their likely route even before they pass the perimeter fence. If you're probably going to arrive home by the front gate, they like to have an emergency exit at the back or at the side.

The first phase is the arrival of their vehicle, which may be a sedan, a minibus or a light pick-up truck with a tent or canopy. To legitimise parking outside your home, they may feign engine trouble and raise the bonnet. At least one of the break-in team stays with the vehicle while the others – commonly two of them – go in. They can break a windowpane and kick in most window bars or front doors 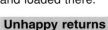 (because they are inadequately made or badly installed) within a minute. Once inside, they try to open a door leading directly to their escape route (most homes have duplicate keys lying about inside). This route may also enable them to load their vehicle quickly. If there are many worthwhile objects, the vehicle may even be reversed into the driveway, and loaded there.

Unhappy returns

Once they've had a really close look at your home's defences from the inside, and inspected your possessions, burglars are quite likely to return within a week or two, so make good any damage as well and as soon as you can. Your second burglars may even be a different team. Word travels fast in the underworld and, having heard that your home is an easy mark, other criminals may decide to try their luck.

Tools of the trade

Most housebreakers carry no incriminating tools such as bunches of skeleton keys or angle grinders. Any hardware they might need – such as a crowbar – is usually passed off as being part of their vehicle's tool kit. Don't make their job easier, though, by leaving your own tools unsecured or lying about for them to use. Ladders, spades, axes, wheelbarrows – almost anything can be put to illicit use.

SIGNS OF A BREAK-IN

If you're at all observant, you'll know you've been broken into even before you let yourself in. It's important for you not only to see, but to register and to associate what you see with possible events. Arrive home alert and on the lookout – the time to relax is when you're inside and find that all's well.

Getting into the habit

Check the outside of your home whenever you arrive there. Start as you approach your gate, or even from the other side of the road, so that an intruder will be less likely to know he's been spotted. If the conditions we describe here are the ones that greet you on your return home, presume that there's an intruder in your home, and get away. Walk, don't run. Don't be tempted to go in after the intruder: he's alert, almost certainly accompanied and probably armed. And as a professional, he's more likely to use his weapon than you are.

Silent signal: fold a piece of paper concertina fashion, with a protruding flap, and close the window over it so that only the tiny flap sticks outside the window. If the flap is not there when you return home, you know that someone has opened the window in your absence.

The street

Note unfamiliar vehicles outside or close to your home, especially those with a large carrying capacity, such as minibuses, trucks or bakkies. The driver may be at the wheel or in a conveniently dark corner, acting as sentry. If burglars have been (and gone again), they may have dropped goods on the pavement or in the roadway, such as an item of clothing or jewellery, a video cassette or even an entire bag of stolen items.

The perimeter

In most cases, burglars on their way in will close gates, doors, shutters and windows that can be seen from the road or from an occupied neighbouring home. They rarely lock them, however, because they like to have readily available escape routes for use in an emergency. But when they depart, they may leave the exit they took open. So the open gate you see on returning home is not necessarily the work of a hawker or vagrant. If you didn't leave it open (and you shouldn't have done) treat it as suspicious. Look out for telltale marks on walls, damage to fences and new holes in hedges.

The garden

Look for broken plants and indented footprints in flower beds, or tracks of mud or earth on paths and lawns. Tools, implements and even piles of bricks or stones, especially near windows, are strong suggestions that you may have had or still have an intruder.

When an open door means 'No Entry!'

From her split-level home in a South Coast village, Susan Gordon noticed one morning that an adjoining plot was being cleared of bush. She didn't think of it at the time, but anyone on that plot had a good view of the back of her house, including the garage. Apart from the garage, which was open much of the time, all ground-floor windows and doors were securely barred.

When Susan Gordon drove off to a lunch date, she closed but did not lock the garage door. She came home to find the ladder from the garage leaning against the wall below one of the upper windows, which had been forced open. Also, the front door was open. Aware that she probably had been burgled, Susan entered her home to find

out what she had lost. Only small, valuable items had been stolen – together with a suitcase in which to carry them. Police questioned the workers on the plot next door, and an arrest was later made.

Police comment: With strangers in the area, Susan Gordon should have practised extra vigilance, especially with regard to keeping the garage door closed and, certainly, locking it when she went out. But seeing the front door open on her return, she should never have entered the house. The burglars might still have been at work and armed. Rather, she should have gone to a neighbour and called the police from the safety of the neighbour's house.

Household goods lying about the garden, such as food or clothing – even if you don't recognise them as your own – are other pointers.

Windows

A shutter that's been left open in your absence is a giveaway. If there are signs of damage to wood or paintwork, especially where two shutters meet, check that they are still locked. In most lighting conditions, glass missing from a windowpane usually shows up as a non-reflective area, but double-check by looking for glass fragments near and under the windows. Where an entire pane has been removed, this may be difficult to detect until you're close to the window.

Damage to security bars is usually obvious, and most often takes the form of a section that has been pushed in, from a lower corner. A set of bars on a particular window may even have been removed.

Security gates and doors

Unless duplicate keys have been used, opened gates and doors will almost certainly show some damage. The most common evidence of forced entry is the splintering of wood caused by the insertion of a bar or lever between a door and its frame, in the vicinity of the lock, or the broken panel of a door that has been kicked in. Typically, gates and doors won't have been closed when the burglars left your house, because having been forced open they may then be difficult or even impossible to close.

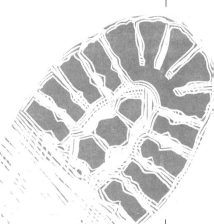

HANDLING A BURGLARY

A break-in is a traumatic event in anyone's life. More than the mere entry of a thief into a building which may be your home, and the loss of your property, it is a violation of yourself and your space, and of a residual faith in human nature that you probably didn't realise you possessed. Anger and a desire for vengeance are common reactions, together with a feeling of insecurity in your own home. The anger and the insecurity will pass. Vengeance, in the form of justice, must be left up to the police and the courts of law.

The discovery

On no account should you enter your home until you're certain that the intruders have left. If you're in doubt, first go to the safety of a neighbour's or friend's house, then call the police and report your suspicions. Your instincts may urge you to go in, but there's nothing to be gained by not waiting for the police, so enter only to prevent further damage – from fire, for instance, or flooding.

Don't touch anything on which intruders might have left their fingerprints, such as doors, door frames and door locks, windows or any other appliance or article they might have used or opened, or that's not where you remember having left it.

DRAMA IN REAL LIFE

Warning from an open side gate

Returning home from dropping her children at a school several kilometres away, Rose Johnson was annoyed to find that the municipal refuse collectors had left her side gate open. At least, that was what she assumed, until she noticed that the refuse bag was still where she had left it. Her suspicions aroused, she walked to the corner of her house and peered down the side that faces a large playing field. All the shutters should have been closed, but those on the furthest window were open. Not quite believing that her house could have been broken into, Ms Johnson walked to the window and saw that it had been forced. On her daughter's bed, open suitcases were untidily piled with clothes. The colour TV set lay beside the suitcases. Thinking that the intruders must have fled on her approach, she turned to go to the front door, but, as she did so, glimpsed a movement inside

the house. Ms Johnson hurried to her neighbour and telephoned the police who, although they arrived promptly, found the house empty and some of Ms Johnson's goods gone.

Police comment: Refuse collection day, when there's more activity than usual on the street, is a good day for housebreakers. Ms Johnson's open gate alone was not proof that anything was wrong, but the open shutters certainly were. She should have gone for help immediately, rather than risk confrontation by looking in at the window. The shock of discovering something wrong – like a burglary – often overrides ordinary good judgment. Work out a plan of action and practise it mentally every time you come home. Then, if the unexpected or unpleasant does occur, you'll be more likely to do the right thing.

No matter what disorder you find, resist the temptation to clean up until the police have finished their inspection. Don't scrub walls or wash floors, for instance, or you may be destroying valuable evidence that the police might be able to use.

The loss

Advise your insurance company of what has happened as soon as you can, even if the police have not yet assigned you a docket or incident number. You can always phone the number through later.

Make a preliminary list of the items missing and check it against the list of contents that you drew up when applying for your householder's insurance (see Insuring Possessions, pp92-3).

Your insurer will send you a claim form to be completed. Find out when it must be returned and, in the meantime, add any items to your preliminary list as you become aware that they are missing or broken. It may take months or years for you to discover exactly what has been taken, and, of course, by then it will be too late to lodge a claim, so take as much time as you're allowed in compiling your list. Don't forget to claim for damage to locks, doors, windows and burglar bars, or for damage to paintwork, furnishings and rugs or carpets.

It may aid your claim if you can supply the insurance company with photographs of the inside of your home showing any of the objects that have been stolen, as well as photos of the damage caused during the recent burglary.

Making good the damage

The first and sadly obvious lesson is that your security wasn't good enough. Once the police have finished their inspection, set about restoring your security measures as a matter of some urgency.

Replace damaged bars, locks, doors or windows, or reinforce them until you are able to obtain new forms of security. Repairing damaged fastenings is unlikely to give a finished product that is even as secure as the previous one.

Ask yourself if the bars themselves were inadequate, or was the attachment at fault? Steel bars or rods of 10 millimetres are the thinnest you should use. If the old bars were attached to wooden window frames, this time round have the new bars made so they can be bolted into the wall. Where locks were forced, replace them with the best you can afford.

What went wrong?

Try to work out what information the intruder had, and how he obtained it, or if he simply improvised as he went along. Security is not a matter of bolts and bars alone, but of defence in depth, of deceiving the criminal and of trying, at all times, to have someone in the house or at the end of an alarm signal on the alert.

EMERGENCY CHECK LIST

YOU'VE BEEN BROKEN INTO –
WHAT TO DO

1. Get away at once.

2. Telephone the SAPS Flying Squad at once; their number is 10111.

3. Give details to the SAPS slowly and carefully. Tell them:
◆ your name
◆ your address
◆ that you suspect the intruders are still in your home.

4. Do exactly what the police tell you to do.

5. Watch the exits of your home, asking neighbours to help you.

6. Write down descriptions and registration numbers of unfamiliar vehicles parked near your home.

7. Write down the description of anyone leaving your home, including details of:
◆ vehicles used
◆ direction taken.

8. Wait for the police. By all means flag them down, but don't get in their way. Again, do exactly as they tell you.

UNWANTED GUESTS

The worst nightmares are those that come true. One of these is waking up or returning home to find an intruder in your home. However you react, your most important aim must be to survive the encounter without serious injury.

First reactions

When you first face an unsuspected intruder you are likely to feel fright and aggression. It's all too easy (and very natural) to shout or cry out, but don't. This reaction may frighten the intruder into using violence.

Regard all intruders as dangerous. They may be desperate to escape and avoid being recognised, and you may just be in the way. Worse, an intruder may be under the influence of alcohol or drugs.

If you can, get out immediately and look for assistance or lock yourself in your 'safer section' (see Windows, Bars and Shutters, pp46-9) where you can phone for help or attract the attention of neighbours. If neither course is possible, and you're left with the intruder, take a deep breath and stay cool.

Seeing it through

Treat the intruder as an equal. Don't be loud, high-handed, bossy or servile. Don't plead with him, except perhaps as a last resort to prevent assault. Keep your hands where he can see them and don't make sudden movements. Don't crowd him, and try to avoid all physical contact. Cooperate and tell him what he wants to know. Deceiving him – about the whereabouts of keys, for instance – may lead to heightened aggression. Depending on the circumstances, though, it might be worthwhile to say that you're expecting a visitor soon.

DRAMA IN REAL LIFE

The eye at the keyhole

Marion and a friend shared a house in a bustling Garden Route town, where a series of burglaries in the district had made her nervous of being alone at night. The house seemed adequately barred, but even so Marion took the precaution of having an extra telephone jack installed in her bedroom. When her friend was away, it became her habit to take the telephone to her bedroom at night, and to sleep with her bedroom door locked and a light left burning in the passage. Alone one night (or so she thought), Marion awoke to hear soft noises in the house. Very quietly she removed the door key from the keyhole and timidly peered through, to see an eye staring back at her from the other side of the door. Shaken, but keeping her head through her terror, she phoned her brother, who lived close by, and the police. In the few minutes before they arrived, she moved a bedside cupboard against the door. Her brother and the police arrived simultaneously, and caught the intruder as he fled.

Police comment: Marion's sensible precautions saved her from an experience that might have been far more serious than housebreaking. However, the apparently 'adequately barred' house did not keep out the intruder, and she should remedy the gaps in security.

Never use a dummy firearm, and be very careful before claiming to have a real firearm when you haven't. Firearms sometimes spark violence, which you should try to avoid, especially in the absence of the protection that a real one might offer.

Call for help – by yelling through a window or pressing a panic button, for example – only if you can do so without attracting the intruder's attention, or if you feel that you are already in grave danger of assault. Whether or not you should attack an intruder depends entirely on your strength and skill, and on seizing a favourable opportunity. Try it only if you're sure you'll win, or as a last resort.

Cooperate!

Unless he's already seen them, the intruder will almost certainly want to know where you keep your gun (whether you have one or not), jewellery and money. Show him what you think he'll find anyway – burglars know all the usual hiding places.

If you're with other occupants, you're likely to be herded together, possibly tied up, and then locked in a room, usually a bathroom or toilet. If this gives you access to a secret panic button, use it only if you think that being caught won't worsen your position. Block the door to prevent his re-entry if you can, but not if the intruder has a member of your family hostage.

When the intruder leaves, stay out of his way. Don't chase him or follow him – there may be an accomplice outside, just waiting for you.

Rude awakening

Some people have slept right through burglaries, some have pretended to be asleep and been left undisturbed. Others, however, have been assaulted. If you're in bed when you become aware that there's an intruder, consider your chances of escape.

Start by calling drowsily to an imaginary male companion. If you're a woman, try to ensure that you can cover yourself from neck to ankles, preferably with a blanket, so that the intruder's attention will not be diverted from burglary to your person. Never make a sudden or silent appearance, except as part of an escape tactic that you are certain can't fail.

Afterwards

When the intruder has left, call for help. Check each member of your household for injuries. Don't move anyone who may have broken bones or who has been struck severely on the head. Keep them calm, keep them warm, and assure them that help is on the way. Memorise the intruder's appearance and anything else about him – scars or gestures, for instance, or unfamiliar words or expressions that he may have used. Write it all down. And don't touch anything that the intruder may have touched – he may just have left his fingerprints behind.

EMERGENCY CHECK LIST

FACE TO FACE WITH AN INTRUDER – WHAT TO DO

1. Get out, if you can do so safely.

2. If you can't get out, lock yourself in a safe room with a telephone.

3. Keep calm, stay cool.

4. Cooperate with the intruder.

5. Be observant, and make a note of his voice and appearance.

6. Call for help only to avert serious assault.

7. Don't block his exits.

8. Don't try to follow when he leaves.

9. Call for help as soon as you can after he leaves.

A STRANGER AT THE DOOR

There are several officials who have the right to enter your premises, but nobody, under ordinary circumstances, may enter your home without showing you positive identification. Most criminals don't look like criminals, and many of them can be very persuasive. That's what makes them so dangerous.

Answering the door

You can identify callers by recognising their voices, or by seeing them through the viewer (see Doors – a Line of Defence, pp40-3) or a side window. If they pass a preliminary inspection (bear in mind that a gang could use a woman to get you to open the door), check that the door chain or limiter is engaged, and open the door only slightly, even if you have a security gate. Whether you open the door further or not depends on the visitor's mission and credentials.

Children answering the door

If you must leave small children alone at home, instruct them not to answer the door, and not to show themselves anywhere else, such as at a window. If they do answer, it will be a very short while before a criminal discovers that there's nobody else at home. You may decide that you would prefer your children to open the door to a limited circle of family members or friends. This raises problems of identification and deception, and even of a casual observer realising that a child is alone in the home. On balance, therefore, it's safer for your children not to answer the door. Friends and family members will understand and appreciate your motives.

Talk right in

As the physical security of homes increases, so it becomes more difficult to break in, and more and more criminals resort to trying to talk themselves in. Their commonest ploy is to pretend to be officials from the building survey department of your local authority, but they may also claim to be calling about the electricity or water, or even pretend to be couriers delivering a parcel. Some will say they are in a hurry, another will be more subtle and merely look at his watch, but all will try to confuse you into letting them in. You may even recognise a uniform as belonging to the electricity department – but uniforms are easily stolen, and admission should be by confirmed identity document only. Don't let anyone in until you've established they are who they say they are.

Checking the story

If official callers don't offer an identity document without your having to ask to see it, close the door at once. Some produce a supposed identity card, wave

Doorstep drill

◆ Don't open your door until you know who is outside.
◆ Don't be impressed or flustered by uniforms or official-looking documents. Check them out with a phone call before letting a stranger into your home.
◆ Don't be lured outside or away from your home by a stranger.
◆ Don't let strangers talk their way into your home.
◆ Don't let in anyone you don't know well if you're at home alone.

it briefly in front of you and return it to their pocket. This is not good enough. Standing behind your security gate, but clear of it, ask your caller to pass you the card. Let him put his hand through the bars and stretch towards you.

It's not possible to recognise the identity documents of all people who may have a legitimate reason for entering your premises. So the safest way of checking whether or not a caller is genuine is to look up the telephone number of his employer and ask whether they have sent a representative – and give his name and staff number – to call on you. Don't ask your caller for the telephone number – he could give you a fake number manned by an accomplice.

Consider allowing yourself until the next day to check your caller's legitimacy. Many supposed officials make their calls late in the afternoon, when offices are closing for the day and it is difficult for you to obtain confirmation of their identity by telephone. Don't be flustered. Simply tell him to come back tomorrow, at a time that suits you.

If you find that his credentials are not genuine, let the police know when you are expecting him to call again.

Admitting a caller

If you're absolutely satisfied that the caller is genuine and on official business, quickly picture the inside of your home before admitting him. Is there anything that you don't want seen by strangers – even if this is an official call? If so, ask him to wait a moment, close the front door and then close the doors of rooms you don't want him to see into.

Make sure no firearms are displayed and, preferably, that items of obvious value are also out of sight. Re-lock the security gate before letting the caller into your home, and then close and lock the front door as well. Follow this procedure even if his visit is scheduled to be a very short one – to read an electricity meter, for instance.

DRAMA IN REAL LIFE

The kindness that kills

Mrs Schwerin, an 81-year-old widow, took pity on a beggar who knocked at her door. He was a local 'regular' whom she must have seen many times before and to whom she offered some hot tea. The mug was too big to pass through the bars of her security gate, so, instead of finding a smaller container, Mrs Schwerin unlocked and opened the gate. It took less than five seconds for the man to overwhelm her and drag her inside. Later that day the body of Mrs Schwerin was found in the passage of her well-protected suburban home. She had been strangled. The security gate was unlocked, and a broken mug and traces of tea on the front steps told the story.

Police comment: Never open your security gate, or lower your defences in any way, to someone you don't know personally, particularly when you are alone. Because the man's face was familiar to Mrs Schwerin, she made the mistake of thinking that she knew him. Clearly she didn't.

WORDS IN YOUR EAR

The telephone has become a wonderfully convenient means of communication and can be a life-saver. Unfortunately, criminals are rarely far behind technological developments, and the telephone has become one of their basic tools.

The right place

Keep a telephone in your bedroom, where it will be handy if ever you need to call for help at night. Your telephone service supplier (Telkom) will install an additional connecting point or jack, if necessary, for which an initial charge and an additional monthly amount are payable. During the day keep the telephone in a passage, the kitchen, study or sitting room, placed so that you can't be seen through a window while you're using it. Keep a pen and some paper next to the telephone.

Cellphones

A cellphone is costlier than an ordinary telephone, but even so it is potentially even more of a life-saver simply because you can carry it around with you. Keep it charged according to the supplier's instructions, and keep it handy at all times. Take great care not to leave your phone switched on with your PIN number dialled into it. Anyone who steals the phone can run up a bill at your expense until you notify the cellphone company of the theft and they cancel the SIM card.

You don't say

Don't give away any information at all when you answer the phone unless you know who is calling. If a caller asks for your number, ask him or her what number he or she requires. If the caller quotes your number, don't even confirm it – merely ask to whom he or she wants to speak. If there's something you'd rather not reveal on the telephone, don't say it.

Anyone else who is likely to answer the telephone in your house must also be taught what not to say. Children, for instance, are inclined to be helpful and want to impress others with their knowledge. It's important they know that the telephone is not part of the performance. They must never tell an unknown caller that their parents are not home.

Teach your children how to pretend to callers that you are at home when you are not. When asked for a parent who is not there, a child should put down the handset without ringing off, walk into an adjoining room and say very loudly, 'Can you come to the phone, Daddy (or Mommy)?' The child should then go back and say that his or her mother or father 'can't come now, but he (or she) will call you back'. It should be unnecessary for the child to remind a caller to give a name and address.

Questions your children shouldn't answer

◆ What time does Daddy/Mommy take you to school?
◆ What time does Daddy/Mommy come home from work?
◆ What's Mommy's phone number at work?
◆ What's Mommy's address at work?
◆ Will Mommy or Daddy be home?
◆ What's your address again?
◆ What are you wearing today?
◆ I want to bring you a parcel. Will somebody be at home?
◆ This is our secret, so you won't tell anybody else, will you?
◆ Guess who's calling?

To any of the above questions, a child should simply say, 'Daddy (or Mommy) will call you back'. If your child doesn't know who's asking the question, he or she shouldn't ask. A genuine caller will be willing to leave a name and number. Especially, a child should not give a caller a lead by asking something like, 'Is that Auntie Joan?' The dishonest or criminal caller will then almost certainly pretend to be Auntie Joan and be in a good position to obtain information.

Beware the cruel crank caller

The telephone rang just before midnight. The caller identified himself as Police Sergeant van der Westhuizen, and asked Mrs Bosman to check whether all her children were home. Just awakened, Mrs Bosman reported that her 18-year-old daughter, Colleen, was not home yet. The 'sergeant' then described a motor accident in which he said Colleen had been seriously injured. He asked more questions, and a shocked Mrs Bosman said afterwards that she didn't realise how much information she was giving him. It was only when her husband took the telephone and began asking questions himself that the caller hung up.

Police comment: Never offer information to a caller whose identity has not been established. If a caller says he is a policeman, ask for his name, rank and telephone number, and say you will call him back. Then phone your local police station and ask them to confirm the identity of your caller and to advise you further. When the police attend an accident in which there is serious injury, they contact the police station nearest to the victim's family and arrange for an officer there to visit the home address to break the news. The police will never pass on bad news over the phone.

No-one on the line

Occasionally, when you answer your telephone the caller will hang up. It just might be a criminal checking whether you're in or out, but there's probably a less sinister explanation. A caller might have dialled a wrong number, realised the mistake only on hearing your voice and, automatically but impolitely, rung off. Double-check your security though, just in case (see Stalkers and Others, pp154-6).

Nuisance calls

Nuisance calls are those that are obscene or just frightening. Most obscene calls are one-off events that result from random dialling. But in some cases, individuals may be repeatedly targeted. Don't listen to this type of call longer than it takes to recognise it for what it is. Ring off without arguing, without asking questions, without saying a word, if you can. Any words or sounds from you are encouragement or amusement to the caller, so don't even bother to be polite.

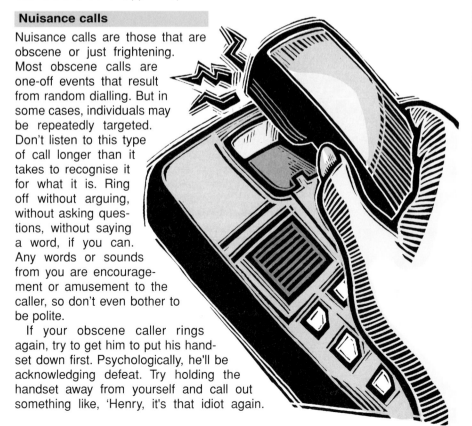

If your obscene caller rings again, try to get him to put his handset down first. Psychologically, he'll be acknowledging defeat. Try holding the handset away from yourself and call out something like, 'Henry, it's that idiot again.

Come and listen to it'. Then put the handset under a pillow or anything else soundproof and leave it there for several minutes.

Obscene callers sometimes introduce themselves as police officers, or as academic or market researchers, but their line of talk soon moves from the apparently innocuous to the lewd. Don't give any personal information over the telephone to a stranger. There is no law that demands that you give information by phone, and it is unlikely that you would be prosecuted for refusing to do so, even if the caller is a state official.

The 'doom caller', who claims to be a policeman or hospital official, is another nuisance, who specialises in giving (false) bad news, usually lurid and detailed. Remember that the police are most unlikely to transmit this type of news by telephone. In the event of a catastrophe, they make every effort to call in person, frequently with a clergyman or medical practitioner.

Telephone sales and surveys

You may receive calls – often after business hours – canvassing your opinion on almost any topic from encyclopedias to time shares. Such calls may be bothersome, but are not classed as a nuisance in the legal sense. However, be on your guard, and make sure as far as you can that the caller is genuine.

An increasing number of organisations, including many legitimate charities, make sales by telephone, and a contract entered into over the telephone may be legally binding. However, the law allows a five-day 'cooling-off' period, during which you may contact the caller and cancel the sale. In practice, it may be difficult for the caller or seller to enforce the contract, whether you avail yourself of the cooling-off period or not, but it's safer to say politely at the outset that you do not wish to take part, and ring off.

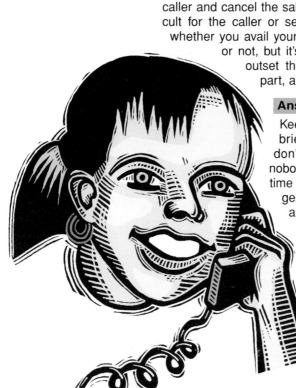

Answering machines

Keep your recorded message brief and noncommittal, and don't tell callers that there's nobody at home. Asking for the time or date of incoming calls suggests strongly that you're out and likely to stay out for a long time. On your home line, it's not necessary to state your own telephone number or to give your surname. A message such as 'We can't come to the phone at the moment, but if you leave your name and number we'll call back' ought to be sufficient. If you're a woman living alone, get a male friend to record your message, using the pronoun 'we' rather than stating your name.

Numbers up

If you have two positions for your telephone, you'll need two lists of essential numbers (see box). Write your lists on a piece of thin white card, cover it with clear plastic to prevent smudging, and tape or tack it to a permanent surface in the position normally occupied by your telephone. See that children know where the numbers are kept. There may be no adult on hand in an emergency to tell them the most appropriate number, so instruct them to call the police Flying Squad at 10111, unless there's another number – of a relative, perhaps – that you are confident will be manned at all times.

Going away

If you are leaving home for a few days or more and there will be nobody at home to answer the phone, make some arrangement for your phone calls. If you don't have an answering machine, have calls to your number diverted to another number – that of a friend or relative, perhaps. About one week's notice is required to implement the service. Details can be obtained from Telkom's toll-free number displayed in the telephone directory. Do not, however, unplug the telephone when you go away, or some well-meaning caller is likely to report it as out of order (see Fooling Some of the People, pp70-1).

If your home number is on an electronic exchange, calls are diverted automatically, but if it is on a manual exchange, callers will be given the new number only when they call your home number. In this case, you may be able to come to an informal arrangement with the operators on your local exchange, whereby, if calls are to be diverted to another local number, they will not reveal the diversion. Only after the identity of the caller has been established should the person answering the diversion decide whether or not to tell the caller that you are away.

LIFE-SAVING NUMBERS

Keep these numbers next to your telephone

Police

Fire brigade

Ambulance

Doctor

Pharmacy

Trauma centre

Poison information centre

Electricity and water supply service

Veterinarian

Schools

Places of work, plus business hours

Your own address and telephone number (in case you forget it in an emergency).

Profile of an obscene phone-caller

Making obscene telephone calls is a form of sexual deviation. It's most likely to be practised by a sexually inhibited male with low self-esteem. He may be married and have a family, but he lacks confidence and social skills. He was probably brought up by a dominating mother in a household in which sex was never discussed and may even have been a dirty word. He has resorted to fantasy, and although he's a nuisance, most obscene callers aren't dangerous. However, some may become obsessive and threatening. It's also thought that some serial rapists and killers may have started at the nuisance level. You should therefore report any incidents of obscene telephone calls to the police. They may be able to trace the caller by tapping the telephone line. A charge of criminal injuria or sexual harassment can be laid, and prosecutions have been successful.

YOUR FAMILY AT HOME

It is vitally important that every member of your family and household knows how your security systems work and takes responsibility for operating them. Your safety depends not only on bars and alarms, but also on one another.

Latchkey kids

Depending on their age, size and understanding, children at home are safer indoors, rather than in the garden. If they have to let themselves in after school, they should not walk home with the keys in their hands. Tell a child to keep keys pinned in a pocket, unpin them on the way home and have them ready in the pocket for immediate use on reaching the gate or door. A child visibly carrying door keys is advertising that there's nobody at home.

Home alone

For the ideal security arrangement, nobody – not even an adult – should be alone. Reality, however, may demand that even children have to be alone occasionally. The most important aspect of their security is that they should not admit the wrong people.

Tell your children whom they may allow into the home while you're out. Give them a list of names, if necessary, and instruct them to contact you before admitting any person not on your list. Explain that they must not be awed by uniformed callers, but, in all cases simply say – through the closed and locked door – something like, 'I'm sorry, Dad says please phone before you come round again' (see A Stranger at the Door, pp80-1).

DRAMA IN REAL LIFE

The bogus baby-sitter

When Marlene and Ted went out at night, their domestic helper, Eunice, usually looked after their two preschool children. But Eunice was on leave on the night they were to dine out with one of Ted's biggest clients. So they called a baby-sitting agency that advertised regularly in their local newspaper and were delighted with the obviously re-spectable and friendly young woman who arrived at exactly the arranged time. Marlene gave her the telephone number of their venue for the evening, as well as the phone numbers of neighbours. They set out relaxed and relieved, and were reassured when the baby-sitter phoned them to say that all was well. When Marlene and Ted returned home, they found the baby-sitter gone and their house stripped of electronic goods, jewellery, expensive clothes and a firearm. The children, unhurt, were asleep in their rooms. Neighbours had seen someone 'coming and going', but hadn't known Marlene and Ted were out. The agency assured them it had checked the young woman's references.

Police comment: The neighbours should have been told that a baby-sitter was in the house, and the parents should have gone to more trouble to check both the agency and the baby-sitter – from references, for example. The baby-sitter could tell, from the telephone number she had been given, how far Marlene and Ted had travelled. Her call to them was just to find out how much time she had to rob them.

If you know you're going to be out when your children are at home, switch on the answering machine if you have one, and tell them not to answer the phone until you return. If you don't have an answering machine, your children should answer calls, pretending that you're there but that it's not convenient for you to come to the phone (see Words in Your Ear, pp82-5).

Empty threats

Teach your family never to get into arguments with callers, whether at the door or on the telephone, and not to utter threats. A child must not say, for instance, as a threat, 'I'm going to call my father'. He or she should say this only if father is actually going to appear. Criminals are quick to sense weakness, and most threats are a sign of weakness.

Closed door policy

Carelessly admitting the wrong people happens when someone leaves a door or gate open. It's very easy to unlock the back door, go into the yard to collect washing from the line, come inside again, put the washing down and then get on with the daily routine. The reminder that you've forgotten to re-lock the back door could be very unpleasant or even fatal. To be safe, always lock the door as you pass through it into the house. Train your staff to lock doors automatically too.

Staff

Be sure that people whom you employ in or around your house are trustworthy. Don't admit or employ any job-seekers unless you have spoken (preferably face to face) to their previous employers. If they are unable to provide contactable references, don't employ them – not even for a day or 'just a few hours'. Generally, it is unwise to issue door keys to your staff. You may trust them, but you never know who they will come in contact with who will take advantage of that trust.

Try to train your staff not to talk about you or your family, your home or your way of life. Inadvertently they may give away information that allows someone else to gain access to your home.

In the case of an emergency

People at home need to know whom to call in an emergency and need to recognise an emergency. For example, anyone who comes to the door and is not on the list of people who may be admitted, but who persists in trying to talk his or her way in, is creating an emergency. It's time to call for help (see Life-saving Numbers, p85). In the case of an internal emergency, such as a fire or flooding, obviously uniformed service officials would have to be admitted. But there is still a need to be on guard against the trickster who will hammer at the door and claim that the roof is alight, in the hope of luring you outside. (If this happens, phone a few neighbours and ask if they can see the smoke.)

Arrest without a warrant

A peace officer may, without a warrant, arrest anyone who:
◆ commits or tries to commit an offence in the officer's presence
◆ has escaped or tries to escape from lawful custody
◆ cannot explain why they are in possession of housebreaking implements
◆ is in possession of stolen property, including livestock or produce
◆ is found at night in suspicious circumstances
◆ obstructs a peace officer in the execution of his or her duties
◆ is a deserter from the South African National Defence Force
◆ has failed to comply with the conditions of a suspended sentence
◆ is reasonably believed to have committed one of a large range of offences, such as assault, forgery, theft, treason, or any crime that may be punished by a sentence of more than six months without the option of a fine.

THE POLICE

The task of the South African Police Service, the national police force of South Africa, is to preserve law and order and to investigate crime, and the powers and duties of the police are carefully regulated by law.

Peace officers

These include members of the South African Police Service, magistrates, members of the Department of Correctional Services and members of a traffic police force. The law requiring that handguns be carried completely concealed (see Firearms, pp258-65) does not apply to peace officers when in uniform or on duty; they must carry handguns according to departmental orders and regulations.

The uniformed members of private security companies are not peace officers and have no more stature in law than the ordinary citizen. According to the law, their firearms should not be visible and they have no authority to carry them openly.

The right to search

Without a search warrant issued by a magistrate, police do not have a general right to search people or their homes. However, peace officers may search an individual or a property (including vehicles) and seize objects without a warrant if:
◆ an individual consents to being searched or has been arrested
◆ the owner or lawful occupier of a property consents to it being searched
◆ the investigating officer believes that a delay in obtaining a warrant will defeat the object of the search.

A forceful but legal search

A peace officer lawfully searching premises may use reasonable force to remove obstacles – by breaking down doors, for instance. But searches must be conducted in 'a decent and orderly manner', and women may be searched by female police officers only.

The police may seize articles for use as evidence if these articles are reasonably believed to be associated with a crime. But the articles remain the property of their lawful owners and should be returned when the case is closed or when there is no further use for them. If the seized articles – dagga or explosives, for instance – may not legally be possessed by an ordinary citizen, they remain the property of the state and may be destroyed.

Powers of arrest

Peace officers have powers of arrest that exceed those of the ordinary citizen (see Caught Up in the Action, pp159-61) and may arrest anyone:
◆ whom they have the power to arrest

◆ whom they suspect of having committed a crime or having attempted to commit a crime

◆ whom they reasonably suspect may be able to give evidence about any offence.

If you refuse to give information, or supply false information, to a peace officer, you may be arrested immediately and taken to a charge office.

Under arrest

If you're being arrested in terms of a warrant, ask to see the warrant so that you can read it for yourself. Where there is no warrant, the officer arresting you must tell you the reason for your arrest while arresting you or immediately afterwards (see box).

If you resist arrest or run away, the officer attempting to arrest you may use the necessary but minimum force to stop you escaping. He or she must inform you that you have the right to remain silent, but that anything you do say may be used in evidence. If you believe you are being wrongfully arrested, say so to the arresting officer. Do not try to fight, or you may be charged with resisting arrest or with obstructing the police. Under the confused circumstances that often surround arrests, you may even be seriously injured. If you think your complaint of wrongful arrest may be interpreted as resistance, it may be safer to state it later, perhaps when you see your attorney.

Making a statement

You cannot be forced to make a confession or admission and you have the right to refuse to answer a question if the answer may incriminate you. If the police question you after arrest, you have the right to have an attorney present. An accused who is under 18 years of age may also be assisted by a parent or guardian. At the police station, your attorney is entitled to speak to you out of the hearing of anyone else. If the police deny you immediate access to your attorney, you have the right to refuse to say anything until you have seen your attorney. No matter how upset you are, make sure you read very carefully any statement you have made that has been written down, and insist that anything you do not agree with is changed before you sign the statement.

Detention

If you are arrested, you must be taken to a police station as soon as possible – unless a warrant specifies some other place. You may be detained for up to 48 hours, or longer if the 48 hours expire on a day on which courts do not sit, before a charge must be laid. Further detention is allowed only if you are brought before a magistrate who orders continued detention on a specific charge, until trial. In certain serious cases, witnesses may be detained if it is thought that they might abscond.

While in custody you are entitled to access to clean water for drinking and washing – it may be brought to you or may be on tap in the cell – and to the use of toilet facilities. However, this access might depend on the availability of a police officer who is not otherwise occupied. You are also entitled to receive adequate food, bedding and a place to sleep. You may request medical attention, and a district surgeon may be summoned to examine you if the police are convinced that you need attention. Lighting and ventilation should be adequate for the number of people contained in the cell. As far as possible, no person should be locked in a cell housing any person who is suspected of having committed a violent crime.

Released on bail

It is more likely that you would be released on bail to await your trial. Bail is money paid to the court to ensure that an accused who is released from custody will appear in court to stand trial.

If evidence produced during the bail application suggests that the accused could interfere with witnesses, a set of conditions to prevent this will be contained in the bail agreement. If the accused does not comply with all the bail conditions, the bail money may be forfeited to the state and additional charges may be brought against the accused.

In minor cases, an accused who cannot afford to pay bail may be released on the understanding that he or she will appear in court when due. The granting of bail is not an automatic procedure, and may be opposed by the public prosecutor.

Helping the police

Males between the ages of 16 and 60 years may not refuse help when a police officer asks them to assist in making a lawful arrest, unless they suspect that the person asking for help is not a police officer or if they believe that there are no reasonable grounds for making the arrest.

In certain cases the police might consider manning a satellite police station where suitable premises are found and paid for by the public. (Such a station, for example, was opened in the nightclub area of Cape Town, but was closed when local entrepreneurs allegedly failed to keep up the rent payments.)

Community policing

Since 1993, the new, 'open' style of policing gives members of every community the opportunity to discuss and decide on their par-

ticular policing needs. A community police forum (CPF) may be established in every area served by a police station, consisting of residents of that area. The frequency of the CPFs meetings with the local police usually depends on the incidence of crime in that area. Several members of every CPF have letters of authority allowing them, without having to give prior notice, to visit any person held in a police cell, to satisfy themselves that he or she is not being abused or unlawfully deprived of his or her rights. Members of the CPF are also involved in all aspects of improving policing, including, in urban or metropolitan areas, the placing of police caravans or substations.

Police Reserve

Any South African citizen – male or female – between the ages of 18 and 70 years, who is reasonably fit and has passed the equivalent of Standard Eight (although matriculated applicants are preferred), may apply at their nearest police station to join the Police Reserve. Successful applicants undergo training and are issued with the standard police uniform, identity document and equipment. Police reservists are expected to do at least eight hours' duty every month, although, to justify the costs of equipment and training, it is preferred that they do up to 32 hours monthly. Being volunteers, they receive no pay, but are covered against death or injury on duty by the same policies as members of the permanent staff. Costs incurred – while attending courses away from home, for instance – are borne by the Police Service.

Calling 10111

Telephone calls to 10111 go directly to the police radio room, where trained personnel summon and coordinate the response they consider most appropriate – such as the Flying Squad, a team specially trained to deal with explosives, or a negotiating team with weapons support to deal with hijackers.

Call 10111 only in emergencies, when a rapid response is critical to save life or property, or to bring about the arrest of a person suspected of having committed a serious crime. If you arrive home and find signs that there are intruders inside, you are justified in calling 10111. A road accident in which property is damaged but in which nobody is injured does not warrant a 10111 call, and should be reported at the police charge office instead.

Before dialling 10111, try to think of sources of help that are more appropriate. For instance, if your cat is stuck up a tree, call an animal-protection organisation (although the cat will probably come down on its own, anyway). If an inconsiderate motorist has left his vehicle blocking entry to your driveway, call the traffic department. If neighbours or vagrants are creating a noisy disturbance, but are not threatening your life or property, report them at the charge office.

EMERGENCY CHECK LIST

WHEN CALLING 10111

1. Give your name and address.

2. Give the number and address from which you are calling.

3. Tell the controller why you've called.

4. Respond, briefly but fully, to the questions you are asked. Keep to the point.

5. Don't hang up until you're told to do so.

INSURING POSSESSIONS

The two most common types of property insurance, apart from motor insurance, are the home-owner's policy and the householder's policy. The home-owner's policy is concerned with damage to the structure of the home, while the householder's or home contents policy covers movable possessions that are normally kept in the home. Rates for the same cover may vary significantly, so it pays to shop around.

Policies and premiums

The usual householder's policy covers furniture and furnishings, electrical and electronic equipment, such as stove, refrigerator and TV equipment, clothing and personal effects. Jewellery, other valuables and cash may be covered up to specified limits. Household items are usually covered against theft, fire, flood and accidental damage, although almost any item can be insured against almost any risk – if you're prepared to pay a very high premium.

The premium, or the amount you pay to the insurance company, usually monthly, is determined in part by the frequency of housebreaking in your area, the type of home and its construction, your security measures (the company may reduce the premium, for example, if you install bars and a monitored alarm system), and the sum for which your goods are insured. If, for instance, you have a range of expensive woodworking machines in your garage, or specialised computer equipment in your home, find out whether these will be adequately covered by an ordinary householder's policy. You may need to take out another policy, relating to commercial or industrial activity, or add a section to your existing policy. The insurer may also require that you take special measures (additional security or approved installation) before he grants cover. The principle remains that the costlier your possessions, the higher the insurance premium.

People aged 50 years and over, and who are retired or in part-time employment, are usually able to obtain reduced premiums through membership of the Association of Retired Persons and Pensioners (ARP&P). The residents of any area and, especially, of any residential scheme, such as a retirement village or an apartment block, may also be able to negotiate a discount on insurance if they use the same insurance company.

All risks

Items temporarily removed from the home, such as jewellery, binoculars and cameras, are best insured under a separate all-risks policy or an all-risks extension of the main policy. Premiums on items insured for all risks are higher than normal, because of the greater risks that the insurer is expected to bear.

Keep your valuables on record

When you make an inventory of your possessions, take snapshots of the more valuable items. Write the value and the date on the back of each photograph. This visual record will aid police and insurance investigators in the event of a burglary.

Risks may include the loss of jewellery through being mugged in the street or even through your own carelessness – leaving your rings in a public cloakroom, perhaps. Some valuables and collections may be the subject of special conditions (relating to storage, for instance), and charged at an even higher rate.

Valuations

To determine the value for which the contents of your home should be insured, draw up a list, with replacement costs, for every room. In the case of items insured under an all-risks policy or extension, your insurer will probably require a valuation certificate signed by an approved expert, such as a jeweller, auctioneer or specialist dealer. This is intended to prevent fraudulent overvaluation by dishonest clients. (Making a fraudulent claim is a criminal offence.)

When applying for insurance, list the contents of your home at their replacement value rather than their market value. Market value will attract a lower premium because of age, depreciation and wear and tear, but you will not be able to replace lost or damaged items if you are paid only their market value.

The perils of underinsurance

Some insurance policies have a clause providing for an annual increase of the premium amount, to keep up with inflation. It's up to you to see that the insured replacement value of your goods is also adjusted from time to time, or you will almost certainly find that you are underinsured. This means that, although it will now cost you more to replace a lost, stolen or damaged item, the most you can expect to be paid by your insurer is the value at the time of your last policy adjustment.

Suppose the contents of your home were insured for R40 000 some 10 years ago, and that today they are worth R80 000. However, you are still paying premiums on R40 000. Despite your best efforts, burglars break in and steal goods that you value at R20 000, and you put in an insurance claim for that amount. But your insurer's assessment shows that the total valuation should, in fact, be R80 000 and you are therefore underinsured by 50 per cent. On that basis, your insurer will pay up to only 50 per cent on any claim, so you will receive a maximum of R10 000 for your loss of value of R20 000.

Claims

Advise your insurer as soon as possible in the event of a burglary, for example, or damage to an insured item. A claims inspector or assessor may be sent to inspect the scene. If a crime is suspected, you will have to quote the relevant police docket number when completing the claim form that your insurer will supply. Your insurer may insist that you improve security measures before renewing your policy.

ON THE ROAD

You and your car are at your most secure from car crimes when you are moving. It's when you slow down or stop that you are most vulnerable to hijackings or car thefts.

The real figures

Statistics of car theft issued by the South African Police Service are based on incidents that are reported to them. Of the number of vehicles reported stolen, the insurance industry estimates that some 40 per cent never existed – they are 'paper cars', fraudulently 'created'. Of the rest, about 45 per cent involve a car that was never stolen. For example, an owner who is in financial difficulties may dispose of the car at a low price to a syndicate that resells it in another part of the country, or even abroad. The owner then reports the car stolen and claims against the insurance policy.

Family favourite

Figures issued by the National Crime Information Centre for Gauteng in 1996 show that high-priced luxury vehicles are not necessarily the prime targets of the thief and hijacker, but rather cars costing up to about R50 000. The next most popular group was those that cost up to R80 000.

In 1996 Toyotas made up 34,7 per cent of hijacked or stolen vehicles (but Toyota also sold more cars than any other make, so this may simply reflect the larger number of Toyotas on the road). The next most-stolen or hijacked makes of car were Nissan at 13,6 per cent and Volkswagen at 8,6 per cent. BMWs constituted 6,2 per cent and Mercedes-Benz models made up only 4,9 per cent of hijacked or most-stolen vehicles.

When and why do they go?

Most cars are stolen from residences or from unmonitored parking lots and while parked on the street. Those stolen from residences are mostly taken at night. Cars stolen from parking lots or around town are usually removed during the day. Hijacking from residences occurs mostly in the early morning and late afternoon.

A small proportion of cars may be stolen to order. Others are stolen because, being popular, they are easy to sell, and a few are stolen simply for the fun of it or because a thief needed a vehicle at the time.

How do they go?

Most vehicles are stolen by breaking into the window or door. The criminal places a towel or thick newspaper over a window, preferably the quarterlight pane in one of the rear doors, and strikes hard with a hammer or half-brick. He reaches in, unlocks and opens the back door, then unlocks and opens the front door.

Some car doors can be simply levered open far enough to insert a wire probe to lift the locking knob. Other doors are unlocked after inserting a flat blade between the glass and the outside panel of the door. This releases the locking mechanism almost instantly. Advanced thieves have special equipment that neatly removes the locking cylinder altogether. Once inside the car, 'hot-wiring' gets the engine going in a few seconds. This involves a length of insulated wire with a small crocodile clip at each end, to bypass the ignition switch and the immobiliser.

Parking

When choosing a parking place, check that there will be adequate lighting if you're returning after dark. The route to your car should also be well lit and safe.

Avoid parking areas that are deserted or remote. A parking area with monitored access is likely to be safer than others, although it cannot offer an absolute guarantee of safety. Try to select a parking bay that you can leave by driving forward, with a minimum of manoeuvring, especially in areas that you don't know well and those you'll be leaving after dark. Once you've parked, remove the key, lock up and go.

Dangerous moments

Be especially alert and anticipate trouble when:
◆ a vehicle obstructs you or wanders about the road
◆ a vehicle stays with you, whether behind, in front or beside you, even if you vary your speed
◆ a vehicle collides gently with yours, usually from behind – this could be the first phase of a hijack.

Dangerous places

Places or areas to approach with anticipation and alertness include:
◆ your own driveway
◆ the street outside your driveway
◆ any road intersection or other place where you're forced to stop or slow down
◆ an overpass/highway bridge
◆ a section of a highway known for incidents of stone-throwing or deliberate obstruction
◆ blind corners
◆ dark or deserted parking areas
◆ apparently deserted picnic sites and view sites.

Invitation to be stopped

Neighbourhood Watch Vehicle Watch is a scheme in which a sticker placed on the front and rear windscreens requests the police to stop the vehicle and check the legitimacy of the car's driver. A member of the scheme who knows no-one under the age of 25 would drive the car may place stickers with a large 25 on the windscreens. This scheme has proved so successful in the United Kingdom that it has reduced car theft by 40 per cent.

CHECK LIST

CAR THEFT PREVEN-TION TIPS

1. Keep all doors and windows locked.

2. Activate the car alarm system.

3. Keep the car in the garage or in a well-lit area.

4. Do not keep spare keys in the glove compartment.

5. Do not tape a spare key to the vehicle's bodywork or use putty to attach it inside a lamp lens – a car-thief will find it.

6. Take all valuables out of the car when you park it. Store them in the boot if necessary.

7. Accessories most often removed from cars are CD players and stereo equipment. Take these with you whenever you get out of your car.

Some consolation

The theft of unoccupied vehicles and motor-cycles dropped from 104 302 in 1994 to 96 715 in 1996. The incidence of car hijacking rose from no reported cases in 1990 to 12 860 cases in 1996. Ordinary car theft is therefore a far more frequent occurrence than car hijackings.

GLASS HOUSES

Your car has an enormous window area, and its contents (including you) are exposed to the gaze of anyone who cares to look inside. Once a criminal sees something of value in your car, it won't be long before he reaches in to take it.

On stage

You and your passengers are on display all the time you're in your car. Always travel with the doors locked and, in town or in any area where you have to slow down or stop frequently, keep the windows closed, or open no more than about four centimetres.

Keep valuables, including handbags, necklaces and other jewellery out of sight. Snatch specialists operate at traffic lights and stop streets, and are quick to grab what they can, including sunglasses, necklaces, bags and even rings and wristwatches. Passengers should hold handbags firmly on their laps, or on the floor next to their feet, towards the centre-line of the vehicle but not so as to interfere with the driver's control. If you are driving on your own and have a handbag, loop the handle over the gear lever and place the bag itself on the floor near the passenger seat.

Articles placed on the rear window shelf may fly forward and cause injuries in the event of a sudden stop or collision, so lock them, particularly larger containers such as briefcases, in the boot.

If you anticipate using a parking meter or buying a newspaper en route, keep small sums of money ready to hand in a pocket or in an outside compartment of a handbag.

On display

Leaving valuables in your car is asking thieves to break in. Sound systems – radios and tape and CD players – are the prime attraction. However, almost all sound systems are available with a bracket that enables them to be removed and refitted easily. So take yours out and carry it with you when you have to leave your car parked outside – even if you intend being away for only a few minutes. Alternatively, consider systems that are uniquely tuned to a particular vehicle, or that have removable control fascias.

Keep keys, registration and identity documents and firearms on your person, not in the car. Consider carrying copies of documents rather than the originals.

Out of sight

It's risky to leave any valuable or attractive item anywhere in your vehicle, but if you must leave it, lock it in the boot. Even a plastic shopping bag of old papers may be presumed to be your week's cash takings on the way to the bank, and an opportunist may smash the window to retrieve it.

Beware of leaving clues to concealed contents: a roll of camera film on the back seat is worth nothing to a thief, but it may suggest to him that somewhere in the car you've also left an expensive camera.

Get into the habit of keeping nothing in the glove compartment, and leave it open so that it can be seen to be empty. Leave nothing protruding from under a seat. It suggests that you may have tucked away something valuable, and this is one of the places that thieves check automatically.

Tinted glass

You may feel safer if people outside can't see in. Tinted glass or tinted plastic film can be fitted to the front windscreen, but it must admit at least 75 per cent of available light. Film fitted to the other windows must admit at least 35 per cent of the available light. Remember, though, that the effect is reversed if you switch on the interior light at night.

Plastic film, of varying grades of toughness, can also be fitted to the inside of the windows to reinforce them in the event of a stone striking them. The window glass that is normally fitted to a car is specially reinforced, but tougher grades can be obtained, all the way up to bulletproof. (The bodywork of an ordinary vehicle, however, is not bulletproof.)

Handing over your property

Before handing your car in for service at a garage, check that there is nothing – valuable or otherwise – in the glove compartment or in the boot. If you are taking your car to a particular workshop for the first time, and if you have had no recommendations, remove the spare wheel before handing it in. Give the garage only your ignition key – it should be all they require.

Lower the profile

Outside mirrors and aerials are often the targets of vandals and, sometimes, even of thieves. When you have to leave your car, especially in a dark or lonely place, lower the aerial and turn mirror housings inwards so that the mirror lies facing the bodywork. Most fitted mirrors rotate through a number of preset stops or 'clicks', so are easy to return to the original position. Remove 'bolt-on' parts, such as the ball of a towing hitch, and fit locking nuts to the road wheels.

SECURITY CHECK LIST

THINGS YOU SHOULD NOT LEAVE IN YOUR CAR

1. The vehicle's registration papers.

2. Documents giving your name and address or those of your family.

3. Family photographs.

4. Firearms.

5. Keys – house keys or vehicle keys.

6. Chequebooks or credit cards.

7. Anything of value that might tempt someone to break into your vehicle.

Easy pickings

In 1995, there were 189 811 reported cases of theft from vehicles. In 1996 this figure had dropped to 180 229.

ON THE ROAD

FULL LOCK

Keep your car locked not only when you're in it, but also when you get out – even if you expect to be away for only a very short time. If an alarm is fitted, see that it is armed when you leave. It's unlikely that any pass-er-by will take action if it's triggered, but it might just discourage an inexperienced car thief.

Manual immobilisers

Manual immobilisers, such as steering-wheel and pedal locks, and handbrake and gear-lever locks, can be more effective than alarms because the car cannot be driven away unless they are removed. Whereas a thief can override an alarm, a well-made road-wheel clamp, for instance, is almost impossible to detach without the correct key. Also, considerable physical effort is required to remove it, an activity that is highly visible. However, this physical effort is also a discour-agement to the legitimate user. A motorist, leaving his car for a minute to buy a loaf of bread at the corner shop, for example, may find the effort too much trou-ble. A proficient car thief should then be able to enter the car and be on his way in only half a minute or less.

Electronic immobilisers

Typically, these disable the engine's ignition system and sound an alarm if parts of the car, such as the boot lid, windows, bonnet and doors, are tampered with. Specific accessories, such as aerials, mirrors and road wheels may also be linked directly to the alarm, and the system may be fitted with a secret override switch, so that it will not be triggered by legit-imate activity, such as routine servicing.

Some immobilisers are set automatically when you remove the key from the ignition, or, together with an alarm, they may be set when the driver's door is closed and locked, and the key removed.

Before having an electronic immobiliser fitted, ask your insurance company for a recommended system and the names of approved installers.

Test your electronic immobiliser regularly by locking your car, and then, from the outside, going through the motions that are claimed to trigger the alarm. Find a safe and remote place to do this, so that the sound of the alarm won't disturb your neighbours. They will probably ignore it anyway if you haven't come to an arrangement about your joint security.

A bit of both

Whether you have an electronic immobiliser fitted to your car or not, keep a manual immobiliser, such as a chain and padlock, to use when you feel that the car needs extra security. If you don't have an electronic immobiliser, confuse thieves by fitting a red, winking, light-emitting diode (LED) on the dashboard. They may think it's the 'armed' signal of a real electronic system, and pass on to the next car. It shouldn't take your garage more than a few minutes to fit, or you could ask help from a friend who knows something about vehicle wiring.

Tracking systems

A radio signal transmitter can be fitted to your car which, when activated (by advising the monitoring company that the vehicle is missing or has been stolen), emits a silent signal that allows a monitoring station to track the vehicle very precisely. The station is operated by a vehicle security company which, typically, notifies the police of the vehicle's whereabouts and also sends its own recovery team to investigate. The tracking system is not part of the immobiliser, and usually cannot be controlled from the vehicle in which it is installed.

If you have a tracking system fitted, make sure that responsible family members or friends will call the monitoring company if you are overdue by a certain time and have not contacted them. The claimed advantage of a tracking system is that it should enable a vehicle to be recovered within a very short time – a matter of hours or less – of being reported stolen.

Anti-hijack devices

There is a type of immobiliser that is activated if you get out of your car with the engine running and close the door. This is effective against having your car hijacked but doesn't protect you in this event. A safer type is activated when you phone the service provider company in the event of a hijack and present your PIN number. This number is transmitted by radio signal and switches on the immobiliser, stopping the car.

Insurance against theft

Insurance companies usually require a certificate stating that the vehicle has been fitted with an immobiliser or anti-theft device. But there are no detailed specifications, and much of the apparatus people use is inadequate, or stops working after a few months. About 70 per cent of 'genuinely' stolen cars were fitted with an immobiliser that was activated at the time they were stolen.

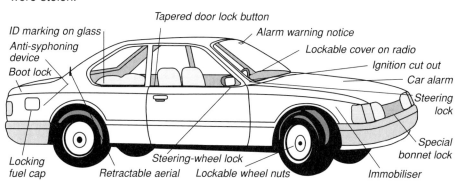

ID marking on glass
Anti-syphoning device
Boot lock
Tapered door lock button
Alarm warning notice
Lockable cover on radio
Ignition cut out
Car alarm
Steering lock
Special bonnet lock
Locking fuel cap
Steering-wheel lock
Retractable aerial
Lockable wheel nuts
Immobiliser

**THINGS YOU SHOULD
KEEP IN YOUR CAR**

◆ spare wheel
◆ jack and wheel brace
◆ towrope
◆ jump leads
◆ fan belt (and perhaps alternator belt as well - ask your garage)
◆ fuses
◆ headlight bulbs
◆ spark plugs and plug spanner
◆ pliers, screwdrivers and spanners
◆ two cans of engine oil
◆ bottle of hydraulic fluid (for brake and clutch systems)
◆ about one metre of binding wire
◆ five litres of water (for the radiator, but drinkable in a stranding emergency)
◆ insulation tape
◆ radiator hose
◆ aerosol tyre-inflater.

As part of your general car kit, also carry
◆ fire-extinguisher (dry powder or BCF type) mounted within reach, not in the boot
◆ warning triangle
◆ first-aid kit
◆ map book
◆ torch.

SITTING TARGET

It's not easy to defend yourself when you're sitting down. It's even less easy when you can't stand up and your arm and leg movements are restricted. This is your situation in your car. Quite literally, you're a sitting target. Be alert and don't sit in a stationary vehicle longer than necessary – it draws attention to your vulnerability.

Look first

Before you get into your car, check it first. It doesn't take long to walk around your car to find out if anything is not as it should be. Have the tyres been damaged? Are there obstacles in line with the wheels? Are there signs of fluid leaks or of illegal entry? Look through the windows to make sure everything is as you left it. If all seems to be in order, unlock the door, remove the key (don't leave it in the keyhole), open the door and get in. Close and lock all the doors immediately.

Carry a small torch at night to make your pre-entry check easier and quicker. If there are suspicious characters nearby when you approach your car, it may be prudent to walk on and come back later. Don't unlock your car door unless you're sure you can be inside, with the door locked again, before they can reach you.

Before you go

Lock your door as soon as you're inside, and instruct your passengers to lock theirs. Start the engine and, while you're fastening your seat belt, see that instruments and warning lights are functioning correctly. Check the alignment of rear-view mirrors. Confirm that passengers are safely buckled in and have locked their doors. If the road is clear and you have the right of way, move off smoothly.

Close the windows

When driving in town, keep windows as nearly closed as you can. An opening of up to four centimetres should prevent anyone from putting an arm inside either to grab you or to unlock your door. Ask passengers not to open their windows further than this. If you drive with windows open in the countryside, close them as soon as it looks as though you will have to stop or slow down substantially, or if there's any sort of obstruction ahead. Also close

them if a stranger approaches while you're stationary. If he has something to say, let him shout.

Many motorists dislike driving with closed windows because they like to be able to give hand signals. The Road Traffic Act neither requires nor recognises hand signals which, in any case, are illegal when you are driving on a freeway.

A hand through the window

If a stranger reaches in through your window, lean away and drive ahead. If he has removed the ignition key or if you're not in the driver's seat, close the window hard on his hand or arm. With a manually operated window, keep up the pressure on the winder handle. Electrically operated windows won't inflict serious injury on a healthy adult, but he'll probably be startled into withdrawing.

Stop and go

If you can help it, don't stop your car in an area where you wouldn't choose to walk alone. Before you stop and park your car, check for loiterers and for places where a thief could be hidden. Hiding places include other vehicles (behind them, or even inside them), bushes, doorways and gateways, pillars and around corners. If anyone moves closer after you pull up, wait a few moments before getting out, to see what they intend. If you're still suspicious and it's a lonely place, drive on.

The time to make sure that no valuables are exposed in the car is when you get in, not when you're about to get out. Any observant bystander will see you putting a wallet in the glove compartment, for instance. Once you're out of the car, stand erect – outside the range of the car door, so you won't be caught if somebody slams it on you. Make sure there's no danger before you lock the door. Collect what you need from the boot, without overloading yourself. Lock up and set the alarm, even if you intend to be away for only a few minutes.

The car that's a nonstarter

If your car won't start, it's possible that it may have been deliberately disabled. Even if you're technically competent, don't bury your head under the bonnet unless you have a companion to keep watch for you. If you can't get it going, lock all the doors and the boot and go to the nearest safe place from where you can telephone for help.

Good Samaritan or bad?

If, while you're still in your malfunctioning car, a stranger approaches who appears anxious to assist you, ask him to telephone a friend, a relative or the police (or the Automobile Association, if you are a member). Tell him you prefer to wait for them to arrive, and stay in your car, with doors locked and windows closed. Attract attention by flashing the lights and sounding the hooter. But if you feel that assault or robbery may occur if you stay with the car, get out. Choose your moment to leave – when there are several potential witnesses passing by, for instance. Find a shop, garage or home from which you can obtain trustworthy help or telephone the police.

Get tanked up

Emergencies are the hazardous occasions that you don't foresee, so try to reduce the odds against you by never letting the fuel tank run below about one quarter full. If you intend to add fuel, do so at the first safe opportunity – don't put it off. The next filling station might be closed. Check oil and water levels and all five tyre pressures whenever you fill up (see Breakdown, pp103-5).

A moving target

If you're being shot at, drive as fast as you possibly can, without causing an accident. Exaggerated swerving is more likely to result in an accident than to save you from being shot. Very few criminals are likely to be skilful marksmen anyway, but where one of them has a fully automatic weapon, such as an AK47 or an R5, the sooner you can distance yourself from the source of danger the better.

Avoiding serious injury from stone-throwers requires a different technique. Suppose a stone has been thrown at your car from somewhere ahead, and it's travelling through the air at about 30km/h. You're driving towards it at 120km/h, so the combined speed at the moment of impact will be 150km/h. At this speed the stone, if it's heavy enough, will penetrate the windscreen, probably take off the head of any passenger unlucky enough to be in the way, and then pass out through the rear window. So, if you see the trouble coming, slow down to about 30km/h. The stone might not even penetrate your windscreen.

If someone suddenly steps out into the road, forcing you to stop, lock all doors and windows as you approach, and change to a lower gear so that you can accelerate away if you have to. Switch on your headlights to get a clear view up ahead. If you must stop, don't switch off the engine, and don't get out of the car. If you're doubtful about the 'emergency', drive past and notify the police from the nearest telephone.

BREAKDOWN

Even the best-maintained car can suffer failure of some minor component and come to a standstill in a situation that may be anything from frustrating to dangerous. But a breakdown is more likely to happen to a vehicle that's poorly maintained, overloaded or badly driven. Do everything you can to avoid being stranded by the roadside and becoming an easy target.

Survive!

A breakdown is not necessarily a life-threatening experience, but your safety counts for far more than the value of the vehicle or its contents. An important aid to safety is to tell responsible people your destination, your route and the time at which you expect to arrive (or to return home). Tell them what you'd like them to do if you don't arrive – advise the police or your family, for instance. Once you've given this information, stick to the route you've described.

If you're travelling an unfamiliar route, look at it on a map to acquaint yourself with the road layout and ask at the local police station whether any section of it is regarded as dangerous or difficult.

What breaks down?

Most breakdowns are caused by the failure of renewable components such as fuel filters, lines and pumps, air filters, radiator hoses, tyres, brake cylinders and linings, electrical wires and connections. Make sure your car is serviced regularly to detect faults before they result in failure. It's worth learning at least the basics of vehicle maintenance and repair, and the significance of all the dials and warning lights fitted to the vehicle you are driving. Recognise your car's everyday sounds and the feel of pedals and steering. A different sound or an unfamiliar feel usually means that something is going wrong.

Reduce temptation

If your car does break down, first take off valuables such as rings and watches, and place them where they won't be seen by anyone who stops to investigate. Remove larger, loose items of value from inside the car and lock them in the boot. If there's anything that identifies you as a long-distance traveller (who is likely to be carrying a fair amount of cash), hide that as well. Don't leave your house keys where they can be found easily, and see that nothing in the car will give away your address.

Roadside repairs

Once you raise the bonnet, you're advertising that you're in trouble. Think carefully before you do this, especially if you're not competent to detect faults or make repairs. Make sure that your car is well clear of

ON THE ROAD

CHECKUP CHECK LIST

Before setting off on a long journey by car, have the following parts of your car checked:

1. Air cleaner
2. Alternator
3. Battery
4. Brakes
5. Carburettor
6. Constant velocity (CV) joints (for front wheel drive cars)
7. Distributor
8. Drive shaft (for rear wheel drive cars)
9. Fan and belt
10. Fuel line
11. Fuel pump
12. High-tension (HT) leads
13. Ignition coil
14. Lights
15. Oil in gearbox (for cars with automatic transmission)
16. Oil level and filter
17. Radiator
18. Shock absorbers
19. Silencer and exhaust
20. Spark plugs
21. Tyres
22. Wiper blades.

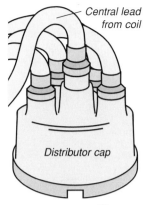

Central lead
from coil

Distributor cap

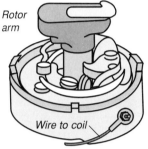

Rotor
arm

Wire to coil

*In case you have to aban-
don your broken-down car
to seek help, immobilise it
further by disconnecting
and removing the central
high-tension lead that links
the distributor to the coil.
Alternatively, unclip and
remove the whole distributor cap, having first
detached the leads from
the spark plugs.*

*Given that the distributor
cap is grimy and bulky, you
may prefer not to carry it
with you but simply to lift off
the rotor arm inside the
distributor body and remove
that instead.*

passing traffic – push it off the road if you will have to
work on the offside. Place a warning triangle 75 paces
behind the car (200 paces on a freeway). Don't smoke
while working in the engine compartment; roll up your
sleeves and remove dangling clothing, such as a tie or
scarf. If you have to abandon your vehicle, and it's not
fitted with an immobiliser, remove the wire between
the coil and the distributor body. If you have the space
to carry it, remove the distributor cap, after detaching
the spark plug leads.

Helping hands

If you have a cellphone or CB radio, call for help
immediately. In a known high-risk area, accept the first
offer of help that you judge to be safe. A vehicle with
all male occupants is the least desirable; one carrying
a young family is probably the safest.

Where you have passengers, and help is offered by
a driver who has room for only one extra person (or
where one would be left behind), stay together and
ask the driver to arrange help for you by reporting your
situation and your location at the nearest police station. Women and children, in particular, should not be
left alone along the roadside. If you don't trust somebody who offers help, thank him and say that help is
already on the way.

To stay or to go

Your assessment of the situation and your proximity to
assistance must guide you. If you break down in a
high-risk area, your first consideration must be to get
out of it. People walking (and showing no valuables)
will almost certainly appear to be a less worthwhile
target than when they are sitting, evidently helpless, in
a broken-down vehicle.

Indecision suggests weakness, and if you stand
around for too long (and 'too long' may be anything
from less than a minute to an hour), you're going to
attract unwelcome attention – perhaps from pedestrians. Your car's best defence is its mobility. Once
brought to a halt, the protection it offers is more an
illusion than a reality, except as a refuge from rain or
extreme cold.

Going at all costs

There are few faults so catastrophic that they will bring
the modern car to a halt with absolutely no warning.
And you must take warning lights and instruments on
the dashboard seriously if you want to avoid a large
repair bill. If your life is at stake, however, disregard
them and keep going – at the most moderate speed
that will keep you out of danger. Your car will eventually grind to a halt but by then you may be safe. These
are a few of the commoner breakdown conditions:

Flat tyre: it will be noisy and uncomfortable, but you
can keep going for as long as you can control the car's
direction. The tyre will soon come off the rim, and alloy

rims will break very quickly. Depending on the road surface, steel rims might last 15 kilometres (front) or up to 30 kilometres (rear);

Oil warning light on: if there is insufficient oil for proper lubrication, your car may keep going for 20-30 kilometres. Shortly before it stops for good, the engine will make loud thumping and grating noises and slow down. Overheating through lack of lubrication causes the engine to 'seize up' – a condition in which parts become melted into one another. Despite the smell and the heat it gives off, the car is very unlikely to burst into flames;

Overheating radiator: if the temperature continues to rise to the limit, and does not come down again, the engine will probably seize up within 20 kilometres. Adding water to the radiator will help if the problem is caused by water loss, but wait until the radiator has cooled before attempting to remove the cap. Adding water to a blocked cooling system (another common cause of overheating) will have no effect;

Fuel warning light on: this depends on the amount of fuel remaining in the tank, and on the car's rate of consumption. You'll go furthest at a slow, steady speed (around 60-70km/h) in the highest gear possible, without causing the engine to strain or shudder, perhaps even 100 kilometres;

Clutch failure: when the car is moving, try revving the engine briefly, and then, as the engine speed drops, gently push the gear lever into the gear position you want. When gear-shaft speed and engine-speed synchronise, it will slip in easily. If you can't manage this, bring the car to a stop on level or forward-sloping ground and switch off. Put the gear lever into second gear and turn the key. The starter motor will jerk the car forward and the engine should fire almost immediately. Remember to push the gear lever into neutral when you stop, or the engine will stall.

Travellers' tool box

Whether you're setting off on a short or long journey, make sure you always have the following in your boot:
◆ Tool box with necessary screwdrivers, spanners, pliers, etc.
◆ Spare wheel, jack and spanner
◆ Spare can of oil
◆ Bottle of battery electrolyte
◆ Jerry can/plastic bottle with 1 or 2 litres of fuel
◆ Piece of suction hose
◆ Spare spark plugs, fuses and globes
◆ Torch
◆ Jumper leads.

DRAMA IN REAL LIFE

Are Samaritans always good?

Eager to get home to Knysna in the car he had just bought, Henry Coetzee irrationally ignored the temperature warning on the dashboard. Several kilometres beyond Port Elizabeth, the temperature gauge needle went to its limit and he regretfully pulled off the road. A glance under the bonnet showed that the water pump housing had fractured. He waited for the engine to cool and then poured water into the radiator, but the water gushed straight out. By sunset, no other motorist had stopped – and then a minibus taxi pulled up. The driver strolled across, looked at the damage and said he would use his cellular phone to call someone in Port Elizabeth to fetch Henry and his car. Henry asked if he could use the phone himself, but the driver said that the phone was with a friend 'along the road', and drove off.

Suspicious, Henry hid in the bush some 20 metres from his car and was roused from a doze by the arrival of a tow truck – belonging to a reputable garage – which the taxi driver had summoned, as promised.

Police comment: Stranded by the roadside as he was, it was a sensible precaution for Mr Coetzee to hide so that he could assess anyone who stopped, before showing himself.

GOING AND COMING

For motorists, safety may end just beyond the garage door, or even in the driveway itself. The statistics for hijacking point remorselessly to home and its vicinity as being the highest risk site. The figures also illustrate that you're most likely to be hijacked while your vehicle is moving very slowly or is at a standstill.

Matters of routine

On leaving home, your mind is filled with thoughts of the day ahead, and your concentration on your immediate surroundings is poor. Similarly, you are likely to be unwinding when returning home, perhaps anticipating a pleasant evening ahead. It's a good time for a hijack, as criminals have discovered. Make a conscious effort to change your attitude at both times of the day, and to be fully aware of what is going on around you. More than that, be aware of the implications of what is going on around you.

Radio silence

It will help your concentration if you turn off your car's sound system. When leaving home, turn it on only when you're about a kilometre from home and when all is going smoothly. Similarly, when you're coming home, turn off the system when you have about a kilometre to go. If you have a cellphone, contact a responsible family member at home, to arrange the precise moment of opening manually operated gates. Do not, however, start up a conversation at this time, or you will lose your concentration.

Can you see?

Lighting outside the gates, in the parking area and along the driveway must be adequate. At night, you should be able to see a person clearly at any point along the driveway. If on leaving home your view of the road outside is blocked by your own high wall, you probably need someone to keep watch for you. There should be no hiding places either along your front boundary wall or fence, or in the gateway. You or some responsible member of the household must watch automatic gates until they have closed behind you.

Setting off

Even before you get into your car, make sure you have everything you're likely to need on the trip – such as money for a newspaper or for parking. If

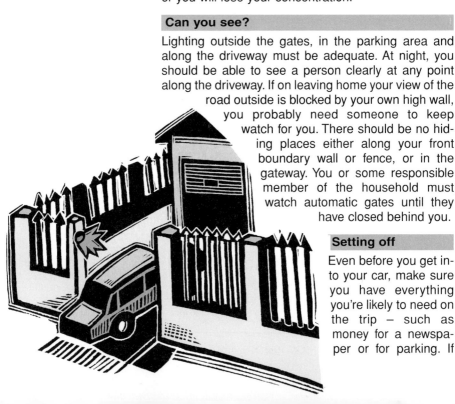

any ice or condensation has formed on the windows, remove it from all the windows – not just from the windscreen – and from exterior mirrors.

Once you're in the car, check your rear-view mirror, and that all doors are locked and windows fully closed. Drive off only when the engine is running smoothly and you are confident it will respond if you have to accelerate suddenly. Open gates for as short a period as possible, starting only when you're already moving towards them. If there are suspicious activities in the street, delay opening the gates until the matter has been resolved. If you feel threatened, call the Flying Squad (10111).

If there is any sort of threat as you are leaving, your only course of action may be to get away as quickly as possible. Seek help immediately if you are pursued, by turning on your car's hazard warning, flashing your lights or sounding your hooter continually, and driving to a police station. If you are not pursued, return home carefully or telephone to ensure that all is well inside.

ON THE ROAD

Hijack hot spots

In 1996:
◆ 42 per cent of victims were hijacked in the street outside their homes
◆ 33 per cent were hijacked in their own driveways
◆ 17 per cent were hijacked at traffic lights and stop streets.
(Automobile Association of South Africa survey, 1996)

Coming home

Start your approach routine about a kilometre from home – or closer, in very slow traffic. Switch off the radio or stereo, and check constantly in your mirrors. Are you being followed? If not, put your gate keys or remote-control keypad where you can reach them easily, to avoid any unnecessary delay at the gate.

As you approach your gate, check the road for suspicious parked vehicles, and examine your mirrors again. If the same car has been behind you for some while and still is, and you're unhappy about it, drive on and then approach home again. If you're still being followed, drive to a police station and report it. Alternatively, drive to a busy shopping centre, and call the police and home from there. Don't go back home until the suspicious car has been dealt with or has left.

Once you arrive at your gate, don't let anything – short of a gun to your head – interrupt your routine of opening the gate, driving in, closing the gate and locking it. Watch automatic gates from a distance inside your property until they are fully closed. If you have gates that require manual closing, stop as soon as you're within your property and clear of them, then close and lock them.

Park your car so that you never have to reverse out into the roadway. Reversing puts you at a great disadvantage. If you can't turn your car around within your grounds, do your reversing at your gateway on your arrival home. (If necessary, park outside and wait indoors until the road is clear of anything suspicious before doing so.)

Opening time

An open gate is an obvious breach in your perimeter security. It's also an invitation to opportunists, vagrants and others, so keep the opening period as short as possible. Don't, for instance, stop the car so that you can chat to someone while you're on your way in or out. And don't open the gate before it needs to be opened. If you have to get out of the car to open or lock the gates, switch off the ignition, remove the keys and lock the doors, even if the car will be in view all the time – a thief could be dropped from a passing vehicle and be off in your car before you could stop him. If possible, check that house doors are locked before you start opening the driveway gates (or other perimeter gates).

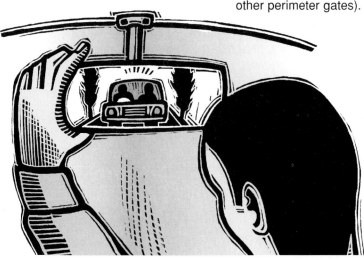

What is suspicious?

A suspicious vehicle is one that doesn't belong to any of your neighbours (see You and Your Neighbourhood, pp16-17) or doesn't normally park in the area. A utility vehicle marked 'Telkom', parked near a telephone pole where men in overalls are working, is probably a genuine telephone service vehicle. An unmarked vehicle parked near your driveway for no obvious reason, and with no recognisably genuine activity going on in or near the vehicle, is grounds for suspicion.

Any strange vehicle is suspect, especially if people start to emerge from it as you approach your home. But even if hijackers arrive by car, the car may drop them off and drive on out of sight, leaving one or two apparently innocent individuals near your gate. If you can't work out what they are doing, don't stop. Consider parking some distance away and out of sight of the suspicious vehicle or strangers, walking home and putting your car away later.

If you notice a suspicious vehicle when you leave home, and if it doesn't follow you, it may be that its occupants are waiting for you to leave. It's worth driving around the block and coming back for another look. If the car is still there, take note of what its occupants look like, the vehicle itself and the registration number. Report their presence to the police and phone anyone in the house to warn them that there are suspicious strangers about.

HIJACK AND KIDNAP

The increasing sophistication of anti-theft devices fitted to motor vehicles has had an unpleasant sequel. Criminals now often prefer to pounce when the driver is in his or her seat and, usually, has the engine running. Robbery of the vehicle's occupants is almost inevitable, and serious assault is a distinct possibility, since almost without exception, hijacking is carried out at gunpoint. The safety of your passengers and yourself should be your first consideration. Your most effective defence is to avoid hijacking, by being constantly alert and suspicious.

Rolling robbery

If you're driving along a fairly lonely street and the car behind you gives you a gentle bump, don't assume that the driver has simply misjudged the distance between you. This could be a setup for a hijack or other theft, assault, rape or murder. The fact that there's apparently only one person in the car that hit you doesn't mean you're safe. An accomplice could be hiding, or in the car ahead of you or beside you.

If you're suspicious, and you probably should be, drive away slowly, checking that all doors are locked and windows are closed. Be prepared to speed up if you're pursued, and head for the nearest police station, hospital, hotel or shopping mall. If none of these is possible, find a busy spot and stop your car so as to block the traffic, without placing yourself or anyone else in danger of injury from a collision. Switch on your lights and lean on your hooter to attract attention. Don't get out of your car until you're sure you're safe.

The static steal

If you're in your car and being held at gunpoint, don't stall, don't argue – just do as the hijacker says. If he

---

What to do if you're hijacked!

◆ Give up your vehicle and possessions without resistance.

◆ Obey instructions, but don't offer anything unless it has been demanded.

◆ Answer questions truthfully if the hijacker will be able to check what you tell him – banking information, for instance.

◆ Don't make sudden movements.

◆ Don't reach for anything without first telling the hijacker what you're going to do.

◆ Tell the hijackers where things are if they ask – don't reach out to give them to them.

DRAMA IN REAL LIFE

Ed's escape

Arriving home after he had just banked his company's takings for the day, Ed pressed the garage door remote control and drove in. As he was getting out of the car, a gun was pressed to his temple and he was ordered to lie on the ground. One man roughly searched him and took his watch and car keys, while another searched the car for money and a gun. Finding neither, they ordered him to get into the back of the car. Ed stood up, and opened the car door swiftly, knocking one of the hijackers aside. He then ran out of the garage, across the road and jumped over a neighbour's fence, shouting for help. His girlfriend, in the house, heard him and called the Flying Squad immediately. They were able to alert border posts but it was too late to track down the car. A month later, however, the car was found in the Free State and returned to Ed.

Police comment: With a gun pointed at him, there was no reasonable prospect that Ed's escape attempt was going to be completely successful – and he was lucky not to be killed. Be aware of this possibility if you're thinking of making an escape. Always assume that an armed assailant will use his weapon if he feels threatened.

wants to know whether you have a firearm or if the car is fitted with an anti-hijack panic button, tell him and tell him where they are. Don't indicate by moving your arm or hand – he may think you're reaching for a gun. Again, if he wants your wallet or watch, tell him where they are, don't reach for them. (For this reason you may consider always travelling with two wallets – one hidden, and one to hand over.)

If he finds your bank card and asks for your PIN number, give it to him – you may be held hostage until he has verified the number anyway. If he wants you out of the car, get out carefully. Use your left hand (the hand furthest from the door) to open the door, and say, before you move: 'I'm going to open the door'. Keep your hands where he can see them and, once you're out of the car, step away from it slowly, so that you don't stand between the hijacker and the car or between him and his escape route. Don't turn away, don't walk away or try to run.

If there are other occupants in the car, ask if they may leave as well and ask the hijacker or his accomplices to open the doors for them. If there is a child strapped into a child seat, tell him that you are just going to get the child out.

Without being obviously observant, note as many details as you can: names, features and markings, clothes and accessories, other vehicles involved. Only when it's safe to do so, call the police Flying Squad (10111) and, if necessary, get medical assistance.

Advise your insurer and follow their instructions concerning attempts to recover your car. Even if you suffer no physical injury, tell your doctor about the incident as soon as you can. He or she may recommend counselling to help you over the tremendous shock of having been in danger of losing your life.

Kidnapped

If you are taken along with your car, keep as calm as you can – your life probably depends on it. Keep your hands in sight and don't make any sudden moves or get involved in a physical fight. Don't try to deceive your kidnapper if there's a chance he may find out that you've lied to him. Try to register the route being taken. Believe that all those involved – family, friends and police – are working for your prompt and safe release (see Abduction, pp151-3).

Aftermath

After you've been held up and robbed, or had a narrow escape, try to think what went wrong with your security arrangements – or were you simply unaware that you were heading into trouble? Next time you may not be so lucky.

You might consider taking out a hijack policy. Some banks offer such a service, which includes a 24-hour toll-free hot line, car rental and psychological trauma counselling.

BENDING THE LAW

If you genuinely believe your life or property to be in danger while you're driving, it is reasonable to take measures to protect yourself or your property. But can the laws that have been designed to protect road-users be turned against you when you believe you are acting out of fear or necessity?

What the law requires

The police are concerned with maintaining the law – that is, seeing that people obey the law. Courts may punish people who do not obey the law, but they are allowed a certain amount of discretion in determining whether a particular act, given the circumstances in which it was committed, amounts to reasonable conduct. The measures that you take must also be 'reasonable', in relation to the threat.

'Reasonable' conduct

Take this scenario, for example. It's night-time and a car that has been obviously following you draws up alongside you at the traffic lights. There are no other vehicles about, and, fearing for your life, you decide to jump the red light to get away. As you pull off, there's the wail of a siren right behind you. The other car was a police patrol car, and you're ticketed for dangerous driving, or alternatively, for failing to heed the lawful command of the red light.

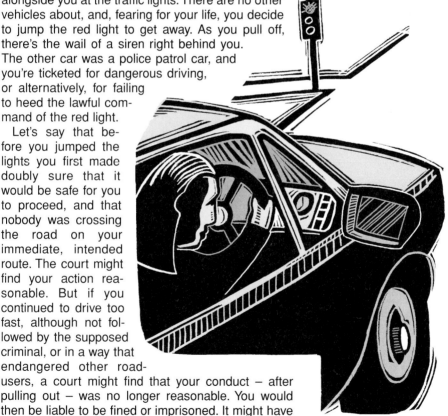

Let's say that before you jumped the lights you first made doubly sure that it would be safe for you to proceed, and that nobody was crossing the road on your immediate, intended route. The court might find your action reasonable. But if you continued to drive too fast, although not followed by the supposed criminal, or in a way that endangered other road-users, a court might find that your conduct – after pulling out – was no longer reasonable. You would then be liable to be fined or imprisoned. It might have been different, however, had you actually been pursued by the supposed criminal.

Spokespersons for several metropolitan traffic police departments have stated that motorists who drive cautiously through red lights because they are in

DRAMA IN REAL LIFE

Incident at an intersection

It was not the sort of place where Sheila Rivers would have chosen to stop an hour before midnight. But as she approached the traffic lights they changed to red. The roadsides were lined with bush, there were no street lights and the only other vehicle was the one that was slowly approaching from behind. Instinct told her to get away, so she eased her car forward, turned left and accelerated – closely followed by the other vehicle, which now drew alongside with flashing lights and a wailing siren. It was a police van, and Sheila was taken to Sandton police station, booked and given a R300 ticket. She contested the charge on the grounds that she had acted with due caution and that her action had been an 'act of necessity'. She had perceived it as being essential to save or protect her life and property. She was discharged in the Randburg Magistrate's Court when, for the second time, state witnesses failed to appear.

Police comment: Ms Rivers was acquitted on a technicality only – she was not found 'not guilty'. It is not advisable to go through a red light – rather take other precautions if you fear an attack: do a U-turn; roll slowly towards the lights so that you don't have to stop; or plan not to go along a route that may be unsafe.

immediate fear of criminal action, might or might not be charged by a police officer, depending on that officer's judgment of the circumstances. If the motorist were to be charged and appeared in court, he or she might not automatically be fined or prosecuted, particularly if the defence was on the basis of a 'sudden emergency', which is when life is at risk. In this case, the motorist might receive no more than a warning.

Other evasions

In the case of a hijack, unless you believe your life or the lives of your passengers to be in danger, it may be safer to stop and hand over your car and valuables rather than incur the risks of racing on a public road. Where you believe that you're being chased because your pursuer intends to kill or injure you or your passengers, on the other hand, it would be natural to make every attempt to get away. Attempting to evade illegal pursuit by entering a road with a no-entry sign is normally held to be dangerous or reckless. However, in the stress and anxiety of the moment, you are more likely to be thinking about saving life than the risk of future prosecution, and a court will almost certainly consider this.

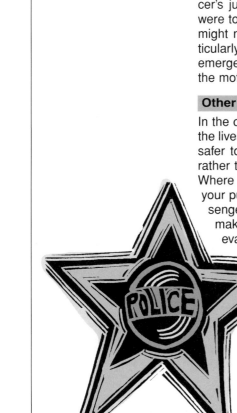

When a roadblock is not a roadblock

A few instances have been reported of criminals manning illegal roadblocks while wearing uniforms and impersonating members of the police service or of the defence force. The object has been to rob motorists of cash and personal goods, and to steal their vehicles. Official roadblocks carry signs warning motorists to stop (and sometimes proclaiming a local speed limit), 30-100 metres or more from the stopping point. There will probably be police officers stationed at this stop sign. Within 100 metres of this point will be a sign advertising POLICE/POLISIE and more police officers. At the stopping point there may be a temporary swinging or lifting bar or temporary traffic lights.

There will always be some uniformed officers at a roadblock. In some cases, defence force personnel and vehicles may also be present. Get to know the uniforms of the police service and the defence force.

Note whether the uniforms at a roadblock fit well or whether they appear to be untidy, too big or too small. Real soldiers and policemen are neatly dressed, carry their weapons in a careful, responsible manner, and don't point them carelessly. A roadblock at which almost nobody is wearing a uniform is suspect. However, consider driving through a roadblock very carefully. Failure to stop at an authentic roadblock may have very serious and even fatal consequences if law officers fire on you or pursue you in the belief that you are a criminal.

Injuring another person

If you injure someone, or damage someone's property while you are escaping from suspected criminals, you may be prosecuted for reckless driving – or culpable homicide if a death is caused – whether the threat was real or not. If a court finds you not guilty, an injured or bereaved party may still institute a civil claim against you for damages, which you may lose. Even when fleeing for your life, you must show due regard for life and property.

People in uniform and the presence of a few cone markers do not necessarily indicate an official roadblock. Look for road signs, a swinging or lifting bar, defence force uniforms and vehicles, and a sign marked Police/Polisie. But even though you may be suspicious, consider your options very carefully before you drive through a roadblock without stopping.

FRIENDS IN NEED?

South Africa's vast distances and relatively underdeveloped public transport systems mean that there will always be people seeking a lift to a destination. Before you offer them a ride, or before you accept a lift, consider the circumstances very carefully.

The roadsiders

Hitchhikers are those people seeking a lift in other people's vehicles. They may be on holiday, or travelling between their home and job, school or college. Some may need a lift because they have been victims of an unfortunate circumstance, such as vehicle breakdown, or even abandonment after an argument. But it is impossible to be sure that any hitchhikers are genuinely what they appear to be, and not robbers, rapists or murderers.

How safe is hitchhiking?

It should be fairly safe to give a lift to strangers when you are already accompanied by passengers known to you. Similarly, if you are hitching a lift with a companion, you should be relatively safe in accepting a lift with people you don't know. But the other side of the story can be so horrific that the lesson is: giving lifts to strangers or accepting lifts from them is risky and is best avoided if at all possible.

For example, there is the case of a motorist who gave a lift to what he thought was a respectable-looking young man in military uniform. The motorist was shot dead by his passenger, who then stole his car. In another incident, two young women were given a lift by a man recently released from prison, where he had been serving a sentence for rape. He managed to rape both young women and stabbed one to death. His second victim, with a lucky shot, killed the man.

Balancing the probabilities

Always weigh up the situation first, before offering anyone a lift. A family standing by a sedan at the roadside, and dressed for an outing, probably have broken down and probably will do you no harm. Similarly, an elderly woman walking in the rain with groceries balanced on her head probably poses little danger. But there are no guarantees.

A criminal setting up a fake family-in-distress might just add all the touches required to make it look genuine. Use your own discretion: do the hitchhikers look convincingly bothered and frustrated, or do reactions (especially those of children with them) seem at all rehearsed? Do the hitchhikers seem nervous, and do they look around as though they are expecting others to appear? How concerned do they seem about abandoning their car, and about removing loose contents?

The dark side of the helping hand

Not everyone who offers you assistance or a lift has your interests at heart. Ask yourself, do those who have come to your aid seem concerned with your whole problem, or do they seem in a hurry to get you aboard and to go? Do they remind you – perhaps more than once – not to leave any valuables behind? Try to gauge whether the attention they pay to the women and children with you merely shows concern, or may be cause for suspicion and alarm.

Try to avoid accepting a lift in a car with only male occupants (see Breakdown, pp103-5). Women, especially, should beware of male drivers who crawl past and then come back for a further look before stopping to offer help.

If you're a male on your own and don't like the look of the people who have stopped to offer you a lift, say that your brother (with perhaps 'two of the guys from the team') will be back at any moment. If you're a woman, say that your husband or boyfriend and his brother are due back.

If you accept a lift, don't let a passenger move to the back seat and give you the seat next to the driver, although this may be a prudent move on the part of perfectly genuine Samaritans. You don't want a stranger sitting behind you from where you can very easily be overpowered or threatened by a gun, knife or strong hands. Say that you suffer from car sickness when you sit in the front passenger's seat and ask if you may sit in the back.

Dress the part

Women who intend to hitchhike, in spite of the risk, are safer in clothing that cannot be described as revealing or provocative. They should wear loose-fitting trousers, and loose blouses or shirts with long sleeves and a high neckline. Having to change your style may seem an irritating interference with your liberty, but the possible alternative is much worse.

Other road-stoppers

The fake accident is a favourite ruse for bringing potential victims to a halt. It usually consists of a motor vehicle that looks as if it has run off the road after striking a pedestrian who is lying, supposedly injured, near the edge of the road. Your safest course is to report the incident at the nearest police station, but if you feel that you can lend substantial help, first make sure that this is not a trap.

Keeping an eye on your surroundings (side, front and rear), and with the engine running and your car in gear, look for signs of recent damage to the vehicle. If there's broken glass on the road, look for broken windows or lights. (Glass from broken bottles and from ordinary windowpanes may be used on the roadway, so get to know what broken motor glass looks like.) Even if the 'victim' is genuinely injured, there may be no point in stopping unless you can render immediate medical assistance. It's safer for you, and probably better for all concerned, to call professional help.

Threatened by a passenger

If a passenger threatens you with a lethal weapon, such as a knife or a firearm, while you are driving, all is not lost. If he wanted to kill you regardless of the consequences, he would have already done so. The fact that he threatened, rather than stabbed or shot, suggests that either he can't drive or that he is afraid of being injured if he kills you and the car crashes.

It may be worth taking the chance that, for as long as you keep going at a brisk pace, your attacker won't dare to kill or injure you. You'll have to stop sooner or later (when the car runs out of fuel), and he might kill you then anyway, so at least try to stop in a place of your own choosing while you can. If you have other passengers and he turns his weapon on one of them, you may have no option but to stop or do as he says – he could kill a passenger without risking a crash.

Attacked by a passenger

If you are actually assaulted while driving, try to bring the car to a halt as soon as possible. Your ability to  control the car is bound to be reduced by the attack and by your instinctive attempts to defend yourself, so do not even attempt manoeuvres such as swerving, especially at speed – they may end disastrously for both of you. Violent braking, however, especially if you have steering control, may throw your assailant momentarily off balance. Do whatever you possi-

Picking up someone else's troubles

She was in a hurry as she strode along Durban's Beach Road, frequently glancing back and, with a raised arm, appealing for a lift. Dave Langley slowed his car, and she tumbled into the seat next to him even before he had stopped. The next few minutes were a blurred nightmare – a powerful truck rammed his car from behind, then pulled alongside and forced him off the road. When this happened a second time, he decided to confront the driver of the truck and got out of his car. As the driver of the truck alighted too, Dave's passenger ran across the road and stopped a car heading in the opposite direction. With a screech of rubber, truck and driver vanished in pursuit, leaving a bewildered Dave alone with his now battered car.

He reported the incident, a docket was opened and his statement was taken. His own evidence was unfortunately not comprehensive – he did not notice the registration number of the truck, for example, and he presented no witnesses. An investigation on site confirmed the apparent sequence of events, and a charge of reckless driving will be seriously investigated when the driver of the truck is found.

Police comment: In this case, the hitchhiker had no criminal intent, but was apparently involved in some domestic dispute. This incident points out the inadvisability of picking up a stranger, and the importance of noting details if a crime does consequently occur.

bly can to attract the attention of other motorists, by hooting, flashing lights or, when travelling slowly enough, colliding with another vehicle. Don't aim at it head-on – just scraping your car against it will probably be sufficient. If you can, bring your car to a stop where it will block the traffic without being struck by another vehicle at high speed – at an intersection, perhaps, or sideways across the lane.

To break from your assailant, try jabbing your fingers in his eyes. Do it hard and do it right the first time, however distasteful it seems. The ignition keys should still be within reach, so use them in your right hand when you punch him or rake his face. (Don't remove them while the car is still moving, or you'll lock the steering.) If you can get out of the car, do so, remembering to take the keys with you. You will then have the option of trying to run away or of continuing the struggle on more equal terms.

If you're sitting behind someone who threatens the driver, try releasing the back rest of his seat and then suddenly pulling the back rest down – being careful not to trap yourself under it. You may be able to overwhelm the attacker while he is off balance.

If one of your passengers is attacked by another passenger (whom you've just picked up, for instance), drive for help if you think there's a good chance of finding it nearby, such as a busy road, a shop or a police station.

It's very difficult to defend yourself against an attack from someone sitting behind you, so don't sit strangers at the back, unless you place a trusted and active friend next to them. The best thing you could probably do, but not while driving, would be to bite your attacker on the arm or bend his fingers back as far and as hard as you can.

LOST OR ALONE

Although it seems so obvious, you're more likely to get lost if you don't know where you're going. In almost every instance, getting lost on the road can be traced to inadequate planning and poor anticipation.

Do you know where you're going?

Most motorists do know where they're going – or rather, where they hope to go. Almost nobody expects to get lost. Being lost at night, or in bad weather, or on a lonely road makes the experience seem much worse, and it may be difficult to control the tendency to panic. Keeping calm, however, is essential.

A good book of maps of the area will relieve many anxieties, especially if it can reveal one of the commonest causes of getting lost – you have gone either too far or not far enough. Typically, the driver who has gone too far keeps going, and the driver who hasn't arrived yet turns back. Knowing the distance to your destination, and watching the time and your odometer reading should prevent this. It's useful to carry a pad of paper and a pencil in the car to make notes of your surroundings in case you do get lost.

Observe

Once you've traced the route on the map, keep a lookout as you're driving for features along the way, such as side roads, intersections, towns, farms, railway crossings, stations and sidings, rivers and anything else that is marked on your map. Conversely, if you note an unfamiliar name along the road, find it on the map to help pinpoint your position.

To avoid getting lost:

◆ always plan your route before setting off, by studying a map of the area you're going to
◆ always carry a map with you in the car
◆ check your odometer regularly to make sure you have travelled the distance indicated on the map
◆ look out for landmarks and try to remember them, in case you have to turn back
◆ check with the local police if you're not sure how to get to where you're going.

DRAMA IN REAL LIFE

A high road to misfortune

Tom and Eve Smart, Scottish visitors and anthropology enthusiasts, came to South Africa in 1992. They knew exactly which prehistoric sites they wanted to visit, and made sure, when they hired a car for the duration of their stay, that they obtained detailed road maps to get them there – and back again. Having visited the Sterkfontein Caves, they set off from nearby Krugersdorp for their hotel in Johannesburg. Chatting animatedly about their interesting day, they failed to notice that Mr Smart took a wrong turn, probably outside Roodepoort. They found themselves on a road crowded with people, in Soweto. Unable to go forward and, soon, unable to reverse either, the Smarts sat in terror as their car was vigorously rocked by a noisy, apparently angry crowd. Mr Smart could think only of producing his passport, but nobody took any notice. And then he noticed that the crowd had moved back, and a man was indicating that he should turn and drive away. The little car, with its occupants shocked but unharmed, shot away down the road and, very much later, the frightened couple found their way to their hotel.

Police comment: This may have constituted a case of public violence – it is a crime not to report such cases to the police. It appears that the Smarts were lost solely through not paying attention to the road and to the map that they had with them. Their adventure illustrates the importance of knowing where you're going, checking your routes and making sure you're on the right road.

Note the position of the sun, and whether trees, buildings or mountains appear on your left or right. Memorise road intersections, and whether you turned right or left. Note the time and set your trip odometer to zero now and then, using prominent landmarks as references, to record your route.

Stop to think

Stop as soon as it occurs to you that you may be lost – don't wait until you're absolutely certain. Keep calm. Note the time and the reading on your trip odometer, remembering where you reset it. If it looks safe outside, get out and get a fix on your surroundings, noting street names and landmarks – anything that can be recognised and identified. Try to work out how long ago and how far back you passed a particular landmark and make quite sure that your destination does not still lie ahead of you.

Go back

Once you've established that you are lost, look around for a passer-by to ask for help, or a public place where you'd feel safe asking for directions or for the use of a telephone, such as at a police station, filling station, shop or hotel.

If you are in the middle of the countryside, turn your car around, facing the direction you have come from, and drive to the first crossroad or intersection at which you can turn. Look for landmarks you may have passed and can recognise. Did you turn here onto the road that you're on now? If it's a dusty road, look for your tyre marks made earlier (but remember that later traffic may have obliterated them). Make a drawing of the intersection, showing where you are and the direction in which you are now travelling. Try to locate the intersection on the map. If you can't find it, drive along one of the roads of the intersection for a set number of minutes or kilometres, and mark the distance travelled on your sketch map.

Try again

If you don't see anything familiar along the first road you try, return to the intersection, reset your odometer and try another road. Eventually you must recognise the right one.

Helpers

Be wary of people who approach and offer advice without your having asked for it. Do not allow them to enter your car – keep the windows up and the doors locked. If you believe you have good reason to doubt the accuracy or honesty of advice given to you by a stranger, don't follow it. If strangers make you nervous, drive away from them, but be careful to register how far and along which road you drive.

SURVIVAL
CHECK LIST

YOU'VE DRIVEN
INTO A RIOT OR
DEMONSTRATION –
WHAT TO DO

1. Turn around and drive away without injuring anyone.

2. If you're closer than 50m, you probably can't turn around. Park your car off the road.

3. Get out of your car and, without panic or undue haste, move to the side or end of your car away from the crowd.

4. Be polite and agreeable, and do not offer any threat or criticism.

5. Do not produce a firearm and do not threaten to do so.

6. If people in the crowd attempt to rob you, it's probably best to let them do so without offering resistance.

7. Let the crowd flow past you and then make your way to safety. Use your car if you can, or walk slowly. Don't run.

PUBLIC TRANSPORT

The most widely used forms of short-haul commuter transport are minibus taxi, train, bus and sedan taxi. The crimes most commonly associated with public transport are theft and assault.

Prepare yourself

Before you even set out, make sure your jewellery is not visible. Remove any jewelled rings or, at the very least, rotate them so that the jewels are on the inside of your hand. Don't arrive at the stop or station so early that you find yourself alone. Stay away from the edge of platforms and pavements while you're waiting, and never turn your back to the railway line or road. If you haven't already bought your ticket, have your fare ready now, so that you won't have to fumble with wallets or handbags in crowded company later.

Travel light

Carry as little luggage as possible, and don't load your arms – you'll need to keep them free for boarding, tendering your ticket or fare, and for balancing. Don't overfill your handbag or briefcase; keep it close to your body and hold onto it securely.

Getting on

Make sure that it's the right train, taxi or bus before you get on, and avoid taxis in poor condition – those with broken windows or missing doors, for instance. When boarding, get a firm hand-hold before starting to step on. If you travel regularly by train, don't always get in at the same door or in the same carriage. Whether travelling by bus, train or taxi, get some useful exercise and confuse the criminal element by occasionally walking to an earlier or later stop.

On board

Try to avoid body contact with other passengers, and, unless you need to hold on, keep your arms in front of your body. If you must put parcels down, put them between your feet. When reaching for a handle or hanging strap, try not to expose jewellery or a wristwatch – use the other hand. Find a seat away from doors or open windows – people sitting near these escape routes are frequent targets of snatch-thieves.

Don't give away any details about where you live or work, or the route you usually travel. When travelling by minibus taxi, if it looks as though you're going to be the only person left, and you're a woman, get out and wait for the next full taxi to come your way.

Train travel

When you're travelling alone, don't sit in an empty compartment, but choose one that has respectable-looking male and female passengers. Avoid eye

Golden rules for train commuters

◆ Avoid travelling alone, especially after hours.
◆ Make sure that you're getting onto the right train so that you don't have to ask a stranger.
◆ If you must travel alone, don't get into an empty carriage.
◆ Don't sit close to the door.
◆ If you're near a window, see that it's closed before the train stops at a station.
◆ Avoid overcrowded carriages.
◆ Don't wear or carry articles of value.
◆ Hold tight onto bags and parcels.
◆ Know your route, and get somebody to meet you at your destination.
◆ Report incidents to a conductor, a security official on the train or at a station, or at a police station.

Be on guard at all stations

They wanted 'the true South African experience', the Dutch tourists told Edna Dumont on the train. It was nearly peak travel hour in the morning, and their video camera was busily recording the crowded third-class carriage. Pulling out of a station, as the carriage doors started to close they came to a sudden halt, and Edna saw that a passenger on the platform had placed a foot firmly between the doors. Then the train began to move, and two men who had got off leaped back into the carriage. One grabbed the camera from one of the Dutch tourists, and the second ripped a gold chain from the neck of the other. The next moment they jumped expertly from the carriage, the doors closed and the train left the station.

Police comment: Ms Dumont witnessed a typical snatch practised on trains. Although she travelled third class daily, she usually wore Bohemian clothes perceived to be 'old' and did not display expensive accessories, unlike the tourists. No-one travelling on public transport should display jewellery, watches, a camera or even an expensive bag.

contact. Keep a book or newspaper open on your lap and read – or pretend to read if you're uneasy – while staying alert to your surroundings.

If you're worried about the intentions of the passenger sitting close to you, get up and move away. Preferably, move to another occupied compartment and to the other side of the carriage, where you can pretend to look at the view. If the passenger has committed no offence (such as molesting you, either physically or verbally), don't express annoyance.

If you are the victim or observer of a mugging or armed assault on a train, consider your response very carefully. Contemplate resistance only if you are certain you will succeed, and by the likelihood of obtaining help from other passengers or railway staff. Above all, don't risk serious injury or death.

In getting away from an assailant don't automatically leave the train at the next station – you may be placing yourself in greater peril and even further from help, especially if your assailant gets off with you. First check that there are people on the platform, preferably police or railway staff, or SOS boxes. These red-painted boxes, introduced on some stations in 1996, provide a link to the station security office and also activate a video camera, to enable police to identify an assailant.

Report any incidents that occurred on the train. You may be able to claim the value of the unfinished portion of your journey, especially if you have the name and address of a witness to the incident.

On arrival

Disembark and walk off purposefully. If you can, avoid walking through subways on your own. Choose someone to walk near, preferably a man and woman walking together, and adjust your pace so that you can walk through with them. It's safest to arrange for someone to meet you at your destination and to walk with you to your own vehicle or your home.

HOLIDAYS, TRAVEL AND RECREATION

The first stage of going away is to make satisfactory arrangements for the security of your home and possessions. The second is to take the necessary precautions for your security while travelling. If you're touring outside your home province or in a rented car, remember that your vehicle's registration probably marks you as a stranger and a likely target.

Know where you're going

Plan your route carefully, especially if you intend to drive, so that you know exactly where you should be at the end of each day's travel and how to get there. If you'll be passing large towns, make sure that you know the through-route or bypass. Book overnight accommodation well in advance so that you don't have to search for a place to stay when it's dark.

Check the areas you intend to pass through. For example, if you will be towing a caravan, are there any mountain passes or other roads on your route that are unsuitable? Are there major road works or other likely sources of delay? For example, if you're travelling in South Africa during the peak period of December-January, allow for a reduced average speed.

Read up on where you're going, especially if you're travelling to another country. Find out about any important cultural differences and social taboos, customary practices such as bargaining or bribery, and the incidence of crime in certain areas. Check the rules of the road before crossing the border – in Zimbabwe and Zambia, for instance, the maximum speed limit is 100 km/h; in Malawi it is only 80 km/h.

As your departure date approaches, check the news every day for anything that may affect your planned route, such as floods or wash-aways, public violence or the threat of violence, and even the prevalence of forged banknotes.

Paper chase

Check documentary details such as passports and insurance well before you need them. If you will be crossing an international border, ensure that everyone in your family has a valid passport and visa for the countries you propose to visit. It usually takes from six to eight weeks for a passport to be issued by the Department of Home Affairs.

If you are taking your motor vehicle temporarily out of the Southern Africa Common Customs Area (South Africa, Namibia, Botswana, Lesotho and Swaziland), ask an official at your bank to help you complete the forms required. In other countries, your car is regarded as a temporary export, together with other items on which duty is normally payable, such as cameras. All of these must be entered on form NEP (Customs). You may need to make financial arrangements, so that you have some currency on hand. Carry most of your money, however, as traveller's cheques.

Check whether your insurance policies are affected by your travel. Will you be reimbursed for clothing stolen from a train, or cameras stolen from a car, for instance? Is your comprehensive motor vehicle insurance policy valid in the countries you will visit? For some countries, you may have to obtain certificates of compulsory third-party insurance.

Taking it with you

The law requires you to have your driver's licence with you when you drive. Any passenger who is likely to drive should also bring his or her driver's licence. It may be useful, too, for you to take the vehicle's registration and licence certificates (you will certainly need them if you drive to another country). If you will be driving in another country, check that your licence is valid there; if not, obtain an international licence.

When you're travelling long distances, take along other forms of identification and a larger-than-usual amount of cash in case of emergencies. If possible, carry these in a securely closed pocket in a garment that you won't take off en route (because you're too hot, for instance). Alternatively, keep documents (or copies of them), cards and cash in a pouch worn round your neck and under your clothing, or in a pouch worn round your waist and hidden under your clothes. Keep original documents and extra cash in a small bag locked in the boot and take it out only when required. A bag with a loop to pass over your wrist is less likely to be left behind in the cloakroom of a roadside service station than one without a loop.

If you take a firearm with you, wear it in a secure holster at all times. This will not only keep it available, but will also prevent small children and criminals getting hold of it. Find a holster that you can wear comfortably for long periods in a sitting position, or you will be tempted to take it off. Take the relevant firearm licences with you. And check before visiting another country that your firearm is acceptable – some countries have their own requirements regarding firearms, and certain types and calibres may be prohibited.

Safekeeping

It is against the law to take a firearm onto almost any passenger aircraft, but there may be facilities for its safe storage if it is declared before boarding. Similar facilities may be provided on some mainline trains.

Generally, while travelling, be as modest as you can in your appearance. Don't display expensive jewellery or items such as cameras. Even if an item stolen is subsequently recovered, you will probably be put to the bother and expense of having to attend court hearings in the district in which the theft occurred.

> **TRAVEL CHECK LIST** ✓
>
> BEFOREHAND, FIND OUT:
>
> 1. The route
> 2. What documents you need
> 3. The luggage arrangements
> 4. How much cash you need
> 5. Your arrival time
> 6. Who will meet you
> 7. The type of area in which you'll be staying.

BEFORE YOU LEAVE

The fewer the people who know your plans to go away, the better. Tell only those whose help will be needed if an emergency occurs in your absence, as well as close family and friends. Also advise someone at your destination when you expect to arrive. You might also consider hiring a cellphone so that you can stay in touch – but bear in mind that there are many areas, especially rural areas, where transmission is poor or unavailable.

Bag and baggage

Label your luggage with the name and number of a friend who can be contacted should your bags be lost and found. Don't forget to obtain the friend's consent beforehand, and to remind him or her shortly before you go away. Using a friend's name and number prevents the casual crook from tracing your probably unoccupied home through your luggage labels. Stick bright bands of tape over your luggage for easy identification, and always memorise how many pieces of luggage you are carrying.

Rigid suitcases generally provide better security than soft-sided ones, which may be torn (or deliberately cut open) in transit. Cases with a zip closure can usually be padlocked. Lock every item of luggage and keep the keys in a safe place.

Pack it in

It's important to pack your car as unobtrusively and efficiently as you can. Some people like to pack everything quickly, at almost the last moment before leaving. This works if you can do it unobserved. But if there is no guarantee that someone will not be watching you, do not stand by the car in the driveway with the boot lid open, waiting for family members to bring you their respective bundles. Family packing sessions attract attention. See that suitcases and bags are packed a day or two before you leave, and placed in a room near the outside door that offers the shortest or least public route to your car.

Before bags are stowed in the car, give family members a last opportunity to check that everything has been packed. Casually put a bag in the luggage compartment one evening, add another after dark, and yet another the next morning. If you space the packing like this, especially if you occasionally drive off and return, it's unlikely that anybody will think you're about to leave on a family holiday.

Keep a list of what is packed in your luggage – this will not only be useful in the event of an insurance claim, but may also save you time looking for an item that you only thought you'd packed.

People in the know

Don't inform people unnecessarily that you will be away. When you have your car serviced just before you leave, for example, don't tell the workshop manager to do a specially good job because you're going on a long trip. The mechanics should do the work properly in any case. Similarly, don't tell your hairdresser that you'll be away for a few weeks. Your neighbour, however, is the ideal person to tell.

She or he may help keep up the pretence that you're still at home when you're actually away enjoying your holiday. Alternatively, you could ask a close friend to live in, or employ a professional house-sitter (but check his or her references first) who will either live in your home during your absence, or visit it at agreed intervals.

Remember to advise your neighbour or house-sitter if other people – such as police or a security patrol – have also been asked to check on your property. Similarly, if you do ask the police or a security patrol to check your home periodically, remember to tell them that you have also asked someone else to assist. In particular, remember to tell them if the neighbour or house-sitter has your key. Failure to advise one group about the activities of another could have embarrassing and even tragic consequences.

Confusing the criminal

There are several ways in which you can bluff or confuse criminals and their spies while you're away. Instead of cancelling your milk and newspaper deliveries for the period of your absence, get your neighbour to cancel his or hers – your neighbour can stroll across to your front stoep or letter box to pick up your milk and newspaper, adding some life and activity to the property. (But advise them to keep an eye open for any suspicious persons watching them when they make the collection.) If you are on good enough terms, exchange garages or off-street parking for a week or two before you go away, and ask your neighbour to continue using your parking place during your absence (see Fooling Some of the People, pp70-1).

HOLIDAY CHECK LIST

THINGS TO DO BEFORE YOU GO

1. Cancel deliveries or switch with neighbour.

2. Arrange to have your letter box emptied daily.

3. Ask your neighbour to watch your home.

4. Inform your Neighbourhood Watch coordinator.

5. See that someone has your contact address.

6. Pay the electricity account for the period of your absence.

7. Advise police or security patrol of your absence.

8. Store all valuables safely.

9. Lock windows, garage and outhouses.

10. Set alarm.

11. Lock doors and gates.

ON YOUR WAY

Cross-country or intercity travel plays an important role in the lives of most of us, whether in business or as part of the annual holiday. Apart from road accidents, long-distance travel is reckoned to be safe, but to keep it that way listen to radio weather reports and news reports as you journey, if possible.

Safe stops

Wherever you stop in a car, keep the doors locked and remove the keys, even if you're getting out for only a moment. See that there's always at least one adult in the car – awake and alert – whenever you make a stop. If this can't be arranged, get everybody out, lock the car and set the alarm.

Roadside picnic sites and view sites are inviting, but if there's nobody else in sight, consider waiting for another arrival before parking there. Some view sites have signposts warning of criminal activities, but most authorities are reluctant to advertise this peril. Park your car so that you can drive straight out, without reversing or excessive manoeuvring.

Watch your bags

Don't surrender your luggage, small items, tickets or vouchers to anyone at travel terminals (airports, railway stations or bus stops), unless you are certain they are authorised to receive them. Uniformed workers operating in or from kiosks in public places are most likely to be genuine. Porters, however, may be less readily recognisable – if you give your luggage to a porter, stay with him until it's safely transferred from his trolley. Watch the transfer closely, to the luggage compartment of a taxi, for instance, make sure the lid is closed and locked, and stay with the taxi until your luggage is unloaded again.

When travelling by bus, be on hand when luggage is being loaded or unloaded – it's easy for opportunist thieves to mingle with passengers at the luggage bay.

It's safest to travel without valuables and with no more money than you're likely to need on the journey and on arrival at your destination. Keep personal items, together with cash and documents, in a money-belt around your waist, covered by your clothing at all times. If you prefer, keep valuables in a permanent or transferable pocket with a flap that closes securely, inside a shirt, pyjama jacket, skirt or pair of trousers.

Train travel

Remember to lock the door if you leave your compartment unattended. When you're inside, improve security by applying a portable door lock or alarm.

If you are sharing your compartment with strangers, be no more than pleasantly polite in greeting them and answering general questions. Don't give away details of your personal life, your job, home address or present destination. Do indicate, though, that you will be met by older brothers (or your father, uncle, sons), and that you will be staying with them. Be polite about not accepting drinks (alcoholic or others) and don't allow strangers to pay for anything for you. The relationship they're trying to establish might be nothing more than friendship, but it might as easily be leading to assault, fraud or theft.

Beware of fellow travellers

Especially in aircraft, there is a tendency to regard other passengers as fellow adventurers and trustworthy friends. Guard against this. Do not give away information about your travel itinerary or advertise that you are carrying valuables or large sums of money.

Make any complaints against a passenger or a member of the crew, in the first instance, to a conductor or member of the cabin crew. Try to obtain the name and address of another passenger who will be prepared to act as a witness. (This does not necessarily mean that the matter will go to court, but the statements of witnesses may be required even for a departmental inquiry.) If your complaint has no effect, you may have to take up the matter with a higher authority at the end of the journey.

If on a train you believe there may be danger of violence from another passenger or of a crime being committed, get off at the earliest safe opportunity. Report the matter to transport authority staff and, if you are not satisfied with their reaction or stated intentions, report it also to the police. Some railway platforms in South Africa have red SOS boxes, which consist of an intercom connected to the security office. A video camera near the box turns on when the system is activated.

Breaking a major journey is a drastic step, to be considered only when you believe the threat to be both real and great. It may be possible, especially if you have obtained the names and addresses of witnesses, to get a refund for the rest of your journey.

Breaking a road journey

If you think you are in danger while travelling in a road vehicle, get out as soon as you can do so safely, first making sure that you will not find yourself in a more threatening position by the roadside. In a minibus taxi, do not criticise the driver (for bad driving or an unroadworthy vehicle) or threaten legal action against a molester or other criminal, unless you feel that the other passengers will support you. Threats may merely lead to aggressive or violent conduct towards you. Just say, in as matter-of-fact a way as you can, that you want to get off. Make sure you have paid your fare, even if you don't get your money's worth. Memorise the number of the vehicle, and the names of any passengers, and report the matter to the police.

AWAY FROM HOME

Without letting it spoil your trip, bear in mind that not everyone in or around your hotel, camp or caravan park is a fellow traveller. Thieves, burglars and con artists find fruitful pickings in hotels and resorts.

On arrival

When you arrive, don't unload your car until you've found out exactly where you must park and exactly where you will be staying. You might have to repack your car, within view of dishonest bystanders.

Take your luggage directly from your vehicle to your accommodation. Where this is impossible – when you arrive by bus, for instance – keep your luggage in sight at all times. If you don't carry your luggage yourself, be sure that the person you give it to really is on the staff (on arrival, ask how you are expected to recognise staff members). Carry valuables yourself.

If the establishment provides safe storage for valuables and firearms, ask to see the storage facility. If it seems adequate and you decide to store items there, obtain a receipt for them.

Where there are no storage facilities for valuables, the boot of your car is usually a safer place than either a tent or a caravan – but bring them in at night. Better still is a car safe fitted into the boot or into a caravan. Never put valuables under a pillow or among clothing. There's a chance that either you'll forget them, or that somebody will find them. Put them in a tie-bag.

Wear your firearm in an adequate holster until you go to bed, and then place it in the car safe or in the tie-bag, or in a night holster (see Firearms, pp258-65). If children sleep in your bedroom or have access to it, unload the weapon and lock the ammunition away or put it in your shoe and stuff a sock in after it.

DRAMA IN REAL LIFE

Two in a room for one

Angela Lake was a 21-year-old student attending a computer familiarisation course at a country hotel in the Eastern Cape. Tired after the first day's activities, she retired early to her single bedroom in a secluded garden annexe, and was soon deeply asleep. She awoke suddenly and, in the dim light from her bathroom, saw a young man – she guessed he might be about 25 – standing on her bed, with one foot placed on either side of her. She lay still for a while, pretending to be still asleep, then loudly said 'Excuse me, am I in your way?' and quickly slipped out of the bed and walked briskly to the door. When she reported the incident, she was told that the

intruder was the hotel proprietor's son, home for the weekend from receiving treatment at a psychiatric institution. After the proprietor pleaded with her, she agreed regretfully to take no action.

Police comment: Ms Lake showed great presence of mind in allowing herself to take in the situation fully before reacting. A cool head in this situation is essential for you to determine what you are going to do. A sudden utterance will often disconcert an intruder, and Ms Lake used that moment to walk – not run – to the door. You have to be aware, though, that this strategy may not work every time.

In self-catering accommodation, see that all the items that are supposed to be there really are there before you settle in. The management should give you a list of the contents on your arrival. If they don't, ask for one, because you'll be expected to pay for anything that's missing when you leave. Read the regulations for visitors, and approach the management for clarification of any aspect that is not clear.

Camps and caravans

When going off the camp site, and before retiring for the night, check that tents and caravans are closed or locked. In parks and nature reserves, learn to identify the uniforms of staff who are authorised to issue instructions to visitors. Always make sure you are in camps before closing time and, if required to do so, report to the person in charge.

Hotels and guesthouses

Request a room between the second and sixth floors. Thieves usually target ground-floor rooms, and fire hoses may not reach beyond the sixth floor.

Before nightfall, check that blinds or curtains cover the windows, and that doors and windows can be properly locked. Always lock windows and doors when you go out.

To ensure privacy and security, especially if you are in the room on your own, apply a portable lock to the door, or place a rubberised wedge behind it. Don't open the door unless you're sure you know who is outside. Verify callers claiming to be hotel staff before you admit them, by calling the reception desk. If you believe you're in danger, follow the procedure that will bring help fastest – shout, telephone the police, hotel security or the duty receptionist.

On the street

Before going out to explore, ask the management of your premises if there are places you should avoid because of crime.

Try not to look too much like a tourist, especially if you're on foot and on your own or with just one companion. You're a tourist if you are obviously carrying cameras, or referring to guide books or street maps. Most tourists carry cash, apart from other valuables, so are considered good targets (see also Reading the Street, pp136-7).

Muggings may take place at any time, but in cities and towns are more likely to occur after about 5pm, when businesses close for the day and most people are going home. If you walk out at night, go in as large a group as you can, and stay in well-lit areas where there is legitimate activity. Be wary of strangers who appear to be going out of their way to be friendly or helpful. If you anticipate returning after dark, make arrangements for your safe return, such as calling a taxi in advance. Carry a gas spray on a key ring.

(see also Reading the Street, pp136-7).

TRAVELLER'S CHECK LIST ✓

SOME POINTS TO REMEMBER

1. Use traveller's cheques or credit cards rather than carry large amounts of cash.

2. If you're in an out-of-the-way place that takes only cash, keep small amounts hidden in different places.

3. Learn to recognise staff and their uniforms.

4. Don't look like a tourist.

5. Don't take unnecessary valuables when you travel.

6. In a hotel or guesthouse, check that doors and windows lock securely.

7. Know the fire drill and the whereabouts of emergency exits.

8. Keep caravan doors locked, even while you're driving.

9. Go sightseeing in a group – never alone.

10. Try to get a recommendation from a friend before booking accommodation.

11. Be wary of overly friendly or helpful strangers – including fellow campers.

12. Wear a fake wedding ring if you're travelling alone and want to suggest that you're 'unavailable'.

KEEP FIT, STAY SAFE

You are less likely to fall victim to criminals if you are fit and healthy. Your responses are quicker, you are more alert, and you are likely to be able to get away faster. But even while exercising you are vulnerable to crime. The most important principles in avoiding the attention of criminals when you exercise are to display nothing worth stealing and never to go out alone.

Stepping out

Many popular forms of exercise, such as cycling, walking or jogging, hiking or climbing – and even golf, on most courses – are likely to expose you to some degree of risk from attack or interference. Join a club or association of people with similar exercising interests to your own – their combined experience and advice alone will be worth the membership fee. Alternatively, exercise with a 'buddy'. Apart from the added security, a companion is likely to increase your motivation to exercise. Choose a busy route or area, if you can, where you'll be less likely to have to call for help or protect yourself.

Always let a responsible person know where you are going and at what time you expect to return. Also let him or her know whom you expect to accompany you on the outing.

Apart from being on the alert for criminals, especially potential muggers, keep an eye on wheeled traffic. You'd probably come off worst in a collision, even if you did have the right of way.

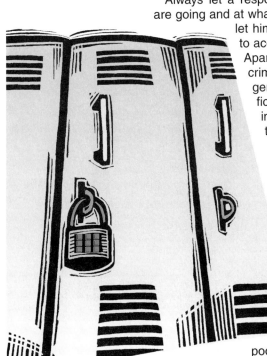

A safe start

Take a minimum of accessories when you go on a recreational outing, because safe storage can be a problem. An inexpensive watch (many of them are very reliable) and an ID disc (not gold or silver), with perhaps a towel and some extra clothing, ought to see you through. If you exercise at a gym or admission-controlled pool, there may be lockers that you can use. Take a small but good-quality combination padlock (no key required) to back up the existing security, which may be poor.

When you're actually exercising – whether swimming, jogging or climbing – try to carry just one key, for your car or your front door. Keep it in a small pocket (which you may have to stitch yourself), inside your shorts, trousers or sweat pants, secured by a zip,

Velcro or a button. Anything else can either be left at home or locked in the boot of your car.

Try to park in clear surroundings, near other people who look as though they are involved in the same activity as you are, and where you have a good view of the area in which you propose to exercise. If you're jogging through a forest, for instance, don't drive to a clearing in the middle and park there – park on the edge, preferably within sight of passing traffic and other joggers. As always, park with the front of the car facing the exit (see also On the Road, pp94-5, and Full Lock, pp98-9).

Prudent precautions

Before setting out, remove jewellery, especially rings, gold necklaces and expensive watches. A pair of cheap sunglasses will protect your eyes just as well as an expensive pair that's likely to be ripped off your face by a mugger.

Ensure that sports equipment – such as golf clubs, surfboards, scuba gear or bicycles – is clearly marked with your telephone code and number, or the name and telephone number of your sports club or association. At least you will have a chance of its being returned if it is recovered by the police. A recovered item with no clues to its ownership will probably just end up on the annual unclaimed-goods sale.

Essential accessories

Carry your telephone number (if there's somebody at home), or the number of a friend or relative.

You could also consider carrying an alarm or defensive spray attached to your waist or wrist (see Non-ballistic Weapons, pp254-7). You could even carry a firearm, but this is likely to be uncomfortable. Carrying – and correctly using – a cell-phone or two-way radio can greatly reduce the likelihood of a thief escaping with his loot, and is invaluable for calling for help should someone get lost or be injured.

Walking or jogging

Choose your time and your route carefully, so that you won't find yourself alone in remote places. (Even a shopping mall can seem pretty remote only 10 minutes after closing time.) Walk or jog so that you are facing oncoming traffic, and stay out of the roadway. Ideally, do all your jogging or walking in daylight and wear the bright-

est colours possible so that there is no doubt about your visibility. Never base your security on the assumption that there will always be other joggers on the route. If you set off in a large group, see that a head count is done at the start and again at the end.

Cycling

Given the price of most bicycles, and their desirability, there is considerable incentive for theft, which may occur when your bicycle is supposedly safely locked up, or even while you are riding it.

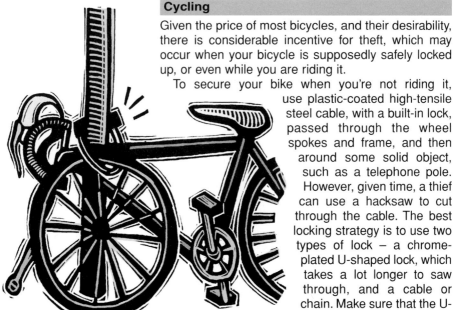

To secure your bike when you're not riding it, use plastic-coated high-tensile steel cable, with a built-in lock, passed through the wheel spokes and frame, and then around some solid object, such as a telephone pole. However, given time, a thief can use a hacksaw to cut through the cable. The best locking strategy is to use two types of lock – a chrome-plated U-shaped lock, which takes a lot longer to saw through, and a cable or chain. Make sure that the U-lock goes round the rim of the wheel and not just round the spokes.

If your bicycle is fitted with quick-release hubs, you can detach the front wheel and lock it with the back wheel and the frame to a fixed object. If your saddle has a quick-release pull, you should consider removing it and taking it with you.

Because cyclists generally travel faster than hikers or joggers, they are less likely to be interfered with while in motion. A thief planning to steal a bicycle is therefore most likely to strike at or near a parking area, where the stolen bicycle can be loaded onto a motor vehicle. Even so, some thieves have halted cyclists in motion, by placing simple obstructions, such as a branch or strand of wire, across a pathway and have used the bicycle as a getaway vehicle. Travel in groups, if possible, but remember to stay in single file so as not to inconvenience other road users. A pepper or gas spray carried round the wrist could be used to incapacitate an attacker, but you must be able to use it properly or you will simply antagonise your attacker and possibly make him become more violent.

In general, increase your safety by wearing bright clothing so that you are clearly visible and wear a helmet to protect yourself should you fall.

Hiking and climbing

These are not solo sports, and numbers, as well as remoteness, tend to keep hikers and climbers fairly safe from criminal attention. Nonetheless, there have been cases of hikers being attacked, possibly for the goods they were carrying. Never climb or hike alone. Before setting out, make sure you are properly clothed and equipped for the undertaking, and that a responsible friend or relative knows where you are going and when you expect to return.

Check the weather forecast for the anticipated duration of your outing. The leader of your party should be properly experienced and should know the intended route thoroughly.

Other people

These are the people who aren't exercising as you are, but are simply enjoying the surroundings at a leisurely pace or, in some cases, looking for someone to rob or assault. Most people dress for their legitimate activities, wearing casual, loose-fitting clothes and stout boots to go hiking, for instance. On a hiking trail, a person carrying no rucksack or water bottle, and wearing inappropriate shoes, is clearly out of place. Steer clear of people who don't 'fit in', and remember that criminals rarely operate alone. Report all incidents, not only to the police, but also to the authority responsible for the area in which they took place.

Secure attachments

It is not always convenient to place sports equipment inside your car – it may be too large or too grubby – and you will have to attach it to the outside. Roof racks that require an Allen key to be fixed onto the car, and racks that are dead-bolted onto the boot or the towbar, and which you lock the equipment to, are the most secure. A sailboard locking system is available that locks the board, mast and boom of a sailboard to a roof rack. If you attach equipment to your car roof, don't travel faster than 100-120km/h, and check every couple of hours to see that it is still secure.

DRAMA IN REAL LIFE

The loneliness of an urban runner

Wanting to keep fit but disliking the indoor atmosphere of a gymnasium, Penny Quick took to jogging, and enjoyed her daily outings through the forest on the lower slopes of Table Mountain. Penny travelled and jogged on her own, although there were usually other joggers to be seen on the paths beneath the trees.

Late one afternoon as she was finishing her usual route, she noticed a group of men standing just off the path, and presumed that they were forestry workers. As she drew level with them, two of the men stepped onto the path, grabbed her and dragged her into the undergrowth, one of

them keeping a knife at her throat. She was raped and indecently assaulted by at least five men, and then stabbed, beaten and finally left for dead. She was found by a couple walking their dog, and eventually recovered, to give evidence at the trial of her attackers.

Police comment: It is almost certain that if Ms Quick had been jogging in the company of another person, she would not have been attacked. The remoteness of certain places makes them attractive to joggers, but it also makes them attractive to criminals.

SAFETY ON THE STREET

It's probable that more crimes against people are committed on the streets than anywhere else. They range from theft, such as bag-snatching and pick-pocketing, to rape and murder. Your safety on the street depends mostly on you and on reducing the opportunities you present to a criminal.

Confront crime

Crime has increased dramatically over the past 10 years, but you must not accept passively that it will continue to get worse. Most people find it easier to accept than to protest, but this attitude can easily become defeatist, and develop into your only response to threats and challenges. Defeatism, or your failure to assert yourself, limits your lifestyle and provides more opportunity for the criminal.

While one of the principles of surviving crime is the avoidance of potentially dangerous people, places and situations, avoiding confrontation at any price must not become a way of life. Even though confrontation with criminals is usually forced upon you, you must face up to it, assertively. If you don't, you will eventually convince yourself that you are no more than a helpless victim.

Before you go out

Try to make do without a handbag or briefcase. If you do have to carry a lot of cash with you, rather take a decoy plastic bag or briefcase, perhaps with a little money in it, and conceal the 'real' money in a belt under your clothes.

Consider carrying a second wallet containing a small amount of money and invalid credit cards, which you can hand over if you are mugged. Place your 'real' purse or wallet in an inside pocket fastened with a zip or button, or in a money belt around your waist. Place your house or car keys in a secured inside pocket, preferably pinned or clipped in place.

Take off or hide jewellery, such as rings, bracelets, watches and necklaces. Remove small change – for newspapers, street collectors – from your purse or wallet, and keep it in an outside pocket.

Tuck away the loose ends of accessories such as scarves and belts, as well as long hair, so that they don't provide a grip for an attacker.

Put on comfortable walking shoes, so that you can walk confidently, or run if you have to.

Assertion, anger and aggression

Assertion is standing up for your rights, and letting others know in advance that you intend to do so. When your rights are infringed, you're entitled to be angry, but don't become abusive. Calling people names or using bad language is not likely to help your case, and will probably harm it. A little aggression can be useful when you're practising your assertiveness and your anger. It starts with a hostile state of mind. Don't, though, be led by aggression into making any sort of unprovoked or ill-considered attack.

Walking tall

This is physical as much as mental or psychological. Show it by walking erect, with your head high and your shoulders straight. Look as if you know where you're going (even if you don't). Walk purposefully, quickly and confidently, even though you may be nervous or afraid. Be alert and look around you – don't keep your eyes on your feet or on the distant horizon.

If you want to avoid eye contact with others, do so completely – don't let your eyes slide nervously across someone's face. However, some self-defence experts believe that full eye contact may put off some potential attackers. If you're confident of your steady, level gaze, look passers-by in the eye, being careful not to look aggressive.

When you speak to someone, especially a stranger, be polite and keep your voice firm and level – don't pitch it too high, don't mumble and don't whisper. Don't feel you have to stop for someone who wants a cigarette, a light or some spare change. This could be a ruse to get you to stand near the person and be pickpocketed or even mugged.

If you have to stand and wait in the street, keep your back to a wall, if possible. Stand firmly on both legs, rather than fidget from one to the other. Hold bags and parcels firmly, without looking as though you're clutching them nervously to yourself. If your hands are free, keep them steady and relaxed – don't fidget or pluck at your clothes.

Don't get your pockets picked

Pickpockets look for easy targets – people who are distracted or concentrating on something other than themselves and their immediate surroundings. Be aware! Don't, for example, wear headphones in the street or in crowded places – the music you're listening to is a distraction from what is going on around you and prevents you from hearing certain telltale sounds such as running feet, or the rustle of clothing as someone approaches you quickly. Similarly, don't window-shop in a dazed fashion on a busy, crowded street, or stop to look at a street address to work out where you are – always find out beforehand how to get to where you want to go.

Keep light fingers off your money by placing your wallet or purse in your front trouser or jeans pocket rather than a jacket or back pocket. Women should hold their handbags tightly and close to their bodies.

If you're carrying a backpack, put any valuables in pockets that can't be easily reached from behind or beside you.

Statistics from the street

The reported cases of robbery, a category that covers street robbery, rose from a total of 117 323 in 1994 to 118 751 in 1996. These figures include robbery with aggravating circumstances (in which a weapon is wielded, for example), which dropped from 84 900 in 1994 to 67 249 in 1996.

READING THE STREET

Spaces to stay out of

Wherever you go, the risk is greater if you go alone and, almost always, if you go at night. Avoid these places if you can:

◆ any thoroughfare you know is dangerous or has a bad reputation

◆ streets in which a parade or demonstration is taking place, or through which a lively crowd is likely to be making its way after a public meeting or sports event

◆ any street that leads straight to a subway

◆ any place where police or security force action is in progress

◆ streets that are poorly lit at night

◆ almost any street after sunset, if you're on your own

◆ cemeteries – they are often situated down lonely roads; don't go alone at any time.

The difficulty of forecasting an attack on the street is that the attack might come from anyone – including someone you haven't even seen. But if you know the likely sources of danger and what quarter it's likely to come from you may be able to prevent an attack.

The attack

It's a route you've walked many times before. There was nobody suspicious in sight. In fact, just where you turned into the pedestrian entrance to the mall, there was no-one at all. And it was as you turned the corner there that the bag-snatcher – probably no older than about 12 years – jumped out at you, grabbed your bag by the strap, tugged until it broke and you fell over, and then ran away. You hadn't seen him because, of course, you can't see round corners, and that's just why you should have noted this site as a danger spot.

Instead of walking right round a corner, consider perhaps stopping, suddenly but briefly, just before stepping round the corner. An assailant, counting your footsteps and waiting to pounce, would almost certainly be thrown off balance, probably to the extent of having to let you pass by unmolested. Or you could walk right past the corner several paces away from it instead of turning close to the corner, to see if there is a potential assailant and stay beyond his reach.

Watch this space

If you walk down particular streets often, get to know where the likely hiding places for muggers are, and avoid them by crossing to the other side of the road. A narrow lane between buildings, for instance, is purpose-made. Perhaps you and others who use your route could ask the owners of the buildings, or the local authority, to consider closing the lane with a high fence, or putting it on the route of a security patrol.

Not every street you walk down, however, is known to you. So watch out for these typical hiding places: the side of gateposts, in doorways and hedges, behind trees and the support pillars of verandas or bridges, around corners of buildings, and in the space between parked vehicles, especially where the one nearer you is tall, such as a minibus or lorry.

Don't get too close to telephone booths, especially where there's one person apparently talking on the telephone, and another just standing by. He may be awaiting his turn, of course, but don't count on it.

Watch these people

Groups of perhaps four or five people, apparently chatting on the pavement ahead of you, may include one who is just waiting for you to come within range. Once he's grabbed your bag and run off, the others are quite likely to run after him as though to catch and arrest him. Give the group as wide a berth as you can, without turning your back to them. Cross the street before you reach them, if necessary. If there's no alternative to walking past them, try to pass so that another pedestrian will be between you and them.

Beware of children

They may not have reached their teens, and some may even be as young as six or seven years old, but the tragedy of their lives is that they have been abandoned and have turned to life on the street, and to crime – chiefly robbery – to provide for their wants. No matter how much you sympathise, avoid becoming one of their victims. Children sitting or lying down and apparently occupied are probably not hunting. Children in a group and moving fairly briskly – whether erratically or purposefully – may be on the lookout for something to snatch. If you're alone, cross the road away from them. If you can't get out of their path, try to find trustworthy adult company or get your back against a wall or shop window.

No matter how safe you feel in a street, you should always look out for potential danger, particularly if you are walking on your own. Give a group of young men walking towards you (1) a wide berth, or even cross to the other side of the road. Walk wide of alleys (2). Be especially alert if you have to walk past a group of young men apparently loitering or hanging about with no purpose (3). Stay clear of dark doorways (4), and of corners (5), walking a couple of metres or so out from them. Beware of walking too close to an occupied phone booth (6) – the 'caller' and an associate may just be waiting for you to get near enough to mug. Be careful too of trees or shrubs (7), and the space between parked cars (8), which may hide an attacker.

NO MUGGERS PLEASE

Like it or not, muggers are around during the day and at night, and there's probably not a great deal that you can do – individually, physically or immediately – to remove them. What you can do, though, is to discourage them from picking on you.

No invitation

It may seem unlikely, but your attitude can actually invite attack. By staring down at the ground or staring vacantly ahead and walking slowly, or hesitating and looking at street names, you indicate that you are not alert to what is going on around you. What you are carrying also identifies you as a potential victim – a camera, for instance, suggests that you may be a tourist who's probably also carrying cash. Break out of this hunter/prey situation by using your best natural defence – an assertive attitude (see Safety on the Street, pp134-5).

What do they want?

Mostly, muggers want money, but some take jewellery and even supermarket purchases. One way of denying them money and jewellery is to carry or wear neither. Instead of cash, carry cheques or, preferably, credit cards.

Muggers may also go for parcels, sunglasses, cameras and expensive clothes (such as leather garments, especially if they are being carried).

Why you?

Muggers like to pick on people who look infirm or undecided, who have something that is visibly worth taking and who probably can't chase them, because they're laden with shopping or looking after children, for instance.

Muggers prefer dark, lonely places, but a mugger who can run fast and has a convenient escape hole to duck into or lose himself in, such as a park, a crowd or a railway station, will strike anywhere.

Hold on

If you're carrying a bag with a sturdy shoulder strap, sling it over one shoulder, and support the bag firmly with at least one hand, like a rugby player holding the ball, but rather more in front of you than at your side. Never wear a strap across the upper part of your body – over your right shoulder to a bag on your left hip, for instance. You may suffer a serious neck injury if a mugger grabs hold of this and pulls hard. If the bag has a wrist strap, use it, but don't let the bag dangle – keep it firmly in that rugby grip. A camera, too, should not be hung around the neck and left to dangle unsupported. Put the sling over one shoulder and keep a firm grip on the camera body.

If you're right-handed, hold objects in your left hand – your right arm is easier to use in an emergency. And if you're left-handed, keep your left hand free.

Don't pretend it's not happening

How many times have you heard running footsteps behind you, but simply carried on walking without even looking back? This may be the polite response, but it's very bad security. Your reaction should be to move out of the way, by stepping into a doorway, flattening yourself against a wall, or by moving so that some object – such as a pole or even another person – is placed between you and your pursuer. (Be careful not to get between your pursuer and the pole – you could be pushed against it and seriously hurt.) The sooner you can begin reacting, the stronger the defence you can build up.

Under threat

You're walking along the pavement when you see a suspicious group coming towards you. Or you're on your way to the car park when you realise you're being followed. Head for a shop, home, office or restaurant, explain your predicament and telephone for help.

If you're infirm or elderly, ask any respectable and robust-looking person for help. Don't start with a long apology or explanation, get to the point: 'Won't you please help me?' or 'Help me, I'm frightened'. Follow up by saying that you'd like to walk with them for a few minutes. Once you've been accepted as needing help, you can explain at your leisure. If you don't want to ask for help, simply move up close to someone (not so close and so suddenly as to alarm them) and match your pace to theirs. Hold your bag so that it's between your body and your new companion.

If you suspect a threat on the street and there's nobody around to help you, cross to the other side. If the suspected mugger crosses over, too, cross back again. This sends the message that you know he's there, you suspect him and he's not going to have things all his own way. Your show of assertiveness may well persuade him to look for a different victim. If you are going to shout for help, don't wait until an assailant has you in his grasp before you start.

Beware of beggars

Some beggars are more than they appear to be, especially those who look healthier and better dressed than the usual local beggar. The very attitude of a beggar – unaggressive, often cringing – doesn't suggest a threat and, too often, stirs you into opening up a handbag, purse or wallet. You're likely to lose it, if not to the beggar himself then to an accomplice you probably didn't even notice. If you're going to give money to beggars, keep small change in a separate pocket so that you won't have to produce your main cash reserve in public.

ASSERTIVENESS CHECK LIST

1. Walk upright, with head high and shoulders square.

2. Walk as though you know where you're going – don't dawdle.

3. Avoid carrying parcels that hinder your movements.

4. Be alert to your surroundings.

5. Walk in company if you can.

6. Look confident, be brave.

7. Remember that your assertiveness when attacked undermines a criminal's confidence, and so reduces his opportunity.

SAFETY ON THE STREET

UNDER ATTACK

Muggers are not out looking for a fight. As a rule, they operate only when the odds are heavily stacked in their favour, so an encounter with a mugger is usually a very quick one. Also, they seldom operate alone.

A typical scene

Typically, a mugger will take hold of what he wants – let's suppose it's your bag – and, as he starts to tug at it, he pushes you violently in the opposite direction. You instinctively let go of the bag and use your arms to regain your balance or to break your fall. Another favourite approach is from the rear. Someone passes close by you on one side, perhaps brushing against you, and as you instinctively look at him, his accomplice puts an arm around your neck from the other side, and pulls you into a head lock. Bent over and firmly held, you're almost helpless. There may be a fleeting kick, a punch or a hard shove just before they run off, to make sure you don't follow.

Are they armed?

Night-time muggers tend to be armed with knives or firearms and may be very dangerous. The chances are that if a mugger has a weapon, and has any intention of using it, he'll have it in his hand right from the start. Otherwise, to deploy a weapon such as a knife later, he would have to release his grip on you, exposing himself to counterattack. If his attack goes wrong, however, and you're holding onto him so that he's in danger of being caught, the chances are that he'll lash out with whatever weapon he has. But whether he's armed or not, he can still inflict serious injury.

Although hurting you is not the object of the attack, and most muggers rely on your fear to make it easier for them to get away with the loot (your bag, wallet or

DRAMA IN REAL LIFE

The tenacious tackle

Janet Stevens was not aware of the knife slashing through the strap of her handbag, but she felt the sharp tug as the mugger jerked the bag from her grasp. As she saw him begin to weave through the crowd on the pavement in Johannesburg's Jeppe Street, she instinctively made a grab to retrieve her bag, and caught her assailant by the arm. Then she noticed his knife and, off balance, released her grip and fell forward. She clutched the man's trouser leg, then his ankle, and held on firmly with both hands. All the while, she shouted loudly – 'swearing, I think, and I also yelled that he'd picked the wrong woman this time'.

During the attack, Ms Stevens was vaguely surprised that nobody had helped her to hold the man or regain her handbag until, after what seemed a very long time, a policeman brought the man to the ground and handcuffed him.

Police comment: In this situation, the person being attacked should always let go of the object being stolen from them. But a person's response to this sort of incident is seldom a reasoned one; Ms Stevens says that she reacted 'instinctively'. She was fortunate her attacker was not quicker to use his knife.

necklace, for instance), they don't care if they do hurt you. So unless you're confident that you can get the better of your attackers in a physical confrontation, don't try to be a hero – don't resist.

The tangled web

You're probably in the greatest trouble when, because of wearing the straps of a bag or camera across your body, it seems to the mugger as though you are refusing to let go. In reality, you have no choice and are entangled until the strap breaks or the mugger cuts it. Until that happens, you're going to be pulled around, shaken about and perhaps even throttled. (You can avoid the worst of this by not wearing straps across your body.)

Calling for help

You have the choice of using your voice or a whistle. (Don't wear the whistle around your neck; carry it on a short wrist loop so that it hangs in your palm.) Some authorities suggest that to yell 'Fire' rather than 'Help' will get more attention, because people will instinctively look to see whether their own property is endangered. Of course, whether they'll actually help you remains in doubt. If you're out of breath through shock or exertion, you'll find that you have almost no voice and not enough 'puff' to blow your whistle very loudly. Consider wearing or carrying a spray or a noise alarm to deter an attacker (see Non-ballistic Weapons, pp254-7).

Freezing

No matter how well you've anticipated an attack, instead of holding tight to your bag and screaming for help, you may find yourself lying terror-stricken on the ground, with the straps of your handbag sliding away through your seemingly paralysed fingers, and no sound at all rising in your throat. You've frozen – and it's no disgrace. Freezing, in fact, relieves you of the urgent responsibility of trying to decide what to do under the awful circumstances. And the chances are that freezing will get you off more lightly – regarding injuries, at any rate – than any other course.

Talk your way out

If it goes the muggers' way, the incident is over in much less than a minute. But if you feel you may be in physical danger, say something to reassure the muggers that you aren't going to give them any trouble. 'OK, it's cool' is short and not easily misunderstood. There is almost no chance at all that muggers will let you keep jewellery or ornaments. Claiming that you can't take off a ring because it fits too tightly will bring the routine retort that they'll take your finger as well. Usually, though, street incidents are too quick and too tense for verbal appeals to be introduced with much prospect of success.

FIGHTING BACK

The likelihood of being able to fight off a mugger successfully is not high. But in certain circumstances you may not have to give in automatically without any resistance, particularly in the rare instance that there is only one person attacking you.

Resistance movements

Since the mugger is working against time, if you're still on your feet after the mugger's first pass and there's no sign of a weapon, holding onto a strap for five or ten seconds may make the difference between losing your bag or retaining it. Don't do this, however, if you have muscular or skeletal trouble, or if your assailant is very large and you're very small.

If you can find your voice at any stage, shout as loudly as you can. Do whatever you can to hinder him as he tries to run off. Push a shopping trolley in his way, trip him, keep shouting after him, 'Stop that man!' You might even let him have your bag now – throw it at his feet to bring him down.

Strike!

If you're going to fight back rather than merely resist, do it with all your heart and energy. Be aware, though, that instead of frightening off your assailant, it may arouse him to greater violence. Most muggers, however, prefer to get away quickly, so they will not spend much time in their attack on you if you fight back.

The mugger is not going to get any closer to you than he needs to, so your reactions must be quick. Grab his hair and hold on tight. Rake his face with keys or shove a key up his nose or in his ear. Knee him in the groin, using an upward and forward movement. (Don't kick at his groin with your foot – he may grab your foot and bring you down.)

If you have an alarm, set it off, or spray gas or even hair lacquer or deodorant into his eyes. A tightly rolled newspaper forms a good club for thrusting at the groin or solar plexus. Remember that once you start to fight, you're going to have to keep it up until you've beaten your assailant or until you can escape from him.

When hurt is intended

You may be able to tell by his language – excessively abusive, aggressive, expressing hate – that your attacker intends to hurt you. Encourage yourself with the thought that he generally has very little time if he wants to avoid recognition and arrest.

If you're on the ground, try to roll or wriggle so that your back is against a wall or even a kerb or motor vehicle. Draw your legs up towards your chest, covering your genital area with the sides of your heels. Use your arms and hands to cover as much of your face and head as possible.

If there is more than one mugger and it appears that you are going to be held by one and beaten by another, simply collapse. You'll probably make it to the ground, where you can assume the protective position just described. Practise this position at home, and practise it well, before you need to use it.

Aftermath

Before you leave the site of the attack, write down the names and addresses of as many witnesses as you can, even if none of them saw the entire incident. Then report the incident to the police, giving them details of the witnesses, but keeping a copy of your notes for yourself.

Try to remember every detail about your assailants – the more closely you can describe them, the better the chances that they'll be arrested, identified and punished (see box).

Mixed emotions

You're going to feel angry, vengeful, frightened, bitter and ashamed. The anger and shame often go together, and are directed against yourself because, somehow, you feel that you should have done better or that you should have stopped it from happening. A portion of the anger and most of the desire for revenge are directed against your assailant, whom it's possible you may never see again. You don't, however, have to live with anger and longings for vengeance. Counselling will either provide an alternative outlet for these emotions or transform them into less destructive feelings.

Fear may keep you from venturing into the street again, in case there should be another attack. You need to overcome this too. Try to walk on the street as soon as you can after an attack, perhaps with a group of friends as an informal escort. You'll find you can gradually reduce the number of your escort and will eventually be able to go out on your own again. Remember, though, shopping on your own is not recommended anyway.

Your bitterness may be directed against the police, a security patrol, your companion, or anyone whom you feel should have been there for you. Worse, your anger and vengefulness may be directed at the class of person whom you hold responsible for the attack. This leads to bigotry, and you should guard against it. But don't pretend that all those mixed feelings aren't there. Discuss them frankly with your doctor, your family or with friends who have had similar experiences. Your local public library may have information about specialised help or counselling.

Remember, above all, and tell yourself and others as often as you need to do so, that no matter what treasure was in your bag when it disappeared, it wasn't worth dying or even being injured for.

ATTACKER IDENTIFICATION

TRY TO NOTICE SOME OF THESE POINTS

◆ SEX: Male or female?

◆ AGE: It's not easy to be accurate, but did you notice, for instance, grey or thinning hair, state of teeth, facial hair, wrinkled skin?

◆ HEIGHT: Was he taller than you? By how much? Compare him with someone of about the same height.

◆ BUILD: Thin, fat, athletic, bow-legged, heavy-breasted, large stomach or buttocks?

◆ FACE: Round, thin, wide, pointed chin, with a beard or moustache?

◆ EARS: Prominent, small, large, with distended or pierced lobes?

◆ SKIN: Colour and condition – spots, acne, scars, moles, warts, hair, tattoos?

◆ HAIR: Colour, long or short, thick or thinning, straight or curly, bald patch, style?

◆ EYES: Colour, clear or bloodshot, squinting, spectacles? Eyebrows – light or heavy, absent, meeting in the middle?

◆ VOICE: Language used, fluency, accent, lisp or stammer, slur, pitch (low or high), unusual or repeated words or phrases?

◆ CLOTHING: Tidy, torn or ragged, uniform, overalls, names or trademarks, colours, tears, cuts or burns, type and colour of boots or shoes?

◆ ODD FEATURES: Purple-stained fingernails, for instance, breath smell, cement or paint stains on trousers.

For counselling, contact one of the trauma centres listed in Useful Phone Numbers and Addresses, pp266-71, or ask your doctor to suggest someone.

No bystander is innocent

If you see someone being attacked, try to end the attack. Shout for help or sound an alarm if you have one, to draw as much immediate attention to the incident as possible. Call the police if you have ready access to a telephone, but try to keep up some form of pressure on the assailant. Be realistic, though. If the assailant is armed, or if you aren't strong enough or skilled enough, don't get involved in a fight. Be aware, too, that killing or seriously injuring the attacker (with a firearm or a sharp instrument, for instance) may result in your prosecution.

If you try to end an attack that is random, and not the result of domestic strife, the assailant is more likely to run away. Unless you're capable of stopping him, don't block the attacker's escape route.

Lending a hand

You may come across someone who has just been mugged and who is in need of help. If it's the quickest way of attracting attention to the victim's condition, shout for help. If the victim is unable to stand, see that he or she is safe from traffic, or very gently move the victim aside, and cover him or her with a coat, jacket or blanket. Assure the victim that help is on the way. Either telephone for help yourself, or ask someone else to do so, preferably someone with a cellphone who can make immediate contact.

If a victim is standing, be careful of causing further injury – by grasping an already broken arm, for instance. Rather let him or her clutch at you and lean on you. If there's a place to sit, ask first, 'Do you think you can sit?'

Apply whatever basic first-aid knowledge you have. Make victims who are bleeding severely or who have bone damage lie down. Unless you are medically qualified enough, don't attempt to reset broken bones or dislocated joints.

To stop profuse bleeding, press any clean, thick pad of cloth onto the wound. Don't lift it up to see if it's working. If the pad becomes soaked, place another on top of it and press on that one. Where an arm or a leg is bleeding, raise the limb and apply a pad at the site of the wound, and, at the same time, locate the appropriate pressure point. This is the place where the main artery above the wound comes close enough to a bone to be squeezed against it. Apply pressure here, as well as at the wound site.

Do not give a victim anything to drink if there appear to be injuries to the chest or abdomen, or if he or she complains of pain in those regions. Do not give stimulants such as tea, coffee or alcohol, but allow victims to moisten their lips with water from a damp cloth.

RAPE – AN ACT OF VIOLENCE

Rape is primarily an act of violence that involves sexual activity of some kind. It is usually perpetrated by a man against women and children, and is a crime that is increasing in this country.

Rape and the law

According to the law, rape is: 'the intentional and unlawful sexual intercourse of a man with a woman'. Sexual intercourse is unlawful if a woman does not give her consent. It is unlawful even if she doesn't resist – she may not resist because she is afraid that to do so will result in greater injury or even in death. Intercourse with a female younger than 16 years is illegal, whether she consents or not, and is known as 'statutory rape'. A male of 14 years or older may be found guilty of rape, and a husband may be found guilty of raping his wife.

Although, legally, only males can commit rape, and only females can be raped, men and young boys, too, are raped. The slightest penetration by the male organ constitutes rape. In cases where penetration is with something other than the male organ or where other parts of the body have been penetrated, the crime of indecent assault is said to have been committed.

Men found guilty of rape, statutory rape, or indecent assault may receive sentences ranging up to life imprisonment, according to the degree of violence and injury involved in the crime, previous convictions of similar nature, the age of the victim and the degree of premeditation. However, even though more rape survivors now come forward to report their ordeals, the number of successful prosecutions is still small.

The victims

Any female, even a baby, is a potential victim. She may be a schoolgirl, housewife, secretary, pensioner or sex worker. Some 45 per cent of reported rapes are committed on women aged between 18 and 25 years. Young women under 18 years are raped in 28 per cent of cases. Women between 26 and 35 years constitute 19 per cent, and women over 35 years are the victims in 8 per cent of reported rapes.

A woman may be raped by more than one man or be involved in a gang rape, having been chosen by a group of men or youths who may also band together to commit other crimes.

Many women are indirectly the victims of rape, whether they've actually been raped or not, because the fear of rape has restricted the way they live.

Avoiding dangerous situations

Stick to the general principles of self-protection and security – especially with regard to travel (see Away from Home, pp128-9), the home (see A Stranger at

Rape report

From a reported total of 20 281 cases in 1990, the number of rapes continues to rise remorselessly.

◆ In 1995 there were 36 888 reported rapes, or 115,2 per 100 000 people.

◆ In 1996 there were 119,5 rapes per 100 000 people.

◆ It's reliably estimated that only one in 35 cases of rape is reported to the police. This represents a real figure of 1 291 080 rapes for 1996, or 2,3 every minute – day and night.

◆ The incidence of rape in South Africa is three times that of the United States, and 12 times that of Germany.

Rape can happen absolutely anywhere, at any time. But there are circumstances, times and places that appear repeatedly in the police statistics. These include:

◆ dates, especially blind dates

◆ home, where not enough attention is given to security

◆ home, where a woman is living with an abusive partner

◆ hitchhiking and pick-ing up hitchhikers

◆ deserted parking areas after hours

◆ waiting areas for buses, trains and taxis, especially outside the busy hours

◆ deserted areas – at any time

◆ driving a vehicle that is unroadworthy or low on fuel.

the Door, pp80-1) and meeting strangers (see Meet You Under the Clock, pp162-3). Relatively few rapes are committed in the street or 'in the veld'; many take place in the supposed security of the victim's home or in the home of the rapist or a friend. More than 80 per cent of rapes are planned in advance.

Blind dates present a problem because you don't know your date, and he may think that women who go on blind dates are willing to have sex with strangers. On any first date, go to the meeting place in your own transport, or get a trusted friend to drive you there – and fetch you. Always let a reliable friend know where you're going and whom you're going to meet – and stick to your planned schedule. Choose a venue that you know well, at which there will be lots of other peo-ple close by – preferably not in the dark, as in a cine-ma. If your arrangements offend your new date, the chances are that your points of view would never have been compatible anyway.

It's unfair that women should have to adapt their clothing and behaviour because of the possibility of male aggression, but it's certainly advisable on a blind date. Wear comfortable shoes so that, if you have to, you can walk home, or run. Avoid revealing clothes, such as short skirts and low-cut tops, that attract attention to your body. Tie back or put up long hair and don't wear expensive jewellery.

If you have a cellphone, take it along in your bag. Decide in advance who you're going to call if things go wrong, check the number and check also that the per-son you may need to call will be available.

Avoid late or cosy scenes on the first few dates, or until you're reasonably confident that he's safe. You can never be sure, but, on the other hand, you can't live your life in a padded cell. Introduce your date to as many friends as you can – this lets him know there are a lot of people who care about you (and who will be able to describe him), and it also gives you an oppor-tunity to find out what others think of him.

Date rape

Also known as 'acquaintance rape', date rape means that the rapist is not a stranger. He may be your boyfriend, or a member of your family, a family friend or someone with whom you thought you could spend an enjoyable and uncomplicated hour or two.

When you go out with an acquaintance, or invite him home, don't drink more than you think is wise. Keep an eye on how much he drinks, too, and watch his moves – is he edging closer, touching you 'by acci-dent', or rubbing against you, for instance? Listen to what he says, especially if it's not his usual line of con-versation. He may be scattering suggestions and if you don't recognise them and turn them down, he may think you're prepared to go along with them.

Date rape may produce aftereffects that are even more serious than those that follow rape by a stranger. The victim is more likely to be seen as having 'asked for it', and her post-rape trauma may be made worse by confusion and unwarranted guilt. In addition, the absence of physical injury sometimes makes it difficult to convince others of what has happened, or, where cases are reported to the police, to obtain a conviction.

Where did it go wrong?

A date or any social occasion ending in rape probably started out pleasantly enough and with no hint of criminal intent on the part of the man. Indeed, it's quite possible that, at the beginning, there was no criminal intent at all. At some stage, the man formed the desire and intent to have intercourse with the woman – this is not criminal. Perhaps because of his interpretation of the woman's attitude, her conversation or even her clothing, he may have come to believe that she would be a willing partner, and he may have genuinely deluded himself. He may even have disregarded her apparent feelings or her statements on the subject altogether – it is here that his intent becomes criminal.

If you form the impression that your date has persuaded himself, or he thinks he has been led to believe, that you have consented or will consent to sexual intercourse, tell him the true situation immediately, clearly, firmly and, if necessary, more than once. Control the drift of conversation, as well as physical nearness and contact.

How to fight back

There is no smart answer that is going to guarantee results, but a few general suggestions may be helpful (see also Physical Self-defence, pp242-8, and Female Tactics, pp249-51).

◆ Shout, kick, bite, or pull his hair if you think you can prevent rape by resistance alone. Women who call for help often attract rescue or at least a witness who can testify against the rapist.

DRAMA IN REAL LIFE

The dodgy date

To widen her circle of friends, Kathleen joined a dating agency and, after speaking on the telephone to a new acquaintance, Tim, agreed to dine out with him.

She made her own way to a restaurant she knew well, where the evening soon turned unpleasant. Tim was good-looking and educated, but seemed to Kathleen – even allowing for the tensions of a first date – to be abnormally anxious and aggressive. He tended to flare up frequently, and then become abjectly apologetic. He became abusive when she declined to give him her address, and when she said firmly that there would be no second date, Kathleen was afraid that he was about to hit her. She excused herself from the table, saying that she needed to go to the rest room, slipped out by the back door and drove to the home of an old friend, where she spent the night.

Police comment: Although her date had her telephone number, it was prudent of Kathleen not to give him her address. Spending the night at a friend's home, in case he had followed her, was a good idea to prevent undesirable further contact.

◆ Talk to him, and try to get him to talk to you. If you reason with him you may be able to change his mind, but don't beg, since this reinforces his power image. Tell him, for instance, that you think you understand his feelings, but that hurting you will not solve his problem. Let him think that you find him attractive, but that his timing and technique are wrong, and that you're sure other women will also find him attractive.

◆ Don't say 'Don't make me do it.' These words reinforce his illusion that you are already in his power and that he can make you do things. Say 'No!', clearly and often, so that he understands you are not consenting.

◆ If there's more than one attacker, address yourself to the one whom you think you'll most likely be able to influence – he may appear shy or even sympathetic, or he may be the youngest.

◆ Tell your attacker you're having a period, that you're pregnant, or that you've just started treatment for AIDS, gonorrhoea, syphilis or herpes.

◆ If you think there's a real chance of making a getaway after a counterattack, hit him hard, stub your cigarette out on him or stamp your heel on his foot (see Physical Self-defence, pp242-8). It's important that you are able to make a getaway after this, because he's likely to be vengeful and vicious.

◆ A well-placed knee to the groin will almost certainly disable your attacker long enough for you to get away.

◆ If he's armed and you're afraid he might use the weapon, it's probably better not to fight back. Resist passively, by simply not cooperating at all – again, until a threat to use the weapon looks like being carried out.

After the assault

In a court of law, a charge of rape is decided by weighing the victim's word, together with corroborative evidence (such as blood or semen from the accused), against the word of the accused.

◆ Get to a safe place as soon as you can. If you're injured, go to a doctor or a hospital.

◆ Tell the first trustworthy person you see what has happened. This person may turn out to be a crucial witness in court, so get the name and address if it is a stranger.

◆ Call a support organisation such as Rape Crisis or RAPCAN (for a child younger than 16).

◆ If you take your clothes off, put them into a paper bag or wrap them in newspaper, for examination by police forensics. Don't put these clothes into plastic.

◆ Do not wash yourself until after you've been examined by a doctor.

◆ Report the rape to the police within three days of the attack. However, even though corroborative evidence after this time may be unreliable, any time within 20 years is still valid.

◆ Insist on your right to report the incident. A police officer may not tell you that you can't report it, or that you don't have enough evidence.

Rape myths: true or false?

The following statements are believed by many people, including women. They are, however, just myths, or lies, that have somehow gained a following. The counter-statements are based on research.

◆ The way women dress is a cause of rape. False: rapists will attack a woman no matter how she is dressed.

◆ Women often use a charge of rape to avenge themselves on men. False: It happens very rarely, because it takes a great deal of courage to report a rape.

◆ Rapists are sex-starved psychopaths. False: Most of them are 'normal' and many are married. Rape is a crime of violence.

◆ Men don't get raped. False: Heterosexual and homosexual men and boys are raped.

◆ If a woman really tries, she can prevent herself from being raped. False: Most men are stronger than most women, and force and the threat of violence are usually sufficiently intimidating.

◆ A woman can't be raped by her husband. False: In South African law, a woman has the right to say 'no' to sex – even with her husband.

◆ A prostitute or sex worker can't be raped. False: Her career is immaterial – she also has the right to say 'no'.

◆ 'Nice girls' don't get raped. False: Any female person can be raped, no matter what her age, upbringing or morality.

◆ If women weren't 'looking for it', they wouldn't hitchhike or go on blind dates. False: Nobody accuses men who hitchhike or go on blind dates of deliberately inviting violence, so it makes no sense to level this charge against women.

◆ You have the right to give your report to a woman police officer. However, if a woman police officer is not available, you may have to wait a long time. You are also entitled to give your statement in a private place – not in a crowded charge office, for example.

◆ When you report the assault, you do not have to lay a charge at the same time. If you wish, you may merely put the incident on record through a sworn affidavit which you can use later, if you find you are pregnant, for instance, or decide to lay a charge.

◆ Make a note of the OB (Occurrence Book) number assigned to your case. If you lay a charge, it will be given a CAS (Criminal Administration System) number – make a note of this as well.

◆ Describe events in great detail, and answer all questions very carefully and fully.

◆ Your statement must be fully written down by the police, and you must not sign it until you are satisfied that it is correct.

◆ A police officer must arrange for you to be taken to a district surgeon to have a medical examination.

◆ Before you leave the police station, see that you have a copy of your statement, both the OB and CAS numbers of your case, and the name and personal number of the officer who took your statement.

Rape trauma syndrome

A survivor of rape and sexual assault is liable to experience feelings of intense shock, which may take the form of insomnia, nightmares, panic attacks, a loss of interest in sex, a compulsion to talk about the attack (or, conversely, a stolid refusal to acknowledge that the rape even took place), feelings of futility and isolation, and anger (often directed against loved ones). The victim may also have to deal with physical damage resulting from the rape.

Guilt is a common emotion, arising from feelings that the victim didn't do enough to avoid or resist the attack. Such self-blame is unjustified. Victims are not to blame for having been attacked – the rapist is the guilty party. A feeling of being dirty or contaminated, and wanting to wash or bath more frequently, is also quite normal.

Reporting a rape often stirs up the distress anew for the survivor. It will certainly help, though, to talk about the events and the fears and depressions they have generated. Talk to a friend or a person recommended by your doctor, or call Rape Crisis or Life Line (see Useful Phone Numbers and Addresses, pp266-71).

Profile of a rapist

PROFILE

Psychologists classify rapists into five different types, but most rapists have in common a childhood in which they were abused, their parents were divorced or never lived together, or they were raised in a single-parent home, usually by a dominating mother.

◆ The power-reassurance rapist is the least violent and aggressive of rapists – at least that is how he starts. He has low self-esteem, probably didn't finish school, is unmarried, and lives with one or both of his parents. He is non-athletic, reserved, has few friends, and is probably a good employee. He probably collects girlie magazines and may be involved in transvestism, voyeurism, fetishism or exhibitionism. He rapes to boost his lowly status, usually choosing victims of his own age and race, who live close to his home or place of work. He does not deliberately harm intended victims, and may even be 'polite' during the rape. He may contact his victim afterwards to find out how she is. This type of rapist is likely to rape every 7 to 15 days, and often travels on foot.

◆ The anger-retaliation rapist actually wants to hurt women. Typically, he likes contact sports, is fairly athletic, socially at ease and, although he hates women, is probably married, although he's likely to have had a number of affairs. After some major incident involving one of the important women in his life, his quick and violent temper may lead to rape. To him, rape is not sexual – it is an expression of his anger, and his aggression may even lead to murder. He will rip off his victim's clothes, beat her and use a great deal of profanity, both to frighten his victim and to gratify himself. He may insist on anal and oral sex, and chooses victims of his own age or slightly older, usually close to his home. He may rape every six to 12 months.

◆ The power-assertive or exploitive rapist is trying to express his virility and his male dominance. He may have had several marriages, and he's a noisy, macho regular at bars, where he's likely to find his victims. He'll probably tear off his victim's clothes, and may even make repeated assaults on the same victim, from whom he will demand oral and anal sex. He may rape again within 20 to 25 days, with aggression and violence increasing each time. This rapist, who makes no attempt to hide his identity, has little control over his impulse to rape, and is probably close to being a sociopath or psychopath.

◆ The sadistic rapist intends to inflict physical and psychological pain. He is probably married, and may even be considered a 'good family man'. He is typically neat and well dressed, well educated, has a white-collar job, and has the planning ability and intelligence to escape detection. He uses his car (which he keeps clean and well maintained) to stalk his victims, whom he drives to a predetermined spot. Victims may be any age, and are likely to be tied, blindfolded and gagged, not only to prevent escape but also to instil terror. This rapist probably has a 'rape kit' containing the accessories he likes to use. Because he is compulsive, the rape must go exactly according to his plan, which may include forcing the victim to say certain words and to perform deviant sexual acts. He may attack the victim's sexual organs and, if not caught, he will become a killer.

◆ The opportunistic rapist is the one about whom least is known, because his attacks are not planned, but arise out of another situation – most typically, a burglary. Having broken into the premises, he encounters a woman alone or sleeping, and rapes her.

ABDUCTION AND KIDNAPPING

The Crime Information Monitoring Centre, which gathers statistics for the police service, defines the removal of someone for sexual intent as abduction, and the removal of someone to curtail their freedom of movement as kidnapping. Classic kidnapping – or illegally holding someone until the family has paid a ransom – is rare. More commonly, hostages are taken to be used as human currency in negotiations, such as gang disputes, or to ensure the success of a crime.

The kidnapped adult

Most kidnappings of adults are incidental to some other crime, usually a car hijacking, where the owner or driver is taken along to ensure that the vehicle will not be electronically immobilised. Children who are kidnapped are usually the victims of a domestic dispute (see Children on the Street, pp180-3). Anyone, however, may be the random hostage of criminals whose plan – to rob a bank, for instance – has gone wrong. In some cases involving the disappearance of adults, it has also been shown that their removal was simply part of a plot to murder.

Nonviolent kidnappings of adults, in which no weapons are used or even displayed, may be carried out by convincing a father, for instance, that his child is already in the hands of his kidnappers and may be injured if the father does not accompany them. Other techniques include impersonating a police officer and forcing a motorist to drive to a particular spot, or simply kidnapping someone at gunpoint.

Basic advance security

Ensure that your home and workplace are secure – that strangers, for instance, are not simply allowed freedom of entry and exit. At home, don't allow staff or family to give away information without first talking to you about it.

In the workplace, see that staff are instructed not to give information about other staff members – such as telephone numbers, addresses and the movements of people – to strangers without first consulting the person concerned. Establish a simple code system to alert staff to an attempt at abduction or kidnapping. It could be as simple as addressing the receptionist by the wrong name. For example, 'I'm just going out, Ms Brown' would alert Mrs Hendricks to the fact that you are going involuntarily, and advise her to set the rescue operation in motion.

The key tactic is to delay departure while the police are informed. That delay could allow another staff member to get ready to identify and follow the abductor's vehicle. But whatever tactics and variations you use, they must not alert the abductor.

Vary your daily routes, so that you aren't always pass-ing the same place at the same time. Even where you have the same set destination, you could vary the places at which you cross a road – the objective is to prevent anyone from being able to set up an ambush, especially one with a getaway vehicle standing by.

Abduction avoidance

◆ Don't arrange to meet strangers in lonely places, or to go with them to places you don't know well.
◆ Make secure arrangements at home and the work-place to exclude strangers, particularly when some-one there is alone.
◆ Drill household members and work colleagues not to give away private information to unknown callers.
◆ Don't indiscriminately or carelessly give out per-sonal information while socialising.

In their hands

If someone does try to abduct or kidnap you and there seems to be a good chance to get away, take it, espe-cially while you're still in familiar territory and where there are people whom you know.

Keep calm, be imaginative and mentally consider ways to escape or to influence your abductors to release you. If there's no evidence of a lethal weapon, and if potential help is within hearing, shout. Even if there is an alleged weapon, if other people are visible and reasonably close – just across the street, perhaps – try collapsing, suddenly and completely, as though you've fainted or had a heart attack. This should both attract attention and unsettle your abductor, who will probably be reluctant to shoot or stab you when you're lying on the ground in full view of witnesses.

Where a knife or firearm is already pressed against you, you must assess whether your abductor really

DRAMA IN REAL LIFE

The kidnapping of an invalid

Norma Smit was literally struck dumb – through shock and fear – when the hijack-ers pounced as she was about to steer her new minibus through the front gate. There was a man on each side, and both had handguns. Mrs Smit was flung to the ground from her high seat in the cab, and it was only as the minibus, tyres squealing, turned the corner at the bottom of the road, that she was able to speak. All she said was 'My mother.' Her mother, Mrs Kyle, aged 84 and unable to walk without assis-tance, had been sitting in the back seat.

Fred Smit assured his wife that no harm would be done to a person so old and helpless, but his wife's worst fears were confirmed late that afternoon when she

received a visit from her minister and the commander of the local police station. Mrs Kyle had been found, dead, beside the burnt-out minibus. She had been shot twice through the head, execution-style. It was presumed that the hijackers had killed her out of fear that she might have been able to identify them.

Police comment: In this situation, Mrs Kyle had no chance, and Mrs Smit was given no opportunity to save her mother. But even if she had been, callous though it may sound, Mrs Smit should not have tried to save her. When you have the opportunity to get away from armed hijack-ers, do so, without threatening them.

will use it if you try to get away, weighing this against the certainty that if you don't do something now you will be taken deeper into captivity, further from help. Protect yourself, but don't fight back unless you have a realistic chance of winning.

No panic

Stay calm. This may be difficult, especially if you're being driven about in the boot or back seat of a car, but it may save your life. Believe that the police and your loved ones, employers or colleagues are working for your release. Staying calm, however, doesn't necessarily mean being inactive. A man being driven away in the boot of his own car was able to loosen the bolts securing the boot lid and make a successful dash for freedom when the car stopped. It may also be possible to kick out the taillight from the inside of a car boot and put your arm or hand out of the hole to try to attract attention. If you are being held in the car, however, trying to attract help is more likely to harm you. It is far better to consider some sort of escape action once you have been taken out of the boot or the car.

Your abductor is probably extremely nervous. Do not challenge him directly unless he can be overcome at the same time. He may be at least as likely to panic as you are. Don't threaten or abuse him. If you become aggressive, it could scare your abductor into being more aggressive towards you.

It will probably not help to fight, particularly if there's more than one abductor, unless you're an expert in martial arts. And even then, if one of them has a gun or a knife, the chances are that you would merely provoke gross violence for no gain whatever (see also Rape – An Act of Violence, pp145-50).

If you're told to do something, such as talk on a telephone, do it. If your abductors ask what measures will be taken to bring about your release, say that you don't know, but that you're sure their demands will be complied with as fully as possible.

Gather as much information as you can, unobtrusively. Your later description of a particular sound or smell may enable someone to pinpoint a locality, and items of conversation that you overhear may suggest the involvement of a particular individual or group.

Friends and family

When you receive a message that someone close to you has been kidnapped, report it to the police immediately no matter what instructions you receive. Handle written messages as little as possible to preserve any fingerprints. If the message comes by telephone, stay calm and take notes of the entire call. If possible, get someone else to listen in or make a recording. Where a ransom is demanded, try to arrange a simultaneous delivery of hostage and ransom money, or make whatever arrangements the police instruct you to make.

Abduction alert!

The reported cases of abduction in 1996 came to a total of 2 019. Reported kidnappings for the same year totalled 4 156. The areas of highest occurrence of both categories were Gauteng, KwaZulu-Natal and the Eastern Cape.

STALKERS AND OTHERS

A stalker is someone who continually follows, watches, harasses and threatens you. Some stalkers mean no harm at all and may be just mild cranks obsessed with another person. Others may not be so harmless. Whatever their intention, stalkers inflict fear and make the victim feel unsafe almost anywhere. Stalking is psychological terrorism.

Stalkers and their victims

Most stalkers are men and most victims are women, but the roles are sometimes reversed, and children are stalked, too. It's estimated that as many as 90 per cent of stalkers may suffer from some form of mental disorder, while the remainder are probably just angry or upset. About 38 per cent of stalked victims are 'ordinary people', 17 per cent are high-profile personalities, 32 per cent are lesser-known personalities, and the remainder are executives or supervisors stalked by disgruntled subordinates.

Stalker at work

Some typical actions of stalkers include:
◆ telephoning, but saying nothing when the telephone is answered
◆ hanging about the vicinity of their target's home, usually where they can be seen from the home
◆ following the target, whether on foot or by vehicle
◆ suddenly appearing close to the target, in a shop, perhaps, or at a theatre
◆ being highly visible in general, but apparently indifferent to being seen
◆ sending or presenting gifts or messages.

When approached or addressed by the person whom they are stalking, stalkers may deny all allegations or become abusive. They may even back off and appear to become shy or withdrawn. This does not, however, mean that they are not dangerous.

Familiar faces

Many victims know their stalkers, a situation that is doubly frightening because the stalker knows so much about the victim. The stalker may be an ex-boyfriend, an ex-husband, a woman who has been rejected, or one who considers her relationship with a lover threatened by another woman – her victim.

If you are engaged in legal proceedings that involve the stalker – a divorce, for instance – report the harassment at once to your attorneys and be guided by their advice. If you think you're in immediate or near-immediate danger, tell the police. On the other hand, it may be worthwhile opening communications with the stalker, but only you can decide whether they should be direct – between you and him – or through an intermediary. Preferably, choose someone who is known to the stalker, to take and receive messages, but make sure it's someone the stalker couldn't reasonably be resentful of, or whom he dislikes. If you're still afraid, tell the police and make sure that you don't go out or come home on your own, especially after dark. When someone escorts you home, ask him or her to wait while you check that all is well inside.

Strange stalkers

If you think you are being stalked by a stranger, compile a good description of him, without letting him know that you are doing so – if he notices you observing him closely, he's likely to come to the wrong conclusions. Get a friend to describe him too.

Ask friends and neighbours if they know him, without saying that you suspect he is stalking you, or that you suspect him of having committed a crime – you might be prosecuted for slander. Say simply that you've seen him near your home several times and that you wonder who he is.

Get a friend – preferably male – to approach the stalker while he's actually stalking. Your friend should ask if he needs help to find a person or place and tell the stalker that he's been seen there before and is making people uneasy. Do not threaten the stalker, at this stage, with legal action or – except as a last resort in self-defence – with violence. The chances are that once he knows you have adequate support from friends, he'll find another target.

If the stalker still persists in harassing you, report the matter to the police. It will help them in their

Profile of a stalker

The immature, romantic stalker is usually a teenager who has developed a 'crush' on an acquaintance or even a stranger. The obsession may involve writing anonymous letters, telephoning without saying anything and watching from a distance.

The dependent stalker is often the rejected lover of the victim. He may go to great lengths to obtain information from the victim's friends and relatives, is likely to send gifts and love letters, and may also visit the victim frequently. He may even break into the victim's home – to watch her sleep, read her mail, damage her property, injure or kill her pets and eventually, perhaps, to murder. This type of stalker tends to adopt a macho attitude along the lines of 'If I can't have her, nobody else will'. Dependent stalkers may have lost a parent during childhood or suffered some other tremendous hurt that they perceive as a rejection.

The borderline-personality stalker is most likely to choose a high-profile victim and may, for instance, come to believe that a film star really is the larger-than-life character depicted on the screen. These stalkers can't always tell the difference between reality and fantasy, and their feelings towards the victim may switch between near-adoration and loathing. The slightest criticism may bring on feelings of rejection, shame and rage, and there is a frightening potential for suicide or murder.

Erotomanic stalkers believe that the victim – often a fairly high-profile person or social superior – is in love with them, usually on a spiritual rather than physical plane, even though the victim may be a stranger. These stalkers see obstacles to close contact as a test of their devotion and believe that the victim actually enjoys their attentions.

Schizophrenic stalkers, being severely mentally disturbed, are likely to contact their victim only where they believe that the victim is 'torturing' them, or when they have been 'commanded' to do so in the course of a hallucinatory state.

information-gathering if you can tell them as much about the stalker as possible: what he looks like, how and when he follows or watches you, including dates.

Stalking and the law

If the stalker has not committed a crime, such as trespassing or threatening you, the police will probably not be able to charge or arrest him. The most they can do is tell him that his conduct is alarming you, and perhaps warn him against illegal conduct in the future.

If he persists with his attentions, you may be able to obtain an interdict or court order against him, prohibiting him from contacting you or from physically approaching you. If he defies the order, he may be charged with contempt of court and imprisoned.

Stalking by post

Writing and sending maliciously threatening letters is another form of stalking. Such a letter may constitute blackmail, and demand money, information or sexual favours, perhaps in return for silence about some supposed misdemeanour on your part. Or the letter may contain a simple threat – 'Beware Tuesday the 15th'.

If you know who is sending the letters, try a direct, stern appeal to the person to stop. If necessary, warn the sender that you will report him to the police. It is unlikely that the police will be able to do much, unless serious threats are being made against you. But it might be possible to obtain a court order requiring the sender to desist. In cases involving extortion or ransom, handle the letters as little as possible and immediately give them to the police. Police interception of postal items may usually be arranged only where national security is threatened. If the letters upset you, get someone else to open your mail, or arrange with your regular correspondents to send their letters or accounts to another address.

will be watching your every

DRAMA IN REAL LIFE

The silent shadow

For some weeks Fiona Scott had been receiving phone calls in which the caller rang off without a word. It was only after she began to notice Rina almost everywhere she went that she had a suspect. Fiona's boyfriend, Max, had formerly had a long relationship with Rina, but had broken it off because of Rina's jealousy and her possessive nature. Rina never spoke to her or threatened her in any way, but Fiona found her constant presence unnerving. Her attorney, however, advised that it would be difficult to obtain a restraining order in the absence of evidence of physical or verbal abuse, and sent a letter to Rina, warning that action would be taken if the stalking continued. After a lull, Rina appeared again, and, a week later, a second letter was sent. In the end, the matter was resolved only when Fiona's employers asked her to take up a position in the United Kingdom, and she left the country.

Police comment: In most instances, the police cannot act until an offence has been committed, such as harassment or assault. However, reporting a case to the police may help a complainant to obtain clarity on the legal position, and may also place the matter on record.

MAKING THAT CALL

Public telephones – or payphones – are usually situated in fairly exposed places, such as outside post offices, courts and shops, and in shopping malls, where you and your money can be seen by many people. They therefore attract hangers-on looking for an opportunity to beg, rob or assault. Be careful not to flash your wallet or purse around, and be especially wary of what you say in the earshot of other people.

Public telephones

Payphones can be operated by inserting a range of coins, or by using a prepaid Telkom phonecard, available from post offices and also from shops and supermarkets. The advantage of a phonecard is that it is quicker to use than cash, and you don't have to rummage in your bag, purse or pockets to look for the right change and so alert anyone watching as to how much money you have on you and where you're carrying it.

While you're using a telephone your powers of observation and your movements are hampered by the instrument, so keep calls short. These are general guidelines for using a public telephone, but many of them also apply when you're using a cellphone out in the street.

◆ Take another adult with you to keep an eye open for likely muggers or other undesirables while you're making your phone call.

◆ Don't take anything with you that you'll have to put down while you're busy making the call – remember, you're going to have only one free hand to guard it with.

◆ Have your change or phonecard ready before you arrive at the booth, so that you don't have to display your purse or wallet.

◆ If you're going to call several numbers, have them written down on a handy piece of paper.

◆ If you're going to call only one number, memorise the number before you start making the call, especially at night or where the number is difficult to read.

◆ If you don't like the look of people 'hanging around' near the booth, walk past. Try again later.

◆ Once you've entered the number, don't stand and talk with your back to the opening of the booth. Turn around and, within the limits of the range of the telephone cord, take note of what is going on around you.

◆ Keep spare change in your free hand rather than build up a tempting pile of coins on the shelf – but don't drop them.

◆ Don't pass on confidential information, such as telephone numbers and addresses, within earshot of another payphone user or someone standing nearby.

Alternatives

If a friend can't stand by while you're making a call, and you're worried about people loitering nearby, ask someone working at the nearest shop if there are usually so many people near the telephone booth. Unusual activity, especially if it's related to potential unrest or violence, means you should seriously reconsider the necessity of making your telephone call at that particular time and place.

If the shop assistants seem sympathetic, ask if they'll keep an eye on you while you use the telephone. If you're really worried about your safety while using the telephone outside, ask if the proprietor will allow you to make use of a telephone in the shop. Make it a rule, whenever you use someone else's telephone, to keep the call short.

Many businesses, such as restaurants, have a table-model payphone (known as the Chatterbox) which is hired from Telkom. The rates, up to a set maximum, are determined by the person or business hiring it out, and are likely to be higher than those of an ordinary public payphone.

Doing the service a service

Report broken or vandalised telephones to Telkom through the nearest post office. If you see someone damaging or tampering with a public telephone, report the incident to the police. Telkom pays a reward for information leading to the arrest and conviction of people who damage or steal their equipment.

DRAMA IN REAL LIFE

Father's night to remember

Driving home from the hospital in Virginia, where his wife had given birth to their first child that evening, David stopped at a phone booth to spread the news. While he was busy, a man slipped into an adjacent booth where he busied himself looking through the directory. His calls finished, David turned to go back to his car, but found himself face to face with a man wearing a balaclava pulled over his face, while the man from the next booth slipped behind him and pressed something against his back. David obeyed the terse command to get into the driver's seat of his own car and then, despite the gun pointed at his head from outside the car, he floored the acceler-

ator, heading for the police station. He didn't hear the shots, but one of several bullets that penetrated his car lodged in his shoulder, and David found himself a patient in the hospital he had so recently left.

Police comment: Alone at a phone booth, and particularly at night, David should have been keeping an eye on what was going on around him. It is possible that he then might have spotted danger approaching and been able to leave immediately. He was lucky to escape with his life during the attempted hijacking. It is not advisable to resist the orders of someone pointing a gun at you.

CAUGHT UP IN THE ACTION

Playing an active part in your Neighbourhood Watch or street committee, or joining the Police Reserve, are the best ways to lend direct help to the country's law-enforcement agencies. However, there may be times when you find yourself more closely involved than you'd expected – perhaps in command of a situation, or simply trying to stay out of trouble.

They need YOU

A police officer may call on any male aged between 16 and 60 years to help him or her make an arrest or to detain someone who has already been arrested. If you have no valid reason for refusing, it is an offence not to assist a police officer when called on to do so under these circumstances.

A citizen's arrest

The law describes when you may make an arrest on your own initiative, but, before you attempt to do so, consider the possible consequences. A criminal, desperate to escape, may be armed and prepared to wound or even kill his pursuer. Your safer alternative is to try to keep track of the criminal while at the same time alerting the police.

You may make a citizen's or private arrest of a person who, in your presence, commits or tries to commit a Schedule 1 offence (see box on page 161). You may also make an arrest on the grounds of 'reasonable suspicion'. Some specific instances include a private arrest where you have a reasonable suspicion that someone has stolen livestock (or is about to steal it), where wilful damage is done or is about to be done to Post Office lines or poles, and where people are brawling in a public place.

Making the arrest

You are required to touch the person you are about to arrest on the arm or shoulder, and you must tell them, at the same time, of the reason for the arrest. You may use force – but only a reasonable amount – only if the person being arrested refuses to submit. If an arrested person comes along willingly, it is unreasonable use of force to twist his arm behind his back, causing pain or injury. The usual strict laws apply to the use of a firearm (see Firearms, pp258-65). You must take the arrested person to a police station as soon as you possibly can.

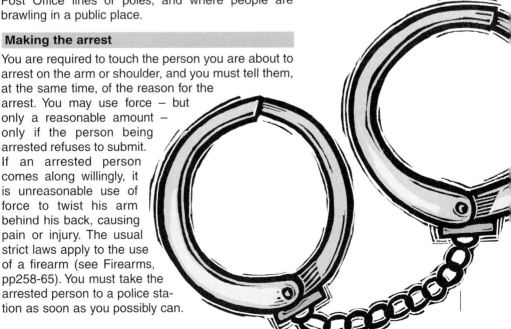

Taxi driver makes a big catch

Taxi driver Joe Msaba had no passengers on board until he stopped outside the town of Adelaide, first to pick up a man and, later, two women. A fare to Grahamstown was agreed, but, once they had arrived there, the male passenger said he had no money. Annoyed, Msaba seized a sports bag the man was carrying and told him he would keep it until the man managed to get some money to pay the fare.

The passengers alighted and Msaba eventually decided to look through the bag. In it, wrapped in a shirt, was an automatic pistol. Msaba's suspicions were aroused, so he immediately drove to where he had dropped his passengers. He confronted his former passenger, who soon became aggressive. Msaba, however, subdued him with 'one big slap on the side of the head' and took him to the police station. At the charge office, the man was soon identified as the alleged leader of a gang believed to be responsible for a series of murders in the Western Cape.

Police comment: The law does not expect citizens to endanger themselves when carrying out an arrest, but if Mr Msaba had not acted as promptly as he did, the suspect might have escaped. Mr Msaba's courage and public-spiritedness are highly commendable.

If you use excessive force on someone whom you're arresting, you may later be charged with assault, whether the person is found guilty of the alleged crime or not. In a case where you arrest the wrong person, that person might be able to claim damages from you.

One of the crowd

Getting caught up in an excitable crowd, such as at a demonstration or in a pub brawl, may result in injury or other misfortune, such as theft or arrest. Avoid unscheduled and unlawful gatherings, and think carefully before taking part in some scheduled gatherings.

The most common unscheduled gatherings are those that form at the scenes of accidents along the road, at fires and at other scenes of disaster or potential disaster. Stay clear of fights, whether between individuals or between gangs. There is always a risk that misfortune will spread, and it may result in anything from pickpocketing to serious injury or death. Unlawful gatherings may be vigorously suppressed by the forces of law and order, and you may suffer injury from gas inhalation or through being struck by a missile – it could be a baton, a brick or a bullet.

If you can, avoid sports gatherings or other scheduled gatherings, such as certain concerts, that have been greatly publicised and have the potential for overcrowding, the widespread use of drugs or inadequate security. Keep away, too, from political meetings at times of political tension or violence. In particular, invalids, small children or any infirm person should not attend these gatherings or meetings. (See also Lost or Alone, pp118-9.)

Staying alive

If shooting breaks out while you're part of a crowd, you're safest if you drop to the ground and lie as still and as flat as you can, covering your head and neck with your arms and hands. Indoors, try to dive under chairs or a table – they won't stop bullets, but they may prevent you from being trampled by the crowd. (Most people tend to shoot progressively higher, especially with automatic firearms.) If you think it will help, yell clearly 'I give up' or 'Stop shooting', without moving your body.

In some circumstances – where mass murder appears to be the object, for instance – it may be better to play dead. If you can reach cover by rolling no more than once or twice, and if you can roll quickly, it may be worth trying to reach the cover. Generally, however, movement is likely to attract fire. Under low cover, you may be able to move farther away by using the leopard crawl: keep as flat as you can and drag yourself forward, using your toes and your elbows. Don't raise yourself until you're absolutely sure that the shooting is over. Even then, let someone else be the first to get up.

The way out

When attending events indoors, note the positions of emergency exits. In most halls, the word 'Exit' should be illuminated above the doorways at all times. Choose an exit other than the main doorway you came through – there may be a crowd of well-meaning volunteers or emergency workers blocking the main doors if something goes wrong. Try to see from the position of the frame and hinges whether the door you're mentally selecting as an exit opens inwards only. An inward-opening door can be a deathtrap for someone trying to get out.

To make sure that you can reach your chosen exit quickly, and to keep it in view, choose a seat on a side aisle, or a place that is no more than two seats from a side aisle, about one-third of the way from the back or front of the hall.

Make sure that you arrive well before the time that the event is due to start. Try to foresee the necessity to evacuate the hall – because of rowdiness or fire, for instance. In the case of an emergency, go straight to the exit, keeping to a wall or other place against which you can brace yourself in the event of a stampede, and prevent yourself falling.

Go with the flow

If you're caught up in a moving crowd, move with them, even if you're frightened and want to get away. Trying to stand still or go against the flow may result in your falling and being trampled or crushed.

To get away, try to work your way towards the edge of the crowd, by moving slightly faster and making your way diagonally past other people. Alternatively, make your way to the rear by slowing slightly and letting the crowd pass on either side of you. Once you're out of the mass, tail your pace off gradually and get as far away as you can.

Schedule 1 offences

You may carry out a citizen's arrest of a person who commits the following offences:
◆ assault and inflicting a dangerous wound
◆ breaking or entering any premises to commit a crime
◆ fraud
◆ forgery
◆ murder
◆ rape or indecent assault
◆ robbery
◆ treason
◆ any crime for which the punishment may be imprisonment for more than six months.

MEET YOU UNDER THE CLOCK

Private and confidential

When meeting a stranger, keep private the following personal information:
- your home address
- whether you live alone
- your home telephone number
- your parents' name, address or telephone number
- where you work
- whether you've been married
- whether you have children.

'The clock' is a feature of many railway stations and, being obvious, is a favourite meeting place. When you're meeting someone for the first time, your rendezvous could be anywhere, but nothing is more important than that the meeting place should be public and on territory that is familiar to you. Remember, you have an appointment with a stranger.

You're meeting who?

You may be meeting a blind date, or someone who has a letter or package to give you from a relative or friend who lives far away, or it may be a business client, or someone who has a job to offer you. Try to find out as much as you can about this person before you actually meet by talking to your friends, family or business colleagues about him or her.

If you're meeting a potential employer, call his business and ask who he is. If meeting strangers in strange places is a part of your job, as it is for an estate agent, for example, make sure you have a cellphone with you at all times. Keeping the advantage is common sense in a new situation, such as the one you're about to enter.

Where to meet

Choose the venue for the meeting yourself – don't be charmed or bullied into accepting a place that isn't safe. Keep to places that you know, dress reasonably conservatively (see also Rape – An Act of Violence, pp145-50) and take a friend. Venues that are obviously undesirable for a first meeting include:
- lonely places, where there is nobody to see you arrive or leave
- remote places to which access is difficult
- places with dubious reputations or a too intimate atmosphere.

When you're meeting someone on business, it may be awkward to include a friend. However, a friend may be able to accompany you to the venue and wait for you there until your interview or meeting with the stranger is over.

Don't change course

Once you've selected a venue, stick to it and don't be diverted from it. For instance, the person you're going to meet may telephone at the last moment to say he can't reach the place you've chosen in time, and ask you to meet him somewhere else. Don't change the venue on short notice – rather change the date, and go some other time.

Another variation may be a messenger sent to you while you're waiting at the original venue, to ask you to meet your appointment somewhere else. Say politely that you're running out of time, or that the new venue makes it difficult to get to your next appointment, and inform him that you'll arrange to meet another time.

Don't wear a rose

If you've never met before, give the person you're meeting a general description of yourself, but don't make it so detailed that he'll unfailingly be able to identify you. Rather ask him to dress so that you may identify him.

While you wait

A person who is obviously on her own and waiting for someone (it shows in nervous or impatient attitudes and gestures) is a good target for anything from a mild flirtation to murder. If you arrived by car, unscrupulous people may use this to lure you outside for their own purposes. Here are some of their lines:

◆ 'I'm sorry, but I've just driven into your car'.
◆ 'I'm afraid you've parked me in, would you please move your car?'
◆ 'The traffic cops are towing your car away'.

Don't respond to any of these lures, unless you're absolutely certain that the person bringing the message is genuine, and that it's safe to go outside. If someone really has driven into your car, all you need is his name, address and details of the vehicle. If you always park legally, as close to the venue as possible, without obstructing other vehicles or any driveways, your car is unlikely to be towed away.

APPOINTMENT CHECK LIST ✓

Before meeting a stranger, make sure that a responsible friend, relative or colleague knows:

1. Where you're going.

2. Whom you expect to meet.

3. What time you're supposed to meet.

4. Any secondary destination – having met someone, you might go on to another place, for instance.

5. How and along what route you intend to travel.

6. When you expect to return.

7. What to do if you don't return when you're expected to.

Profile of a serial killer

There are several classifications within this group of bizarre and terrifying criminals, but their most significant aspect – in almost every case – is that serial killers are strangers to their victims. The victims are targeted by the killer and then make the mistake of allowing themselves to be drawn into his 'comfort zone', a place where he can kill them at his leisure, in the knowledge that he will not be disturbed.

Serial killers have been classed as organised or disorganised, according to characteristics of their personalities, differences in their methods of killing and details at the scenes of their crimes. The organised serial killer is of average to high intelligence, socially competent, probably lives with a partner and shows great interest in published news of the murders. Stress may precipitate his actions and he is likely to use alcohol before the murder. He makes carefully planned attacks on selected strangers. A disorganised killer, on the other hand, tends to make spontaneous attacks on random victims. He's likely to be of below average intelligence, socially ill at ease, probably lives alone and takes only minimal interest in news of his crimes. The organised killer demands submissive victims, and will use ropes or handcuffs to control them, later transporting and hiding the body, and removing the weapons that he used. The disorganised killer, relying on sudden violence, rarely restrains his victims and leaves a scene of chaos, with the body displayed and weapons left behind.

Other categories on which the classification of serial killers may be based include: the pattern and method of murder; characteristics of the victims and their relationship to the killer (they may all be prostitutes, for instance, or remind him of a particular person); the location of the murders; the background of the killer, including his childhood, current behaviour and likely social patterns.

There is no instant way to recognise a serial killer – the way to avoid becoming a victim is to take sensible precautions, especially where strangers are involved.

STREET CONS

Fraud figures

There were 61 016 cases of fraud, forgery, embezzlement and cons of different kinds reported in 1995 in South Africa. This figure went up to 62 186 in 1996.

Nobody has reliably reported having been sold high-density building rights for the top of Table Mountain. But some of the fraudulent transactions that take place – many of them on the street – are only a little less amazing. Be on your guard whenever anyone approaches you in the street with a story about how you could help them or make yourself some quick money – it is bound to be a con.

The attraction

You may be offered the opportunity to buy something, supposedly of immense value, at just a fraction of its worth. You may be invited to join a pyramid scheme, a card game, or some other game of chance. There is only one certainty, and that is that you are going to lose your money. You may be beaten up as well.

Fraudulent practices range from sales of nonexistent computer courses and the collection of money supposedly 'owed' to the government by someone masquerading as a government official, to sales of fake tickets to sports events and concerts, sales of blank paper claimed to be dollar bills treated with a special chemical and worth R1,5 million, and any number of sleight-of-hand tricks whereby gullible people have lost watches, cash, rings and other jewellery.

The basic con

Wristwatches and jewellery are the favourite goods of street con men. Most of the items sold by them are factory-made copies of famous designs or have a well-known and reliable brand name printed on them. The vendor's story – usually concerning 'a batch uncleared by Customs', or 'an insolvent estate' – plays only a small part in making the sale. You believe that you are buying the object at a bargain price. But in fact you are being offered a markedly cheap item at a hugely inflated price. And if you buy it and have regrets soon afterwards, it's unlikely that you'll be able to recover your money. The chances of acquiring an honest bargain for this sort of item are very low indeed. It's safer to buy from a reputable source.

Gambling games

These may involve cards or, popularly, a mysterious pip that appears and disappears under three bottle tops. (The pip may be a small stone or coin, and the bottle tops may be enamel mugs, but the principle is the same.) A stranger is attracted by bystanders betting on which bottle top conceals the pip. The tops are moved around by the operator, and one of the bystanders, having guessed correctly, is paid a large sum of money and goes off with a smile on his face. The operator, by sleight of hand, may allow strangers to win at first, to build up their confidence until they make a large bet. This, of course, they lose. It's quite likely, too, that the original bystanders and the happy 'winner' are part of the con team, working to draw curious passers-by into the scam. They also may be busy picking the pockets of newcomers watching the game.

Donations

Unscrupulous people sometimes use schoolchildren or students (who are invariably acting in good faith) to solicit donations to support their worthy 'cause'. The organisation for which the money is allegedly collected may be represented as any quasi-charity, from a nature reserve to a society helping orphans. A touch of authenticity is sometimes lent by giving donors a brochure or bumper sticker.

Collectors of this type often operate in the car parks at shopping centres. Other collectors, encountered both at the front door and on the street, may present a photocopied 'letter of authority', usually with an official-looking stamp on it, and a notebook containing the signatures or initials of reputed earlier donors and the amount of their 'donations'. Unfortunately, the money you give does not go to charity, but to the bogus collectors or the people who employ them.

Instead of handing out sums of money to collectors whose integrity is not established, consider making an annual donation to a charity that you know is genuine. This way you have plenty of time to decide which charity to support and to establish its authenticity.

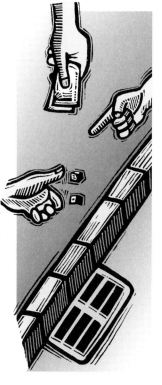

Fake investments

The principle of all of these – whatever the amount of money involved – is that you are asked to part with money in return for a profit that you will receive later. One example is the pyramid scheme. Remember that if it really is such a good scheme, its promoter should be able to raise the money without approaching strangers. Another notorious example is the Nigerian '419' scam, so named because it is referred to in Section 419 of the Nigerian penal code. Investors are offered a chance to participate in a lucrative contract that will see the transfer of millions of US dollars into their bank accounts. They are required to provide blank invoices and information concerning their bank accounts, which are then emptied by the swindlers. Investors may also be asked to provide goods, such as gold watches, for use as bribes to secure the contract, and may even be asked to attend meetings in Nigeria (where they are likely to have to bribe their own way out of detention).

Don't sign, don't pay in advance

Unscrupulous people will try to trick you into signing away your money or rights by claiming, for instance, that they need your signature to prove to their employer that they have called on you. Or they will try to hurry you by claiming that the offer is about to close or that you will regret not signing. You will almost certainly regret it if you do sign, so tell them that you never sign anything without your attorney's approval.

A scheme intended to take your money may not be strictly illegal. But once you've signed an undertaking to pay a lump sum, or even to make regular payments, you may find it difficult and costly to withdraw from the arrangement. So don't sign any contract or other undertaking unless you've read and understood it yourself – and, preferably, also given it to your bank manager or attorney to approve.

What to do

Be wary of anyone who comes up to you and tries to persuade you to buy something, or to give a donation. If something unusual is being offered for sale on the street, smile politely and say something like 'No thank you, not today'. And beware of another operator who may be trying to get into your pocket or your handbag while the first is talking to you.

If you're offered a study course, check that the institution offering the course is genuine before you enrol, sign anything or hand over your money. Write to the Correspondence College Council, PO Box 84448, Greenside 2034 to check the institution's authenticity. Also ask for the names and addresses of successful students in your area to find out how highly regarded the institution is.

If you have been the victim of a swindler, or if you suspect that someone has tried to con you, report the incident to the police. In many cases, however, it is difficult to obtain a conviction because of lack of evidence. (See also A Stranger at the Door, pp80-1, and Words in Your Ear, pp82-5.)

DRAMA IN REAL LIFE

When a green light meant danger

In several towns it has become customary for people with vehicles to sell to park them in a certain public place on Sundays, with a sign showing the price and other details. Piet Vosloo's four-wheel-drive truck had attracted no firm buyers until the end of the day, when someone said he would like to make an offer. He was an Angolan, he said, and had no money, but he had brought 'things' from Angola Mr Vosloo might be interested in. When Mr Vosloo was non-committal, the Angolan drew him aside and produced a small parcel wrapped in animal skin and tied up with leather thongs. He opened the package to reveal a number of glittering green stones that he said were emeralds – some of them cut and others in the 'raw' state. He poured an effervescent liquid, that he claimed was acid, over the stones and said that the fact that it didn't etch the stones showed they were genuine. He added that he knew an expert who could value them, but Mr Vosloo decided not to proceed.

Police comment: Many people fall for scams involving bits of coloured glass, and amounts of up to R250 000 have been handed over for 'stones'. Only about two out of ten victims complain to the police, because most of them believe they might be prosecuted for dealing in illicit stones. In fact, most of the 'stones' are fragments of glass from traffic lights. It would have been helpful if Mr Vosloo had made an arrangement to meet the vendor later, and, in the meantime, had contacted the police. The police could then have investigated the matter and taken appropriate action.

WALKING IN HIGH-RISK AREAS

You may live in a high-risk area, you may have to visit one, or you may find yourself stranded in one. Given the strong likelihood that you may be a target while walking through it, consider taking a few precautions to avoid becoming a victim.

What is a high-risk area?

There's no firm definition, but a high-risk area is one in which there is a relatively high number of attacks on people or on particular types of people, such as tourists or members of different political or religious groups. These people may be strangers to the area or residents. The area may have a steady flow of pedestrian traffic, which attracts muggers and other criminals. Or it may be the territory of gangs and drug rings (see High-risk Living, pp64-5).

Gross violence is frequently committed in broad daylight in these areas, often in the knowledge that no witnesses will dare to report the incident, and that because of lack of evidence, convictions may be difficult or even impossible to secure. Particularly where large-scale violence has recently broken out, as in a riot, there may a great deal of resentment that could simply find an outlet in an attack on a defenceless, innocent passer-by.

Don't go alone

If you absolutely must walk through a dangerous area, then don't walk alone. If you can drive through it rather than walk, then drive – but again, not alone – or accept a reliable lift, preferably right to your front door.

Try to go in a group of at least three (preferably four) able-bodied adults. Muggers usually operate in hit gangs of up to three, which means that their loot has to be split three ways. Increasing the hit-gang size reduces the individual's loot to an uneconomic low, so your group of three or four is relatively safe from a full confrontation, although snatch-and-run specialists may still try their luck (see Under Attack, pp140-1). Some child gangs commonly consist of a dozen or more members, but even they will be reluctant to tackle four adults (see also Reading the Street, pp136-7).

Since muggers are no heroes and prefer to pounce on the solitary person or the couple who looks least able to resist them, walk assertively to give them the impression that they can anticipate serious resistance if they try to tackle you (see Safety on the Street, pp134-5).

On the other hand, if you're walking through territory that you know is 'claimed' by a gang, walking in a group of, say, four or more, may lead to aggression if the gang is large enough and sees your combined presence as a challenge to its authority. In this case, choose a smaller number of companions, even if you will still be outnumbered.

Don't go at night

Most criminals, including muggers, prefer to work at night, because the darkness provides them with cover both before and after the attack. It also makes it difficult for you to recognise them during the attack and, in particular, to distinguish the colour of their clothing. In addition, fewer people are likely to see an attack at night, so your chance of receiving prompt help is greatly reduced. Therefore, if you can, avoid walking through high-risk areas at night.

Getting ready

Carry a mobile alarm and whatever legal weapons you're competent to use (see Non-ballistic Weapons, pp254-7). Knives are considered to be an exclusively offensive weapon, and using one on another person – other than in self-defence in your home, perhaps – is likely to land you in trouble with the law. A lighted cigarette is a useful asset, even if you don't smoke (see Everyday Items as Weapons, pp252-3).

Keep your weapon in your hand as you walk. Just having your gas spray handy, for example, with your finger on the button, will give you confidence and an air of all-important assertiveness, even if you don't use the spray. Whatever your weapon, make sure it's ready to use, because there's likely to be almost no warning of an attack. But remember that, under most circumstances, a firearm may not be exposed in a public place.

Having said this, if you're likely to be confronted by a gang, it's doubtful whether carrying a lethal weapon, such as a firearm, would be of much value. You're unlikely to be able to shoot all of them before one of them shoots or stabs you, and just the presence of a weapon will almost certainly invite a violent reaction.

Dressing the part

Dress down, without any obvious expensive items, so there's less motivation for robbing you. Avoid carrying large sums of money, and divide what you do carry among your clothes and – for example – a bag of vegetables. Keep an old wallet with mugger's money – a few rand – where they'll find it fairly easily.

If you normally receive your salary in cash, ask your employer to assist you in opening a bank account into which he or she can pay the money direct. You will then be able, in turn, to arrange regular and direct bank payments from your account for money owed, such as rent and electricity.

Danger zones

◆ Dark or lonely alleys
◆ Paths or short cuts across parks, veld, wasteland or fields
◆ Dark or lonely stretches of beach
◆ Subways
◆ Overhead pedestrian bridges
◆ Cemeteries, even at normal visiting times
◆ Dark areas beyond the street lamps
◆ Any areas of political tension
◆ Any areas of gang warfare
◆ Places where alcohol and probably drugs are consumed, such as nightclubs and bars
◆ Parked vehicles with people sitting in them
◆ Building sites after working hours
◆ Around any street gambling or 'game of chance'
◆ In street crowds that may have assembled to see an accident, to watch a fight, to take part in some activity. Apart from con men and pickpockets, a crowd may be targeted for an attack motivated by vengeance
◆ Around a supposedly injured person, who may be a decoy in a plan to mug you.

A warning unheeded

The elderly German couple had spent a quiet day at the beach and were looking forward to a lively dinner at Cape Town's Waterfront. After freshening up at their city hotel, that evening they enquired at the reception desk for a map showing them the route to the Waterfront. They were given the map, but the receptionist warned them that they should rather take the Waterfront Shuttle, since the entrance to the Waterfront was notorious as a mugger's hang-out. Ignoring the warning, Klaus and Juta decided to go on foot with the map in hand. They took a wrong turning and found themselves wandering under a flyover bridge. They stopped to look at their map,

and then they were attacked from behind by a group of about 10 children. Some threw Juta to the ground, kicked her and pulled off her jewellery, camera and handbag. The others held Klaus by the legs, pulled his sweater over his head so that he couldn't see, and tore at his pockets to get hold of his wallet. 'We had no chance. They were professionals', Klaus said later.

Police comment: It is not advisable to walk around a city alone at night, particularly in an area known for attacks on pedestrians. The couple should have ordered a taxi, or waited for the Shuttle, to take them to their destination safely.

Coping with provocation

Many street kids and gang members are unemployed in the conventional sense. Their days spent hanging about on the street soon become very dull, and the presence of a stranger on 'their' turf presents a chance to relieve their boredom. This recreation usually takes the form of teasing, humiliating or challenging the intruder – not, as a general rule, with the intention of leading to violence.

As you pass a group hanging about, they may demand to know who you are and where you think you're going. Answer truthfully and politely, without being servile. If you're a woman, there will probably be crude sexual comment. Don't ignore what they're saying and doing, but be wary of answering back sharply. Put your hand to your face, for instance, to indicate shyness or embarrassment, and to suggest that their comments have got through. If you reply to them, don't threaten or criticise.

If thugs do block your way and seem determined not to let you pass without some sort of conflict, rather turn around and go away. Gangs don't pick fights unless they know they're going to win, so if you stay to argue, you will probably be beaten up and robbed. You may be sure that anyone trying to pick a fight with you will have a backup of several cronies waiting to lend a hand if you look like coming out on top.

OUT SHOPPING

We do most of our shopping in malls or shopping centres, where the large numbers of shoppers and the adjacent parking areas attract thieves, muggers and con men. Stay alert and do not be distracted.

Getting ready

Prepare your shopping list in advance. This doesn't mean that you can't browse for bargains, but it will give you an indication of how much money you should carry. Also, if your time and shopping route is planned, you're less likely to be distracted.

Wear comfortable, casual clothes with at least one pocket on the inside of the garment, which you can secure by zip, button or Velcro. Remove jewellery and expensive accessories – they suggest that you're carrying a lot of money and are a worthwhile target. If you're wearing a ring that you normally take off when you wash your hands, take it off before you go out – many rings are permanently lost in the rest rooms of shopping malls.

Accessories such as a wheeled shopping basket indicate that you're probably carrying money and that your home is likely to be unoccupied long enough to be broken into. Try to do without them. If you're elderly, arrange shopping outings with two or more friends. You're safer in company.

Your handbag

There are few more tempting targets than a handbag. If you can get by with your purse, credit cards or chequebook, identity document and door keys, leave your bag at home and carry the items you need inconspicuously in your pockets or under your clothes. If you must take a handbag, use a small one with a short loop to pass over your arm, and make sure it has a positive fastening such as a zip or spring clip to prevent pickpockets getting into it. Hold onto it tightly.

Keep it safe

Take as little cash as possible, and keep cash and credit cards in a securable inside pocket. Don't put them in an outside pocket. Never place your bag or purse in your shopping trolley or basket – it's an easy target. When paying for your goods, whether by cash or card, don't put your wallet or purse on the counter – hold it in your hand until you've put your change or credit card back into it, and then return it to your inside pocket. Don't go out of the shop until you've put it away, and you have a firm grip on your purchases.

Keep small change, for newspapers or street collectors, separate from your main money supply. This way you won't have to produce your purse or wallet in front of pickpockets and snatchers, who often position themselves near street vendors and collectors.

Always buy the most expensive items last, so that you can take them straight home, rather than risk leaving them in your car – car boots are not impregnable. Try to avoid going to a rest room or toilet with your purchases. If you must, though, don't put your parcels on the floor near a door, where they might be snatched. Also, keep your bag off the floor when you're inside a toilet cubicle – someone in an adjoining cubicle may be waiting to snatch it.

Stay alert

With your arms full, your mind on shopping and perhaps on the whereabouts of other purchases and your children, you may be less alert than usual to the activities of pickpockets and con men. One con man who got away with his misdeeds for several months was a respectable-looking young man who told well-laden shoppers that he had been sent to call them back to the cash desk because there was something there for them. He offered to look after the shoppers' purchases while they went back to the cash desk, where they found – nothing. Hurrying back to where they had left the obliging young man, they again found nothing. He, and their shopping, had gone.

Park close by

In a busy shopping centre or crowded parking lot you are unlikely to fall victim to violent crime. Even so, try to park as close as possible to the store you're going to. You won't have to carry your parcels so far and your car is less likely to be broken into. The sooner you arrive after opening time, the more likely you are to be able to park close by. Criminals may go to work anywhere in a parking lot, but are most likely to be near the edges where there are bushes or a shrubbery, where fewer people can see them and from where they can get away more easily. On returning to your car after shopping, have the keys ready before you reach the car.

Shopping services

The easiest way to shop is to get someone else to do it for you. You could ask a trusted neighbour if he or she would shop for several neighbours, for a fee, or you could use a formal shopping service. Draw up your shopping list and give it to your shopping service, either over the telephone or (preferably) in writing, and let them know when you require the goods. Your instructions must be precise, stipulating the brand name of a tin of beans, for instance, and an acceptable alternative if that brand is not available. Once your purchases are delivered, check them. If you are satisfied that the service has carried out your instructions, pay them the cost of the goods plus an agreed service fee or commission. Deal with an organisation recommended by a friend or your supermarket manager, if you can.

SHOPPING OVERLOAD

When out shopping, limit your purchases, not only to what you can afford, but to a weight you can carry fairly comfortably for as far as you're going. You are an easy target if you are overladen.

Beware overload

It can take several seconds to disentangle yourself from plastic shopping bags, particularly if someone tries to snatch your bag or wallet, so don't carry too many bags. As a general guideline, if your bags tend to bump against your legs as you walk, and you can't hold them clear, you're carrying too many.

Safe storage

When shopping in more than one store, return regularly to your car and lock your purchases away in the boot – don't merely put them on the back seat, where they will attract thieves. Alternatively, leave them at the parcels counter in a shop, to be picked up later. Remember, though, that security at these counters is not high. It's too easy for someone else to present a wrong or fake ticket and be handed your goods.

Don't lose your grip

After shopping, particularly if you're elderly, hot or not in good health, you may want to sit and rest, or wait for a friend. To make sure that you don't leave a bag or two behind when you get up, run loops of strong, brightly coloured wool through the handles – one for the bags you're carrying in your left hand, another for the right. This way, if you pick up one bag, the others will follow. Similarly, anyone trying to snatch a bag will find himself unexpectedly weighed down by the drag of the others. And if you do sit, sit indoors.

If you're walking home, stay alert – don't plod along staring fixedly at the pavement. You're vulnerable when your hands are full and your eyes are not on what's going on around you.

Bringing home the goods

Decline offers of help, unless they come from someone you know personally. It's too easy for goods to go astray, even under your nose and in the short distance between the trolley and your luggage compartment.

If you have an adult companion, take it in turns to put the goods into your car while the friend keeps a lookout. Don't both bend over the trolley or have your hands full or have your heads in the boot at the same time. Trouble could be muggers hiding behind the car next to yours, or it could be a carload of youths who will simply stop, snatch and drive on. Keep a lookout in all directions. If somebody suspicious approaches, stop loading, close the door or boot, stand erect and close together, and face them. Take the same precautions when unloading.

Unless it's to put children or goods into the cab of your car, don't unlock the doors until you're ready to get in. Use the rear door on the passenger's side and keep the other doors locked, to reduce the chance of anyone slipping into the driver's seat. (Now is the time to reward children with a snack that will keep them happily occupied.) Lock this door, too, once you're ready to get in and drive off.

If a thief strikes

Shout as loudly as you can. 'Help' is a word most people understand and it lends itself to really loud use. Your instinct probably will be to hold even tighter to the parcels that the thief is trying to snatch. But rather let go. Unless you feel you are fit and strong enough to sustain a vigorous defence, don't fight back. Remember, the thief's main objective is not to hurt you, but simply to take your goods and clear off. Fighting back will make him feel threatened and may trigger gross violence.

The aftermath

You're going to be shocked and perhaps physically injured. Don't wait for somebody to come along and offer assistance. Ask for help, find help and make sure you receive help at once. You should certainly be examined by a doctor as soon as possible. If you aren't able to do so yourself, see that somebody informs the police of the crime, and see that close family members and your children are advised about what's happened to you.

DRAMA IN REAL LIFE

Assault in a multistorey car park

Mr and Mrs Howes pushed their shopping trolley to their car in a multistorey car park after late shopping on Friday night. Because Mrs Howes is unable to lift weights, she sat in the car while her husband – with his back to the most likely direction of assault – transferred their purchases to the boot of the car. Mr Howes never saw the man or men who knocked him down, held him face-down on the floor and rifled his pockets, also taking his expensive wristwatch. He was aware that they got into a car that had stopped behind his own, and that it drove off slowly. Mrs Howes knew nothing of what had happened.

Police comment: This seems to have been a purely opportunistic attack, particularly common on Fridays. The thieves knew Mr Howes hadn't seen them, and that there was no witness to identify them, because Mrs Howes was facing forward. If she had been visibly keeping watch, however, the chances are the thieves would have driven past. After all, she might have been able to describe them, their car, perhaps even remember the car's registration number.

Anyone who is preoccupied in a public place – as Mr Howes was – should have at least one extra pair of eyes, and should also use his own. The lookout should regularly scan through 360 degrees.

Remember that while you're busy guarding the rear, criminals can approach you from the front of the car, where they are conveniently screened for at least some of the way by the open boot. Mr Howes didn't see them, but his attackers could easily have been children in their early teens or even younger.

AS SAFE AS FORT KNOX

Don't take safety at the bank for granted, either for yourself or your money. Although the big gangs who raid banks are after the big money deep within the vaults, there are many smaller operators just as happy to take your relatively modest amounts and leave you penniless (and possibly lifeless) at some spot nearby.

Going to the bank

Whatever it is you want to do at the bank, try not to go alone, even if it's just to find out your balance, to ask for a new chequebook or to arrange a transfer. The thug who sees you going into the bank doesn't know that you're not coming out carrying a lot of money, but he'll be much less likely to attack you if you're accompanied by someone. And if there are two of you, he won't even know which one to attack.

If you can avoid it, don't go straight from the bank to some remote area – a semi-deserted car park or a public toilet, for instance – where you're at increased risk of attack. If you do some shopping first, anyone still shadowing you will probably become discouraged because you're spending the cash he thinks you've just drawn. Chances are that he'll return to the vicinity of the bank and wait for another victim.

No slips showing

Don't advertise by means of the things you are carrying that you're going to the bank. Keep all deposit slips, bankbooks and bundled documents out of sight. If there are a lot of them to carry, divide them between yourself and your companion, then put them in a couple of bags that suggest you're each carrying something else, such as groceries. Never display any bag with a bank's name printed on it – even when you're not going to the bank.

Wait until you are well inside the bank before you start taking out your documents and papers and, when you have completed your banking business, you should not even start heading for the door until you have put everything away again and have a firm grip on your possessions.

Carrying cash

If you have to carry a large sum of money, split it up in as many ways as you can. Carry it in supermarket bags or divide it among your pockets. But be careful not to put loose banknotes in the same pocket in which you keep other articles that you might need to use – keys or a handkerchief, for instance –since the notes may fall out.

Avoid putting anything valuable in rear trouser pockets. If possible, use only inside pockets or pockets that have a firm closure by zip, stud, button or Velcro. Sew a secret pocket to the inside of a garment, if neces-

ATM CHECK LIST

1. Check your surroundings. If there are suspicious people loitering about, come back later.

2. Make sure you have your card ready and your handbag, if you have one, securely held in the other hand by the time you step up to the ATM.

3. Stand close to the keyboard, so that people behind you and to the sides can't see the number you key in.

4. Don't place your bag or anything valuable on the counter. If you do have a parcel that you have to put down, place it on the ground in front of your feet.

5. If a stranger speaks to you while you are busy at the ATM, press the CANCEL key and keep your hand over the slot through which your card will be ejected. Take the card, check it and put it in a secure inside pocket.

6. If the transaction has proceeded too far to be cancelled, carefully and firmly take your money and card (don't snatch) and put them in your secure inside pocket.

7. As your transaction draws to its close, keep your hand over the slot and remove your card as soon as it is released. Check to make sure it really is your own.

sary. A money belt around the waist is also recommended. If you wear one, cover it with clothes that allow you to reach it and remove or open it easily.

Using an ATM

If you need to be shown how the machine works, ask a bank official or a trusted friend to show you. Never ask a stranger standing in the queue – ATMs attract criminals and con artists. Although banks advertise a 24-hour service, use ATMs during daylight hours when other shoppers and bank-users are about. If you must use an ATM at night, go to one in a mall where there are security guards and ample lighting.

Banking from home

Most banks offer a range of home-based electronic services. To take advantage of them, you need a tone-generating telephone (the type with press-button pads), a cellphone or a computer, and a modem with access to the Internet. If you do not have a tone-generating telephone, your bank will usually supply a supplementary tone pad free of charge. You are allocated – or select for yourself – a secret PIN, or Personal Identification Number, without which you cannot gain access to your account in this way, or use the service. If you have a link to a fax machine, it is possible to have replies printed.

The service, which is inexpensive and is open at all times, typically includes balance enquiries, account queries, utilities account payments, such as electricity and telephone, inter-account transfers, provisional statements, chequebook requests, and currency exchange rates.

Inter-account transfers are electronically possible only between accounts linked by one of your bank cards. For example, you can transfer money from your current account to your credit card account or savings account. It is not possible to undertake electronic transactions involving cash or cheques from home.

ATM do's and don'ts

◆ Don't go to an ATM laden with parcels and shopping. You can't concentrate on them, your transaction and bystanders all at the same time.
◆ Don't be distracted by other ATM users – this is invariably a preliminary to a con.
◆ Don't accept help from strangers, especially the first one to offer assistance.
◆ If someone tries to push in front of you while you are at the ATM, shout loudly and resist – he has probably seen your PIN and is after your card. Pull his hair as hard as you can.
◆ Never operate an ATM for a stranger. At the most, offer brief verbal advice once you're sure that your card, cash and parcels are safe. Smile politely, say 'I'm sorry, but I don't know', and walk away, even if you think the appeal is genuine.

DRAMA IN REAL LIFE

The ATM cardsharp

After making sure that she was alone at the ATM, Mrs Haig – a pensioner – inserted her card and punched in her PIN number. Nothing happened and, when she pressed 'Cancel', her card still did not emerge. She went into the bank to report the incident and so didn't see the young man approach the ATM after her. He inserted tweezers into the card slot, swiftly retrieved her card, reinserted it and drew a large amount of Mrs Haig's cash. When she came out with a bank official, it merely seemed as though the machine was working normally again – which, of course, it was.

Police comment: Mrs Haig should have looked behind her before keying in her number and asked the thief, who was obviously standing close to her, to move away a little. When the thief removed her card, he also removed the paper or matchstick with which he had blocked the card rollers. If Mrs Haig had had a friend with her when her card disappeared, her companion could have watched the machine while Mrs Haig was inside the bank solving her problem. To avoid losing a lot of money this way, ask your bank to lower your daily limit.

PAYING WITHOUT RISK

Many people find that it is safer and more convenient not to pay with cash, but rather with credit cards, ATM (automatic teller machine or autoteller) cards, debit cards or charge cards. Because these cards represent cash, the power to purchase, and access to your bank accounts, take good care of them and be aware of how other people could use them to rob you.

Credit and debit cards

These magnetically encoded cards can be used for making purchases (although traders are not compelled to accept them) up to a set financial limit. Purchases made by credit card are charged to a credit account and can be paid off completely or in part when you receive your statement. Interest is charged on any unpaid amounts. Purchases made with a debit card are paid off immediately from your current account and don't attract any interest at all.

Used with a personal identity number (PIN), most credit and debit cards (except for department store charge cards) serve also as ATM cards for carrying out banking transactions at an ATM or over the counter at a bank.

Secret numbers

Your PIN is your secret. Without it, anyone who steals your card will not be able to draw cash or transfer large sums from your account. It is best to remember the number and not to write it down, because having to read out the digits while actually using the ATM is asking for trouble.

Some people who do write down their PIN write it backwards as one of a list of phone numbers. A PIN usually consists of four or five digits, so to bring it up to the six or seven digits of a real phone number, they add the year of their birth (54, for example, for 1954). To make sure they'll recognise the PIN number, they write it down on the list next to the name of someone they don't know. However, even this code can be cracked by a sharp con man.

If you do forget your PIN, go to your bank – preferably the branch at which you keep your account – and explain your predicament. You will need to produce adequate identification, as well as the relevant card. Since banks do not keep lists of PINs, the card will have to be cancelled and a new card will be issued.

Using your credit card

When paying for purchases, don't let your card out of your sight. See that only your charges are entered, that no other purchase forms are validated with your card, and check the total before you sign. If possible, fill in the total yourself.

Although it's safe to make purchases by credit card over the telephone with businesses that you know, problems may arise when dealing with concerns that do all or nearly all of their business by telephone and credit card. Without there being an intention to defraud, errors may arise whereby clients are billed more than once for the same article.

In terms of exchange-control regulations, you may no longer use credit cards for occasional purchases from abroad, but must obtain a bank draft or bank cheque. However, there is no really effective way of controlling this rule.

Lost cards

If your credit or ATM card is lost or stolen, inform your bank immediately, quoting your account number. Most banks have a 24-hour toll-free line for such emergencies. Make sure you are given a reference number that includes the time you reported the loss or theft.

If it's quicker – where your card is stolen just outside the bank during business hours, for instance – go in and report the loss at the counter. You will be liable for withdrawals or purchases made by the fraudulent use of your card up to the time you report its loss, after which the issuing company usually carries the loss.

You may be able to avoid loss through unauthorised use of your credit card by obtaining lost-card insurance, for which a small premium is debited annually to your credit card account.

Money in thin air

Paying by credit card over the Internet is as insecure as handing your credit card to a waiter at a restaurant or paying over the phone. Advertisers on the Internet have been known to take money, close their e-mail address and simply disappear. But it is usually safe to send credit card details to known, reputable companies – your number is normally securely encoded when you send it, making it very difficult for hackers to access it.

The cheque

When issuing a cheque you (the drawer) must write the date, the amount to be paid (spelled out in full, and written as digits), the name of the person to whom it is to be paid (the payee) and sign the cheque. Don't accept a cheque that doesn't have all these elements on it – the bank won't honour it.

Crossed cheques

Cheques have the words 'or bearer' printed on the line on which you write the name of the payee. As the drawer, you should normally cross this out, so that the cheque can be paid only to the named payee.

To cross a cheque, draw two parallel lines anywhere across the face of it. (It is not necessary to add the words 'and co' between the lines.) The effect of crossing a cheque is that the bank will not pay out the amount as cash over the counter. The payee or endorsee usually deposits the cheque in his or her account and waits for payment in due course of the bank's business.

Endorsements

These are usually written on the back of a cheque. For example, a cheque in favour of 'J Jones' may be used by Jones to pay someone else, by writing on the back 'Pay T Smith' and then signing 'J Jones'. The effect of a blank endorsement – where the payee signs the back of the cheque but does not specify to whom it should be paid – is to make the cheque payable to the bearer, or whoever holds it at the time.

Not negotiable

A cheque that has the words 'not negotiable' written between the lines of the crossing may still be endorsed and transferred – that is, passed to another person. The words affect legal right to payment in the event of a cheque being stolen.

Suppose a thief steals a cheque marked 'Not negotiable' from the payee, endorses it and passes it to an innocent third party. The third party's right to payment is no greater than that of the person from whom he received the cheque. In this case, that person was a thief, so the third party would have no right to payment at all. Do not accept an endorsed cheque marked 'Not negotiable' unless you know that the person passing it to you has the right to endorse it.

Not transferable

The words 'not transferable' written anywhere on the face of the cheque – not necessarily between parallel lines – mean that the cheque may not be endorsed or transferred to anyone alse. To ensure this, also cross out 'or bearer'. Then, only the payee may receive the amount for which the cheque was drawn. Don't accept a cheque with these words on it unless you are also the person to whom the cheque has been written out. The words 'a/c payee only', written between the parallel lines, do not have the same effect. A cheque marked in this way may still be endorsed to another party, as the endorsement merely changes 'the payee'.

Cheques lost or stolen

Advise your bank as soon as possible on discovering that your chequebook has been lost or stolen. If you don't know how many blank cheques were in the book, stop payment on all the cheques in the book. Stopping payment usually involves going to the bank and giving them written instructions not to meet or pay any of the missing cheques. However, this will inconvenience anyone who was legitimately entitled to payment. Contact them to explain what has happened, and issue new cheques as soon as you can. There is a charge for stopping cheques.

Forged cheques

The most common forgeries on cheques are alterations to the amount and to the signature of the drawer. When writing the amount spelled out in full, start as far to the left on the cheque as possible, to prevent unauthorised insertions being made later. Always write the word 'only' after the spelled out amount, or draw a line through any unused space. And when filling in the amount as figures, start as close as you can to the printed 'R' and try to fill the block.

If you write the cheque carelessly, enabling a forger to alter the amount, the bank may not be responsible if it pays out the wrong amount.

Dishonoured cheques

When a bank stops or refuses to pay a cheque, the cheque is said to have been dishonoured or to have 'bounced'. There may be several reasons.

◆ The cheque may be incomplete – that is, it lacks a date, the name of a payee, the amount in words or digits or the signature of the drawer.

◆ The cheque may be stale or 'out of date'. As a rule, a personal cheque is valid for six months from the date of writing, and a company cheque for three months. A postdated cheque – one made out with a future date – will not be paid until that date.

◆ The cheque may have been visibly altered.

◆ Payment has been stopped, because the drawer has ordered his bank not to pay when the cheque is presented.

◆ The drawer has insufficient funds to meet payment.

◆ The drawer may have died or become insolvent.

◆ A signature or the account may have been faked.

Before you accept a cheque, always make sure that it has the necessary elements and that the date is correct. Make sure that any alterations are signed in full by the drawer.

If you deposit a cheque that is later dishonoured, the cheque will be returned to you, marked 'refer to drawer' or simply 'R/D'. A printed slip stating particulars of the cheque may be attached. Contact the person who gave you the cheque and demand payment. You may also instruct your bank to return the cheque to the bank that dishonoured it. The cheque is then presented by the bank for payment again, and if the reason for its having been dishonoured no longer exists (temporary shortage of funds, for instance), payment will be made. In the event of a drawer having died or become insolvent, you would have to apply to the drawer's executor or to a curator appointed by the court to obtain payment. Your bank will be able to advise you of how to do this.

CHILDREN ON THE STREET

Their trusting natures, lack of experience and obedience to elders are among the factors that make children easy prey to criminals. Although it is impossible to guarantee a child's safety outside (or even inside) the home, risks can be reduced by teaching children to recognise danger and to protect themselves.

Accidents

Make sure that perimeter fences are in good repair (children can fit through very small gaps), and that gates are closed and locked as part of your ordinary security precautions.

A safe start

By the time your children start to lead their own independent lives – when they start going to nursery school, for instance – they should be able to state clearly their full names, address, telephone number and where their parents may be contacted. They should also be able to use a telephone, and should know which of their parents' friends or neighbours they can go to for help. They should know – because you have told them – who is part of the trusted close circle (see below), and that others are strangers.

The close circle

These are the close friends, relatives and, possibly, employees whom you trust fully, and to whom you would entrust your child's life and welfare. With you and your partner, they form a ring of protection when your children need it. Other people are strangers.

Watch over your children

Until your children are old enough to reason astutely (and to outrun adults without endangering themselves in traffic), don't let them go out – to shopping malls, for instance, or even to and from school – on their own. Never leave your children alone in a car, outside a shop, or playing alone on the street.

Check whether school playground gates are kept locked at break times, and if there is a security guard present. If you are concerned about a lack of security, talk about this with the school principal, and tell your children not to play close to the gates or the fence.

Don't write your child's name on the outside of a satchel or any other place where a passer-by (or potential kidnapper) can read it. It is not advisable either to give a child a necklace, bracelet, T-shirt or jacket with his or her name on it.

Who's bad and why

Explain that there are bad people in the world, but don't create in the children's minds caricatures of brutish, sly or slovenly people as representing those who are best avoided. Be sure to explain that bad people may be young or old, male or female, and that they may be friendly, well dressed and say kind or amusing things. Warn them about the typical baits of sweets, toys, money, secrets and small animals that are offered by strangers.

Playing the part

The best way to teach children information that may be outside their experience is by acting the parts of the various people involved. Present the situations you're warning them against, with yourself in the role of the stranger and your children being themselves. You might say, for instance, 'Let's pretend it's a very hot day, and a man or a woman who's a stranger comes to you and says "Would you like an ice cream?" Now, show me what you're going to do, or what you're going to say'.

You might take them to your car, sit yourself in it and take the part of a stranger trying to lure them into it. Make sure that the words you use are not taken too literally, that 'ice cream' may be any type of sweet or toy; that a 'lost puppy' they're invited to look for may be a lost kitten, a lost purse or even a four-leaf clover. What you are warning them against is the association with the stranger, by presenting examples of how the stranger may try to start it.

The meaning of messages

Children may be lured by false messages that require them to act immediately, usually by accompanying the stranger who brings the message. Here's an example: 'Your Mommy had to go to hospital and she sent me to fetch you'. With the members of your close circle of friends and relatives, devise a simple code word to insert into any important message that has to be given to your children. This code should be known only to them, you and your partner and your children.

A code is especially important where a child is being asked to go with someone he or she doesn't know. Keep it simple, or it will lead to confusion. For example, instead of using a title – like 'Mommy' or 'Auntie' – in a relayed message, use the name of the individual. The sentence used above would come out like this: 'Cynthia had to go to hospital and she sent me to fetch you'. Or a code name could replace a noun, as in 'Your Mommy had to go to the plaster palace and she sent me to fetch you'. Your children must be taught to go only with members of the close circle or those who use the correct code.

Safety strategy

Teach your children that when they are accosted by people in cars, they should move away from the kerb, preferably in the direction from which the car has come, so that if the stranger wants to follow, he'll have to drive in reverse or on the wrong side of the road.

ANTI-ABDUCTION CHECK LIST

STAY ALERT – DON'T LET YOUR CHILD BECOME A VICTIM

1. Make secure arrangements for your children between home and school.

2. Check that proper security measures are applied at their school.

3. Teach your children not to go close to strangers, and to tell you about strangers who approach them.

4. Ensure that your children are always being cared for by people whom you trust.

5. Don't leave children alone in a car without adult supervision.

6. Don't indiscriminately give out personal information.

7. Don't let children go to meet strangers in lonely places, or in places outside your known territory.

8. If you or your family are involved in an abduction, keep calm – panic will only make matters worse.

9. No matter what instructions you receive, inform the police at once of an abduction.

They should be ready to run. If they have to reply at all to the stranger's invitation, they should say 'No thanks. My dad's coming now'. Explain to your children that it doesn't matter if their words or behaviour make an adult feel insulted or embarrassed. What matters is that they should be safe.

Adult authority

Your children need to know that there are circumstances under which they are allowed to defy adults. Let them know that the one time they're really allowed to scream – as loudly as they can – is when they're afraid or distrustful of someone. Encourage them, if they're touched by that person, to keep shouting, and also to bite, hit, scratch, kick and run away, especially in public, when there's a chance a potential molester will be frightened off by attention from passers-by. This defiance also applies to members of your close circle. Your children must know that they're allowed, in certain circumstances, to say 'No'.

Your children will need assurance that they won't get into trouble with the adult they've defied, and especially with you as a parent. Encourage your children to tell you if they have defied an adult and why they did it. You may have to straighten out affairs with an indignant teacher or other adult on occasion, but give your children this assurance and stick to it.

Out and about

As they get older, your children will want to actively assert their growing independence. Notwithstanding this, explain that it makes good sense, for the security of the family, that you should always know where they are and how to contact them. Similarly, assure them that they may call on you for help at any time if they're in an awkward or frightening situation. The 'no secrets' principle carries over into young adulthood. Tell your children that you want to know about unpleasant experiences they have, and that you won't blame them. Tell them, in the absence of other indicators, such as another person's experience, to trust their instinctive misgivings about strangers, and, on the other hand, to be wary of instinctively trusting someone. Tell them that where new friends and strangers are concerned, trust must be earned by proving reliability. They should never, for instance, accept lifts from strangers, or accompany strangers anywhere on foot.

Out walking

Depending on their ages and on where you live, try to ensure that your children are indoors or, at least, on your property before dark. This becomes more and more difficult as they get older. Tell your childen that if they're being followed while they're out, to stay on a busy route and head for any public place such as a shop, or a police station. Taking short cuts will generally not shake off pursuers and may land children in trouble. If they know there's nobody at home, they should stay away. There's safety in numbers, and your children are safer going out – and returning – in a group. Rather than walking, it's safer if you can arrange a reliable lift.

Missing children

Most children return home safely, unharmed, within 24 hours. There is seldom reason for panic if a child is late returning home. All the same, as soon as you're concerned by a child's absence, report it to the police.

Some daycares and schools arrange for an ID card to be created for each child, which carries a recent photo of the child together with his or her name, parents' names, fingerprint, blood group and identifying marks. One copy of the card is carried by the child, pinned inside a pocket or hung around the neck, and a copy is given to each parent. The child's details are entered into a database monitored by a private company. If a child is reported missing, this information can be given immediately to the Child Protection Unit or National Bureau for Missing Persons, instead of these organisations having to wait for up to two weeks for adequate information to be provided.

Why are children abducted?

Babies and very young children may be at the centre of disputes between unmarried or divorced parents who disagree with the ruling of a court, and who may decide to retrieve their children in their own way. Babies, especially, may be stolen by women unable to bear their own children, by childless women who desperately want to have a child, or by women who have suffered the death of their own child. The kidnappers may not necessarily be the people who want the child, but may be paid agents acting on their behalf.

Children around the age of the onset of puberty may be abducted by paedophiles or (especially girls) sold into a form of sex slavery. In a few cases, children may be murdered for ritual reasons involving witchcraft, but here it is their death that is desired, rather than the living child.

The greatest threat of abduction for sexual reasons comes from strangers who may have been watching you and your family, and learning your routines. They probably know your children's names, their class in school, where you work and a lot of other information. But strangers aren't the only villains: even relatives are known to have abducted young people in South Africa.

SHOPPING WITH CHILDREN

The preoccupied crowds in a shopping centre or mall make it an ideal place for criminals – including abductors and child molesters. Do not leave young children alone anywhere. Warn them to stay close to you, and see that they do so.

The children with you

If you take your children shopping, go when the crush is not so great. Consider fitting toddlers with reins and harness so that they won't be separated from you or get lost. Don't tie the reins to your shopping trolley, keep them firmly in your hand. Make small children walk immediately in front of you and just behind the trolley. A child on the far side of a full trolley may be invisible to a motorist making a tight turn.

Make sure that children accompanying you who can walk about independently are able to give their full names, address and telephone number. Train them to link hands with one another, forming a chain with you as its pivot, to stay close and not to spread out at arm's length. Give them a task to do, such as carrying a light, indestructible parcel, to keep them interested and alert. If your children are not old enough to help you load your car, put them safely inside the car before you pack your purchases.

Don't keep your purse or handbag tucked into your baby's pram or pushchair, and keep baby and vehicle within arm's length at all times.

Stay aware

You obviously need to examine goods before you buy them, but don't let this absorb all your attention. If you're with a partner and small children, let one of the adults examine the goods while the other sees that the children are safe. Keep children clear of people whom you've seen repeatedly, perhaps near the public toilets, who are not obviously shopping and are apparently waiting for someone. They might be innocent; they could be pushing drugs. Never leave your children alone, especially in toilets and rest rooms.

Hanging out

In many urban areas, young teenagers hang out at malls, socialising. It's a part of growing up and it's also, unfortunately, an opportunity for teenagers to become too closely acquainted with undesirables who may be drinking, selling drugs, or just generally disrupting the ordinary flow of events. Warn teenagers against people they don't know in shopping malls.

Talking to strangers

Dishonest people have many ways of getting close enough to make off with your purse or wallet without your being aware of it. A favourite trick, which almost always works, is for one operator to pay flattering attention to your children, drawing your attention while an accomplice robs you.

When it comes to crimes against children, however, the perpetrators may even be children themselves. A horrifying case was recorded by video camera at a shopping mall in Britain, when two 10-year-olds led a toddler away while his mother was finishing her purchases. Her child was later found dead on a railway line, having been beaten and stoned and then left on the tracks.

Entertainment

Some mall managements and shopping centres provide entertainment for children while their parents shop. It may be a concert or a supervised play area with magic shows, drawing and painting or story-telling. There is usually a responsible person in charge of the children being entertained. However, if your child needs to go to the toilet halfway through the show, while you're still shopping, the chaperone cannot leave her other charges unattended to accompany your child. In most such arrangements for children's amusement, however well meaning, security is inadequate. Unless you're going to be present all the time, there's no certainty that your child will still be there when you've finished your shopping.

The lost child

If you lose a child in a crowded place, look for an obvious attraction close by, such as a toy shop or a display of animals that may have drawn the child away from you. Alter your vantage point so that you can look among legs rather than the solid mass of torsos, or by finding a high point from which you can look down.

Ask people around you whether they have seen your child. Walk in the direction you were walking when your child disappeared, for a short distance, looking into shops or along passages as you pass. Then retrace your steps to beyond the point where you remember last seeing your child, again looking into likely places and asking if anyone has seen him. (On shopping expeditions, children are more likely to lag behind than to go ahead.)

Ask at the security kiosk or manager's office if a message could be broadcast over the public-address system. Follow their instructions. Telephone the police to advise them that your child is missing. It is unlikely that they will consider mounting a search immediately after a disappearance not associated with suspicious circumstances, but at least they will be able to contact you if they receive reports of the child's whereabouts.

If possible, arrange for a responsible person to stay at home in case the missing child should arrive there. Once the child has been found, remember to notify – as soon as possible – all the authorities you alerted when you discovered the child was missing.

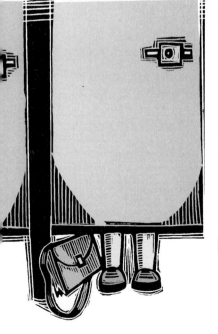

PUBLIC PLACES

A public place is any place that the public is invited or permitted to use: a cinema or picnic ground; shops and banks; showers and toilets. Many of these places are also hunting grounds and hang-outs for a range of undesirable people.

Lifts

The lift that stops at your floor, when you are the only one there, may contain muggers. Don't stand close to the lift-shaft doors while you're waiting for the lift to arrive. You'll have enough time to get aboard even if you're a few metres back – and you'll be out of reach of anyone who might lunge at you from the lift.

If you don't like the look of anyone in the lift, don't get in. Take the stairs or another lift. Where the only other person waiting for the lift is someone you don't trust, and the lift arrives at your floor empty, make a quick excuse not to get in: 'I've forgotten something' or 'What am I doing here – I'm just not thinking'.

If you're a woman alone in a lift with a man or a group of men, stand at the control panel, facing the men but without establishing eye contact. Note the position of the alarm button. If you're attacked, press the alarm button and any others you can reach and shout at your assailant. Sounding the alarm might discourage him and, having pressed the buttons, the lift is bound to stop fairly soon. Get out and run at the first opportunity. If you don't know the building well, get off at ground level and shout loudly to the security guard. You should also inform the police.

Possessions in toilets

Try to arrange your outings so that you don't have to visit public toilets or rest rooms. Possessions are frequently left behind in public toilets and quickly removed by someone else, and toilets are hang-outs for criminals. Never place goods or your handbag on the floor – it's too easy for someone in the next cubicle to remove them. Rather hang bags on a hook on the door or place them on the cistern lid. Avoid the basin nearest the door (it's too easy for someone to snatch what you put down), and choose one about halfway along the line.

If you're wearing a firearm on a belt holster, remove it, make it safe and hold it in your hand before you loosen your belt. Don't put the firearm on the floor where someone in the next cubicle might just scoop it up. A firearm in a well-fitting thigh holster should not need to be removed.

People in toilets

Public toilets, however elegant they may be, are often home base for someone you'd rather not know. Especially in strange areas, you're unlikely to be aware that a particular toilet has the reputation of being a sales point for drugs, for example. Avoid going to the toilet alone, and you and your companion should use adjacent cubicles simultaneously, so that neither of you is left alone in the general area. Never allow young children to go to public toilets alone.

When you enter a public toilet, push the door open all the way, unless you can see in a mirror that there's nobody behind it. Check behind all other open cubicle doors as well.

You almost certainly won't be able to distinguish a pervert, drug dealer, thief or con artist from a law-abiding citizen, so don't get involved in conversations with strangers. If anybody does attempt to molest you, shout and get out. Where the building's security staff are readily available, tell them what has happened, and if the perpetrator is still in the toilet, offer to accompany them to detain him. Also inform the police, even if you feel that the incident was trivial. Criminals who are not reported are unlikely to be arrested, and usually go on to commit more serious crimes.

At the show

At any public gathering indoors, whether it's a political meeting, church service, live theatre or cinema, look for illuminated 'Exit' signs above the doors, or doors that you can reach easily. If seats are unreserved or have been reserved for you unseen, you may have no choice, but try to sit at the end of a row about one third of the way down the hall. (Sitting near the middle of a row means you may be less disturbed by late patrons, but you won't have a clear start in an emergency.) See also Caught Up in the Action, pp159-61.

Avoid being over-friendly to people you've never met before. Where enthusiasts are gathered – say, to view a particular genre of movie – it's easy to slip into the start of a relationship with someone you know nothing about at all. Don't be sidetracked into going to a lonely corner or to a new friend's car – to look at something they claim will interest you, for instance.

Keep your handbag on your lap when you're seated, or on the floor with the handle looped around your foot. Tucking it next to you works only if you remember to keep sitting up against it and not to move your arm. Better still, don't take a handbag.

Waiting in the queue

Most of us don't like to have strangers pressing in on us too closely – it's a situation that provides opportunities for pickpocketing and sexual harassment. To give yourself more space, don't stand too close to the person in front when you join the queue, and stand sideways rather than face the front. If you're still crowded, don't move forward when the people in front of you move, until you have enough space. In a shopping queue, place your basket or goods on the floor between you and the person in front.

UNWANTED ATTENTION

Unwanted attention or comment of any kind amounts to harassment. The country's common law, which is more widely based (on custom and precedent, for example) than parliamentary legislation, gives everyone the right to live their lives free of bullying and of unreasonable threats and intimidation. Sexual harassment may be any of these.

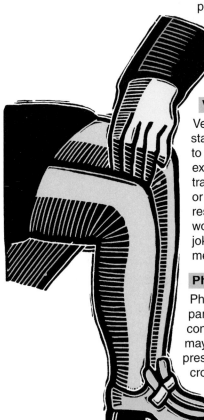

Indecent assault

The reported cases of indecent assault rose from 3 874 in 1994 to 5 220 in 1996. Incidences were highest in the Western Cape, followed by the Northern Cape and Gauteng.

What is sexual harassment?

Sexual harassment is almost always inflicted on women by men, although there are a few incidents when women harass men. It is an infringement on a person's dignity, but is not regarded with the same seriousness by all societies. Sexual harassment in the workplace (see pp201-3) is a form of manipulation. It may also be so in a public place, but is more likely to be a form of 'catching a thrill'. Wherever it is practised, sexual harassment is always part of a power game in which the harasser sees himself as having the greater power, and the effect is to make the victim feel humiliated, embarrassed, afraid, anxious, resentful or angry. Many women, accustomed to entrenched beliefs in male superiority, do not realise that they themselves are victims.

Verbal harassment

Verbal harassment includes sexual words, statements or jokes made directly or indirectly to a woman, but intended for her to hear. For example, men sitting opposite a woman in a train may comment to one another on her body or on her 'availability'. Men in a group in a restaurant might make sexual comments on women coming in, or they might tell sexual jokes denigrating women. Insulting racial comments may be included in the harassment.

Physical harassment

Physical harassment includes touching any part of the person being harassed, but typically concentrates on legs, buttocks or breasts. It may involve touching with the hand or simply pressing the body against the victim's, often in crowded areas such as public transport, supermarket aisles and queues. More violent and obvious sexual contact involves grabbing or clasping, flashing or attempting to remove clothing.

The harasser may use his body to dominate the space around him and his victim, by crowding his victim or preventing her from moving away – often pretending to be unaware that his actions are having these effects.

Eye contact can convey a great deal that is insulting and disturbing, through leering and 'undressing with the eyes' or attempting to peer down a woman's blouse or up her skirt.

The threat

Sexual harassment by men carries all the overtones of potential rape. Supposedly 'harmless' harassers may become obsessive, or they may employ more sinister forms of harassment – culminating, perhaps, in stalking (see Stalkers and Others, pp154-6). Someone who harasses you on the morning train, for instance, may start appearing on the evening train as well. A harasser's excuses for his conduct, typically including claims that he 'was only teasing', or 'meant no harm', do not disguise the fact that harassment is psychologically harmful, could lead to a violent crime, and should be taken seriously.

Harass the harasser

Most of us are too shy to create a disturbance in public, and we often lack the confidence to protest when we are wronged. Many harassers take advantage of this, trading on it as a form of immunity for themselves, and deliberately operate in crowded public places. But nobody has the right to touch you without your permission, or to deliberately and maliciously offend you. You are entitled to protection even if, in the first instance, you have to provide it yourself.

If you're in a public place and a stranger touches you, slap his hand away, point him out and say loudly and angrily 'Take your hand off me' or 'How dare you put your hand on me.' If you're in a darkened cinema, you could make a loud request for someone to call the management because you are being harassed. Like most bullies, the harasser will probably stop what he is doing once he realises that his action has been made public and he is up against some resistance.

If you are standing in a queue or in a crowded place and someone presses himself against you, press or stamp your heel hard on his foot or scrape your heel down his shin. At the same time ask him loudly to please leave you alone.

If he denies having touched you, ignore him. Where the harassment takes other forms, such as verbal abuse or eye contact, get away as soon as you can. People who openly behave offensively are unlikely to be cowed by angry words. Report all incidents to the police or, at the very least, complain to the management of the premises or the public transport on which they took place.

FLASHER!

The act of indecently exposing parts of the body – usually the genitals and usually by males – is known as flashing. It is a form of sexual harassment and is one of the crimes classed as criminal injuria, or an act that deliberately, unlawfully and seriously impairs the dignity of another person.

The act

It could be a man unzipping his trousers and displaying his genitals in a public place. He might be blatantly masturbating at an upstairs window and be visible from outside. A male passenger in a train might expose his genitals beneath a raincoat or partly conceal them behind a briefcase on his lap. A young woman responding to a motorist's appeal for directions may find, on reaching his car, that he is exposing himself, although only to someone standing close to the car. (She should not have approached a stranger's car at all.)

Many flashers pretend to be unaware that they are exposing themselves, such as the man who regularly stood on a table, naked, changing a light bulb while placing himself in full view of pupils in the playground of a girls' school. (The frequency of light-bulb failures led to a charge being laid against him.) Another flasher's tactic is to wear loose-fitting shorts, without underwear, and to pretend that the indecent exposure is unintentional. Flashers may be furtive or they may draw attention to what they are doing, by hand movements or by calling.

Genuine accidental exposure – when a towel is blown off a man who is changing on a beach, for example – may be impossible for the observer to distinguish from a deliberate act. Streaking in public, usually on a sports field before a large crowd, is not generally considered as seriously impairing the dignity of others, but it may also lead to conviction on a charge of criminal injuria.

The places

Flashing may occur in any public transport or place, from a church to the corridor or laundry of a block of flats, from a park to a railway embankment. Some flashers expose themselves indiscriminately; others may select particular individuals to whom to expose themselves. A flasher may even operate in the premises where he is employed, despite the likelihood of being recognised and identified. He will probably deny all charges.

Most flashers have a regular beat, and likely places are the vicinity of women's residences, girls' schools or any place where women or girls congregate or pass by, or from where they may be seen. Similar places may also be chosen by Peeping Toms, who derive their pleasure from secretly watching other people, rather than from exhibiting themselves engaged in a sexual act.

Who is flashed

Most indecent exposure is done in the presence of women or girls, but the homosexual male flasher prefers to be seen by young men or boys. With its suggestions of rape and violence, flashing by a man is likely to cause fear and distress.

What to do

Ideally, pretend that you haven't seen him, that he simply doesn't exist. Unfortunately though, you're almost bound to be taken by surprise and to react. If you're alone, overcome your reaction as quickly as you can and simply carry on with what you're doing.

Don't say anything unless he asks you a direct question and you can't avoid answering – by walking out of the room, for instance. Keep your replies calm and fairly noncommittal. Leave it up to him to make the next move at conversation. Tell him you're 'surprised', if he really wants to know, but don't be critical or tell him you're shocked, disgusted or frightened. If he insists that you watch him, try suggesting that maybe this isn't the right time or place. He's likely to want to know whether you're going to tell anyone about this encounter. Ask if he wants you to tell and, if he doesn't, say that you'll think about it. Even if you say you won't tell, you can't be bound to keep a promise made under duress. He may be blocking your way, and although it's unusual for flashers to be violent or to seek actual physical contact, find another route or wait until he moves away – which he will do. In a lonely area, whether you're on your own or in female company, get away from him, without obviously turning and fleeing.

Tell your children to keep away from any man whose penis is visible. They shouldn't laugh, point or say anything loudly – just get away and inform the nearest trusted adult. Report all flashers – to the police, the management of the area or building, or his employer.

Profile of a flasher

Unlike stalkers, flashers don't besiege people – they have their thrill or orgasm and then go back to their 'normal' lifestyle until the next time. A flasher may come from any level of society, any race or religion, may be married and may have children. He almost certainly has a low self-esteem, he may have difficulty in establishing relationships with women and he's probably sexually inhibited. He has turned to a form of sexual deviation (paraphilia) for his satisfaction, and although he's a nuisance and probably harmless, a small proportion of flashers may become dangerous. Most people practising a form of sexual deviation tend to be drawn to others, which means that flashing may lead to other antisocial or criminal acts. Flashers are not usually certifiably insane, but many will benefit from psychotherapy.

THE WORKPLACE

THE WORKPLACE

Employers need to protect their staff, their staff's possessions and their company property from strangers with criminal intent. But, unfortunately, most organisations also need to set systems in place to prevent or monitor theft and fraud committed by employees in the workplace.

Basic duties

It is obviously advisable for the owner of a business to install the necessary systems to protect that business and its assets (see Perimeter Alarm Systems, pp30-2, The Alarmed House, pp50-3, and Security Services, pp54-5). But in addition, the law expects employers to do all that is reasonable to provide safety in the workplace, to identify, remove or reduce hazards and to provide safety information and training for staff. Failure by the employer to adhere to labour safety regulations may lead to legal action.

Employees' duties include obeying lawful and reasonable requests to maintain the security of the company they work for. As an employee, you should look on company security systems as a means of protecting you and your job rather than as an expression of management's mistrust. Where an employee does not honour the company's security policy, the result may be dismissal.

Personal security

If you are threatened in any way – by structurally unsafe premises, dangerously worn equipment, exposure to criminal activity or improper conduct, such as sexual harassment (see Sexual Harassment at Work, pp201-3), make a complaint. Direct it to an appropriate senior staff member or follow the set procedure laid down in company regulations. Note that following company regulations does not prevent you from reporting criminal activity to the police.

Exposure to risks

The acceptability of risks depends on the type of job you do. If you are a bomb-disposal specialist, for example, risks are a normal part of your work, but if your duties are those of an office clerk, then physical risks should have no part in what you do. Some jobs require you to meet strangers regularly as part of your duties. For an estate agent, for instance, meeting strangers – often at out-of-the-way venues – is a normal preliminary to doing business. If you are exposed to risks such as these, find a way to reduce them.

Reducing the risks

Identify the risks involved in your own job and try to find solutions through consultation with your colleagues and your employer.

Once you've found that colleagues share your concern for the safety of the staff, see that the management is informed – they may be unaware that a problem exists. Notice of a security problem will carry greater weight if it is written, includes specific incidents that illustrate a lapse in security or dangers to the staff, and is signed by all staff members who support your action. Management should have its own stand-by plans ready, and should assure staff of its support.

These are the basic steps for staff and employers in identifying problems and finding the solution:

◆ Collect as much information about the problem from colleagues as you can.

◆ Encourage colleagues to report ongoing incidents.

◆ Devise and employ preventive measures.

◆ Monitor the efficacy of the preventive measures, and, if they don't work, change them. It may also be advisable to call in outside assistance, from a security firm or a security consultancy.

SECURITY QUIZ

How secure is your company?	Yes	No
1. Do you control entry into your premises?		
2. Do you monitor on-site staff vehicles?		
3. Do you monitor staff between on-site vehicles and the workplace?		
4. Do you have an effective identification system for staff and visitors?		
5. Do you have an alarm system?		
6. Does your receptionist know what to do if faced with an armed intruder?		
7. Does your telephonist know what to do in the case of a bomb threat or threat of attack?		
8. Do you know if your company is currently affected by fraud or stock theft?		
9. Will you be able to tell the difference between arson and accident?		
10. Is your company safe from industrial espionage?		
11. Do you have a security officer or a member of staff dedicated to security?		

Score one point for every 'yes' answer, zero for 'no'.

11/11: A perfect score, and you are to be congratulated on taking your security seriously. However, a score of 100 per cent is not necessarily a sign of perfect security, because the need to be on guard, and to improve and update, is constant.

If you scored less than full marks, you may already be suffering losses that you don't even know about. Find out what other businesses in your line are doing about security, or call in a security consultant.

THEFT IN THE WORKPLACE

Your need for protection doesn't end when you walk into your office, where the most frequently committed crime is common theft. The dishonesty of its employees can cause a company to collapse, thereby also bringing about the loss of jobs.

What is taken?

Thieves on the staff in an office or factory will steal anything for which they can find a buyer. The preferred loot is cash, stolen from an employer or from a colleague, because it is difficult to prove unlawful possession of cash and it can be disposed of easily. But whether people empty the till, make false entries in the books or merely take home a pencil sharpener, the crime is theft.

Theft by employees often takes place after normal business hours, when goods that have been hidden on the premises are removed. This two-stage theft may be operated by a staff member in conjunction with an outsider, the staff member 'placing' the goods and the outsider making the collection.

Company security

To protect the interests of both the company and its workers, restrict and control tightly after-hours' access to the premises (see also Perimeter Alarm Systems, pp30-2, and Living Alarms, pp33-5). For example,  the only staff members to be admitted after hours should be those who are on after-hours' duty or whose type of employment requires them to work at night. Some form of official, checkable identification must be produced by everyone claiming admission, without exception. A card, for instance, should carry a photograph of the holder, and a copy of the same photograph should be in the security admission file.

An after-hours' register should be completed and signed by everyone claiming admission, on arrival. Keep locked any sections of the premises to which after-hours' access is not required, but with cameras and intruder detectors switched on.

Anybody who does not qualify or who cannot produce the correct identification should not be admitted, and a record of their attempt to enter should be noted. Registers and records are of value only if they are examined and analysed by a competent authority, such as the company executive in charge of security.

Security on the job

You're more likely to suffer from theft if you work in a building where the staff members are strangers to one another, than if all the employees know each other, even if only by sight.

Don't leave anything valuable – including your wallet, keys, credit cards or cash – in any garment that you're likely to take off at work, such as your coat or jacket, or in a bag that you leave unattended at your desk. Instead, keep valuables in a secured inside pocket in a garment you won't take off (see Out Shopping, pp170-1). If you have a handbag or valuables that you don't want to carry around with you, place them inside a filing cabinet or drawer and lock them away. The simple locks in doors and drawers in much office furniture can be opened with easily obtainable keys – those from kitchen cupboards, for instance – but if locked they will discourage the casual pilferer.

If you're provided with a locker fitted with a combination lock, ask if the combination can be changed, as it's quite likely that others will know the existing combination and be able to get at the contents. If you're given a key-actuated padlock, replace this too.

It's not only your property that may be stolen. Your employer's property, such as calculators or specialised instruments, clothing, computers and stationery, may all disappear while in your custody or from your desk or office. To prevent your involvement in a theft – even as an innocent party – see that small valuable items are cleared off your desk and locked away whenever you go out of the office. Larger items, such as typewriters and computers can be secured with equipment locks and special adhesive pads designed for desktop fitting.

Protected information

Information is also a desirable possession for casual thieves and for the professional spy in commerce and industry. Paper – and even carbon paper – on which confidential material has been recorded, should be effectively shredded before disposal. Accessibility to computer files should be strictly limited. Ensure that important documents are locked away when you're out of the office. Take care not to make casual remarks about confidential information – they may be overheard by the wrong people.

Information about staff movements, especially absence from home or office, should also not be divulged, except to people who have established their identity and their need to know. Telling a stranger that the manager will be away until next week, for instance, may help to set up a burglary at his home.

Beware strangers

An offer to help is a good deterrent when you see a stranger in your office, either walking through or apparently waiting but not obviously involved with another staff member. Those strangers who are on legitimate business will be grateful for the offer. Others, knowing they have been observed, might decide to go away. If the stranger does ask for help – to remove an item of equipment, say – check his or

Business break-ins

The reported incidence of burglaries, or housebreaking, at business premises dropped from 89 058 in 1994 to 87 863 in 1996.

her identity and then confirm with an appropriate person that the caller is expected and is entitled to remove the particular item.

Stop thief!

Theft by an employee provides the strongest grounds for summary dismissal – that is, instant dismissal without serving notice. As soon as a theft is discovered, a disciplinary hearing must be convened within the company, and the worker must be allowed to put forward his or her case. The onus is on the employer to prove that the dismissal is fair. The value of the stolen goods or money is not necessarily relevant. For example, a waiter who stole a cold drink from his employer was dismissed after a disciplinary hearing. The Industrial Court ordered him to be reinstated, on the grounds that dismissal was too harsh, given the low value of the stolen goods. The Labour Appeal Court, however, found that what really mattered was that the waiter had stolen from his employer's stock in trade and so could not be trusted. The order for reinstatement was overturned.

Get details of the procedure to be followed from the company attorney, labour consultants and the industrial council for the particular industry. In serious or repeated cases of theft, call the police. The thief is then likely to be prosecuted in open court.

Working late

The main safety consideration when working late is your safety on the premises and while commuting. If your employer can't ensure your safety after hours, at least to a reasonable degree, tell him or her that you are reluctant to work late, and give your reasons. (Workers have the right to refuse to work overtime.) It might be unreasonable, for instance, if your employer expects you to make your way home late at night by public transport, and then to walk through an unsafe area to reach your home. Ideally, your employer should provide or arrange safe transport.

It is unreasonable for your work premises not to be adequately secured against intruders who might molest or injure you. If you cannot avoid working after hours, make sure that you are not alone and that, at the very least, you will be able to contact the police or a security service. It is also advisable to identify a room, preferably with a telephone, in which you can lock yourself as a last resort.

Once you know you'll be working late, phone a friend, tell him or her where you are and that you'll call again when you get home. Ask the security guard employed by the company to call on you on his or her rounds. Try to think of alternatives to working late, such as starting early the next day, or taking work home. Avoid working late when you are dealing with large sums of money.

SMALL FIRMS

The need to protect yourself, your business and your stock is a real one, particularly if you run a small business. Although statistics may show that most crimes committed against businesses occurred in cities, any premises, from an inner-city jewellery store to a remote farm shop, may be targeted by criminals.

Business Watch

Introduce yourself to other business proprietors in the neighbourhood and find out if there is a local traders' association. It will almost certainly be to your advantage to join such an organisation, as it may already operate a mutual protection scheme. Get advice about forming a local branch of Business Watch from your nearest police station. Business Watch is a cooperative security arrangement concerned with the observation and reporting of unusual or suspicious characters or events.

Danger periods

The times when robbers are most likely to strike – at a shop, for instance – are around opening or closing time. You are particularly vulnerable while locking and unlocking the premises, because your back is almost always to the street and there are usually very few people about. See that you have an alert and reliable person with you at these times. Without establishing an obvious routine, check outside the premises, and be especially wary of occupied vehicles parked close by. An occupied vehicle parked so as to face the exit of a parking area is doubly suspect. Apart from watching from outside, criminals will probably come in as legitimate customers as well, where they quickly become aware of routines in order to turn them to their own advantage.

Bars and alarms

Security gates, locks and bars may prevent criminals from entering a business, but they also prevent a free flow of the customers and clients on whom the business largely depends. Turnstiles or other means of control, apart from being disliked by customers, may also contravene local fire regulations. To help overcome customer resentment when you introduce security measures, display signs pointing out the new system. For example, 'For your protection, we have installed closed-circuit TV'.

Fit master-keyed locks (see Keeping it Locked, pp44-5) to reduce the time you spend locking and unlocking doors on your premises.

If a burglar succeeds in breaking in, an alarm will at least limit the time he is prepared to spend on the premises. A simple form of alarm, called the 'buddy buzzer' is believed to have reduced shop hold-ups in the United States. A battery-operated bell unobtrusively sounds in the shop next door, advising the neighbour that a hold-up is in progress and the neighbour immediately contacts the police. Take great care not to arouse suspicion when operating the bell.

Caring for the cash

If your business depends largely or exclusively on cash transactions, it's likely that somebody will plan to steal it. Find out from brokers or insurance companies what policies they can offer to cover its loss by theft. Typical multiperil policies offer (usually limited) cover for money, cheques and notes, stamps and postal orders. Knowing that your money is insured may dissuade you from risking your life in the event of a robbery. (See also Insuring Possessions, pp92-3.)

To keep large amounts of cash safely on the premises, you will almost certainly need to invest in a safe (see Keeping it Safe, pp66-9), unless you have a bolted-down, well-built cabinet with an adequate lock.

Where cash represents only a small part of the turnover, or where only petty cash is kept on the premises, a lockable cash box kept in a locked filing cabinet may suffice. Depending on the type of business, a hideaway safe may be adequate, blending in with the general office background. Choose one that looks like, say, a tin of floor polish or a box of paper clips, rather than a can of cool drink, which a burglar might just fancy in the middle of the job. But make sure that your choice of hideaway safe doesn't look out of place.

Good money and bad

Today's sophisticated computer equipment makes possible the production of highly deceptive forged or counterfeit banknotes, usually of a face value of R50 or more. In the first six months of 1996, close to R6 million – most of it in counterfeit R200 banknotes – was seized by the police in Gauteng and North-West Province. Irregularities in the forged notes most often show up in the metallic strip, the watermark and the type of paper used. Train your staff who regularly handle the cash to look for irregularities such as these. People attempting to pass forged notes are most likely to do so when shops are busy, or late in the day when the light may not be adequate for examining a watermark.

Handling the cash

Keep no more cash on the premises than you need for ordinary working and, especially, don't allow excess cash to accumulate in the cash register or till. Counting the takings is likely to tempt others – strangers as well as staff – so do it where you aren't in full view or readily accessible – in an office at the end of a long corridor, or up a steep flight of narrow steps, for example.

Banking

Bank takings as frequently as reasonably possible, to avoid having to carry very large sums of money. However, if carrying large sums is inevitable, consider engaging a security service that specialises in cash transfers. Ask your bank manager to recommend one. Arrange to have your staff's wages paid straight into a bank account.

If you carry the bank deposits and wages yourself, and you have other calls to make on the same trip, go to the bank first. Never leave the money in your car, however well you think you may have hidden it. Try to avoid going to the bank on your own, and vary your time and route so that you don't establish a routine. As far as you can, distribute the money throughout your pockets or under your clothes rather than carry all of it in a single container, such as a briefcase. If precautions fail and you are robbed in the street, at least you probably won't lose everything.

Firearms

Don't rely on firearms to keep your cash safe. The robber who is coming after it is probably armed, and he'll have his weapon out and ready to use before you've even reached yours. He's almost certainly nervous; he may be callous – either way, it will take little encouragement to start him shooting.

Unless you wear a firearm on your body, which may be uncomfortable or impractical, or unless you keep it locked in a secure place, where you probably can't get to it in an emergency, a firearm in the workplace is generally a greater danger to law-abiding citizens than it is to criminals. Even in the hands of experts, firearms used in public places have the potential to produce unforeseen and tragic results.

Almost the only occasion on which a firearm may give you equality is when you recognise an armed criminal and his intention before he has produced his gun, or when you are alerted by the sounds of a break-in (see Firearms, pp258-65).

Admissions and intruders

Ideally, strangers should be admitted to a business premises by appointment only, but shops, for instance, would suffer severe disruption if this was applied. In other businesses, however, do ask all strangers to identify themselves before letting them in (see Theft in the Workplace, pp194-6). If their identification is unsatisfactory, or if they appear suspicious in any way, deal with them at the security gate rather than admit them to the premises. Officials requesting entry should be in possession of formal identity cards (see A Stranger at the Door, pp80-1).

BUSINESS PRECAUTIONS

1. Be wary of issuing duplicate keys. Collect them from staff before they leave your employment.

2. Don't leave office keys lying about.

3. Keep all bank account documents, cheques, cards and references securely locked away.

4. Don't discuss business affairs where you can be overheard by strangers.

5. Don't discuss your banking procedure in front of anyone other than those who need to know.

6. Be especially alert on opening up for the day, and just before closing time.

THE WORKPLACE

Shoplifting shocker!

There were 62 198 reported cases of shoplifting in 1996 as opposed to 67 059 reported cases in 1994, the highest incidences occurring in Gauteng and KwaZulu-Natal.

Alert and attentive assistants offering help to strangers who appear undecided will help to avert hold-ups or shoplifting by letting those who are criminals know that they have been seen and will be recognised.

Challenge strangers who are out of bounds on your premises assertively rather than aggressively. The best approach is to ask 'May I help you?' and, if no satisfactory answer is received, firmly show them out or consider calling the police. (Deciding to call the police or not might depend on the nature of your business and on whether you think that the intruders may have committed a crime. They might be making off with jewellery, for instance, or with confidential plans.)

Decide in advance on your security policy and tactics when dealing with intruders. For instance, alert your staff by the use of a particular phrase, such as 'order from Exco'. Staff would be alerted by the warning, 'I see we've got an order from Exco', while 'I think we've got an order from Exco' informs them that you are suspicious of a stranger. You or another staff member (or both of you) detain the intruder while the receptionist telephones the police or the building's security guards.

If you are unable to physically detain the intruder, you will have to let him go, but write down a description of him as soon as possible. The unjustified use of force may lead to action against you in court, so you must be fairly sure that anyone whom you attempt to detain really is a criminal. Signs advising that you have no jobs vacant may help to reduce the number of non-clients who enter the premises.

Bomb threats

Take threats of bombs and other violence seriously: evacuate the premises and get away from the building immediately. Contact the police as soon as you can. Once outside, don't stand opposite windows or doors – shards of glass and splinters will scatter over an increasing radius – and keep away from rubbish bins, parcels, and motor vehicles that you don't recognise.

Have a plan in place, just as you would in the need to evacuate a building on fire, with marshals responsible for groups of people, a safe area identified to marshal the staff to until the building is declared safe, and a system of accounting for all staff.

Working at home

An obvious advantage of working at home is that your home is not left unoccupied as often as it would be if you worked elsewhere. The ordinary householder's protection of bars and security gates should be adequate in this case. If you work in a room with an outside door, make sure that the security gate over the door is locked at all times. Devise a system whereby deliverymen and other frequent callers, other than clients, don't need to be admitted to the residential portion of your home.

SEXUAL HARASSMENT AT WORK

Sexual harassment in the workplace is more about power and domination than it is about sex, and is almost always committed by men against women. Even when no physical injury is caused, sexual harassment is nevertheless an act of aggression, and may be severely damaging to the victim. Many women workers mistakenly see it as a normal part of the job.

What is harassment?

Sexual harassment exists when somebody repeatedly, deliberately and seriously infringes your dignity – that is, your self-respect, composure and privacy – with actions or words that have sexual overtones. The nature of the harassment might range from the romantic (sending you love poems) 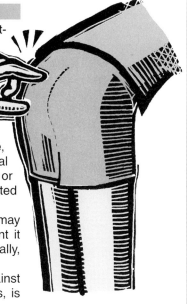 to the tease (running a finger down your spine, or verbal sexual teasing), to the explicitly sexual touch (kissing on the mouth, fondling the breasts, or requests for sexual favours). (See also Unwanted Attention, pp188-9.)

A single incident may not be harassment – it may offend you and you should take action to prevent it from happening again (see p203). But essentially, harassment is repeated and unwanted.

Any sexual harassment, whether directed against males or females, homosexuals or heterosexuals, is against the law.

Harassment of males

Men also suffer unwanted sexual attention at work, although much less commonly than women do. The motivation – power and domination – is the same, and the victim may undergo all or most of the ordeals experienced by female victims. He is, however, more likely to be ridiculed by his colleagues because of the old-established culture of supposed male superiority which demands that he should be able to 'handle' women. However embarrassing or humiliating, sexual harassment of men does not contain the element of terror, associated with rape, that it does for women.

Harassment of homosexuals

Homosexuals may be harassed in the workplace by other homosexuals, or, more often, by heterosexuals. Harassment by a heterosexual person may take the form of taunting, insulting language or behaviour, or the use of obscene language or actions.

The problem

Sexual harassment among workers is a subtle and widespread phenomenon that is not easy to resolve, although the increasing national concern for human

Sexual harassment – typical examples

◆ Violating your personal space by touching, crowding or pressing against you
◆ Asking about the intimate details of your life
◆ Leering or staring at you
◆ Telling lewd jokes or stories in front of you
◆ Passing lewd or suggestive pictures or reading material within your sight
◆ Making lewd comments, whether directly to you or to another person in your hearing
◆ Persistently sending you notes or letters after you've indicated that they are not welcome
◆ Adopting sexually suggestive positions or gestures
◆ Persistently asking for a date after you've indicated that you are not interested in one
◆ Waiting for you, or following you, after being told to stop doing so
◆ Making threats if demands for sexual favours – kissing, touching, even intercourse – are not met
◆ Demanding sexual favours on the grounds of high position in the company
◆ Promising promotion if you submit to sexual demands, or threatening to hinder promotion if you don't submit
◆ Making sexually explicit remarks
◆ Touching, clutching or fondling you, especially at the breasts, thighs or genital area.

rights has helped to bring it to prominence. The problem for the victim is acute – she fears further harassment but also fears that her reactions to prevent it may damage her career. The harasser usually feels protected by his more senior position in the company. Behind harassment there is always the terror and threat – whether real or imagined – of rape.

Harassment in action

A man who habitually touches you, for instance, although you dislike the contact, may say that he was unaware that you objected. Unless you have expressed your objection, it's possible that he will be believed. If you're not sure that the way a man touches you is sexual, ask a few trusted colleagues for their opinion, and also note whether the man touches men the way he touches you. If he doesn't, you're probably right in thinking that it's sexual. But whether it is or isn't, you have the right not to be touched if you don't want to be touched.

Participant or victim?

Suppose you're hurrying through a doorway and you bump squarely into a pleasant male colleague heading the other way. You apologise and, in response, he gives you a friendly smile and says 'No problem, it's a pleasure bumping into you.' You find the words inoffensive because they come from a friend, but if they had been said by someone else they might indeed have been suggestive and offensive. An observer may see no difference between your encounters with one or the other. What makes the difference between ribald exchanges and sexual harassment is that the woman (or victim) is not a willing participant and is made to feel uncomfortable.

Keeping quiet

Many people suffering sexual harassment at work have difficulty talking about the problem and, ultimately, doing something to put a stop to it. Common reasons for this reluctance, which may be part of the debilitating psychological effect of the harassment, include: fear of retaliation by the harasser; fear of ridicule or disbelief; lack of confidence in their own case; lack of support among friends and peers; and the belief that nothing will change. The only certainty about keeping quiet is that nothing will change – except perhaps to become worse.

Fighting back

Especially when you're young and new to a job, it may be hard to imagine that your protest will actually change anything. Also, you may actually like knowing that you're sexually attractive, although you may not like the way it's expressed, and therefore think that somehow it's your fault. You may be afraid of being labelled a prude. You may feel that it is probably meant as a joke and that you should accept it as such. But it comes down to this – if it bothers you, it must stop.

Find out if the harasser has bothered other women, or whether he has been the subject of other complaints. Even if you find no other evidence, have faith in yourself and don't give up.

As soon as you're aware of being sexually harassed, start keeping a record of harassing incidents. Include the date, time and place, the names of others involved, whether as participants, witnesses or simply as being present, and where and how your harasser touched you, or what he said.

Confrontation

Tell the man who is harassing you that his actions upset you, but first plan what you're going to say. In the emotion of the moment you may not stress your concern strongly enough. It is essential that you be firm about what you say, so that he can be in no doubt that his attentions are unwelcome. It may help to take a friend with you, for support. Ask him to stop his behaviour. You don't have to offer any reasons or explanations. Speak to him (with your friend) in privacy, if you can, although a spontaneous outburst in mid-office will give him the message and provide witnesses too.

If you can't bring yourself to confront your harasser, send him a note – but make sure that he gets it, and keep a copy yourself.

Help from above

If the direct approach doesn't stop the harassment, contact your human resources manager, or any senior woman colleague who seems sympathetic. If you are a member of a trade union, a union official should be able to help you. Ask to speak to the company's lawyers, if necessary. As a final resort, consult your

DRAMA IN REAL LIFE

The price of ignoring harassment

Pauline Clinton, a 40-year-old technical supervisor, suffered months of torment at the hands of a colleague. In court, Ms Clinton said that at every opportunity Hans Botha would lean against her and touch her, and had also put his hand up her dress and made crude sexual suggestions. The situation worsened after she had been promoted. In terms of an agreement negotiated by a labour consultant, Mr Botha resigned from the company and Ms Clinton agreed not to take action against him. But the harassment continued, both on the premises and off. Finally, Ms Clinton had no option but to resign, fearing for her own physical safety, and took the matter to court. The Pretoria Industrial Court ordered the former employers of Ms Clinton and Mr Botha to pay Ms Clinton the sum of R730 000, having found that the employers had 'repudiated their obligation to Ms Clinton' by refusing to sever ties with Mr Botha.

Police comment: Mr Botha's persistence suggests that, despite the outcome of the case, he may try to continue harassing Ms Clinton. If he does, she should report it immediately to the police, and consider taking further action in a court of law.

FAMILY VIOLENCE

Most people believe that even if home is not a castle, it is a safe and private place. What happens there, or between members of the family, is often seen by family, friends and the police as a domestic affair only, to be sorted out by those involved. This attitude not only conceals a great deal of violent crime, but makes it difficult for victims ever to seek help.

Why violence?

Every family comes under strains of some sort – unemployment, overcrowding, frustration at work, exhaustion, financial difficulties, inadequate housing, the demands of elderly or ill parents, the loss of family ties – and many find an outlet for these strains within the family itself. Consequently, very few marital or parent-child relationships run smoothly all the time and bickering is a normal part of family life. However, ordinary bickering is often taken to unreasonable lengths, when angry words and deeds become abuse. And unfortunately, this abuse seems to be increasing.

Living in one of the most violent societies in the world, many South Africans believe that violence, if not actually respectable, is at least acceptable as a means of asserting authority or solving problems. It is not. The law does not prevent you from disciplining your children, but unreasonable or violent behaviour towards children, or towards a spouse – causing injury, for instance – may be criminal. It should always be reported.

Keeping it in the family

Where violence exists between spouses or domestic partners, it is almost always the man who commits it. Similarly, sexual crimes against children are more commonly committed by the man, but both partners may be responsible. Child abuse of any sort, as well as spousal abuse, is grossly under-reported. This silence almost becomes a secret agreement to perpetuate abuse within the family, since physical and sexual abuse often occur because of similar events in the childhood of the abuser. Precipitating factors, not causes, may include alcoholism, drug addiction, financial hardship and insecurity, or any threat to the man's authority.

Extreme violence

Family violence may include the murder of the entire family – usually by the husband/father – followed by the suicide of the murderer. Even where there has been little or no history of violence, family murder and suicide may result from the effects of the man's upbringing on his inability to cope with failure or misfortune in his life as an adult. Many men are brought up believing in some inflexible and strictly regulated pattern of life – often with religious overtones – that seldom exists in reality. And in almost all societies, many males are taught that they are the 'natural' leaders. When misfortune strips them of status, power and faith, some of these men try to punish those whom they see as the cause of their misfortunes, and still assert their authority – by killing their own families. Such people are frequently described by those who knew them as 'religious', 'church-going', 'a model for the community'. They are rarely remembered as 'cheerful', 'unselfish' or 'adaptable'. Divorced parents – both mothers and fathers – have killed themselves and their children out of self-pity and as an extreme way of punishing the surviving ex-spouse rather than for any other reason.

Drug and alcohol abuse

Many substances are abused by people who turn their backs on problems, rather than facing them and looking for solutions. However great or tragic a problem or sorrow may be, a mood-enhancer will not make it go away. Nor, in the long run, will it make the pain or conflict more bearable. Drugs and alcohol often make an abuser violent, and in turn invoke antagonism from the family towards the drug abuser, leading to the disintegration of family relationships.

Getting help

If you never talk about the problem, you'll never sort it out. Once you realise that you can talk about your fears and anger to someone who cares, you won't feel so helpless. But the decision to find someone to talk to about the problem must be yours – a counsellor can't make up your mind for you. A counsellor is any person to whom you can talk about your problem and who will help you decide what to do about it. Your counsellor may be a psychologist, a social worker or even a family friend, and may suggest other people and organisations that may be able to help you.

The first step towards solving family violence is for partners to try to talk the problem out between themselves. In many cases, however, it's often gone too far to be settled without help. Where both partners accept that violence is a problem and the abuser is willing to take responsibility for the abuse, the couple may seek counselling together. However, the more common scenario is that only one partner is willing to seek help. Then, the only solution lies in obtaining a court interdict that prohibits violence between the partners.

Violence against children or even family elders is perhaps the most pathetic, because they lack the physical and emotional strength, and economic independence, that might enable them to cope. In many cases, adults must make decisions on behalf of abused children or elders, whether they are their own or those of a neighbour, and report the incidents to the police or a social worker.

WIFE-BATTERING

An abused spouse or 'battered woman' is one who is hit and assaulted – even raped – or who is verbally abused by being grossly insulted and sworn at by her husband or boyfriend. It may happen at home or when they are out together. In South Africa, it happens to at least one woman out of every six.

The problem

Most of our home lives and our domestic problems are hidden from the outside world, even from friends and relatives. Home, the one place where we should be safe, is too often a place of dark secrets and of violence. The victim who keeps quiet protects the man who assaults her, in the belief that battering is a family matter. But such violent assaults are also a crime. Talking about them in the community breaks the shroud of silence, and is the first move towards making your personal world a safer one.

Why are women battered?

In many countries and cultures, boys are brought up to be strong and aggressive, ambitious and unemotional. Sexually, economically and physically, they expect to control women. But most of them do not achieve the ideals of strength and authority they expect, and so some may try to compensate for this by trying to control people whom they consider to be weak or inferior – such as women.

In addition, South Africans have lived through very violent times, exposed to images of, and enduring, political violence and faction fighting. Our society,

Q U E S T I O N N A I R E :

Check your man

This questionnaire will help to determine whether you're in a relationship that is, or could turn, violent. Remember, violence takes many forms – threats and verbal abuse may sometimes be as devastating as physical assault.

1. Does he object to your having close friends and to your friends visiting you at home?
2. Does he swear at you, or criticise you unfairly in company?
3. Has he ever beaten you, smacked you or thrown things at you when he's been angry?
4. When he hurts you, does he say 'sorry', but hurts you again the next time he gets angry?
5. Do arguments end up with your getting hurt?
6. Does he leave it up to you to make the relationship work, and then blame you for not doing enough?
7. Has he ever hurt you, or threatened to do so, without your knowing the reason why?
8. Are you or some outside influence always blamed for his bad moods?
9. Do you sometimes feel you must be the only one this has ever happened to?

If you've answered YES to most of these questions, you're no stranger to physical assault or verbal abuse. But you can change the situation.

which taught that men were superior to women, seemed also to be teaching that violence was acceptable as a means of solving problems and disputes.

Many women are economically dependent on their male partner, because they are paid less or because they look after the home and receive no income, or because their partner will not allow them to work. Many men therefore believe that they own their female partner, that she is his and that he can do with her whatever he likes.

The man's state of mind and behaviour towards his female companion are also influenced by his own situation. He himself may be unemployed, underpaid, discriminated against or even humiliated. Dominating 'his woman' – sometimes beating her – gives him back some of his sense of control. Control equated with physical strength is appealing to him. Economic and social factors, alcoholism or drug addiction do not, on their own, create a man who will beat his female partner (see Profile of a Wife-batterer, p209), but they will certainly influence his behaviour.

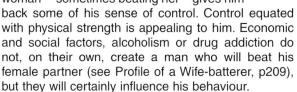

Wife-battering myths – true or false?

◆ Wife-battering is caused by drugs and drink – false. The same man who beats his wife when he is drunk will also beat her when he is sober. And some men who beat their wives don't drink or take drugs at all.
◆ Battering happens mostly to black or uneducated women, or to those in the low-income groups – false. Women of all races and from all levels of society are beaten up, although only those with lower incomes are likely to ask help from welfare departments.
◆ Women get beaten because they ask for it, or they like to be shown who is the boss around the home – false. No woman asks or wants to be beaten.
◆ Battered women are always a bit mad, anyway – false. They certainly live in a state of acute fear and anxiety, for themselves and for their families. They may be depressed or seem a bit odd, because of the stress and the terror that they try to hide. They're probably trying to think of a way to leave the man, or, at the very least, to get him to stop beating them.

Why women stay

Here are some of the answers that women give when asked that simple question, 'Why do you stay?'
◆ I'm afraid of the future.
◆ I have nowhere else to go.
◆ I have no job, no money.
◆ People will think that I'm a bad wife.
◆ It's like he said. It's my own fault.
◆ Maybe I can change him if I stay.
◆ I must stay for the children.
◆ I don't know where to go for help.

◆ I can't be bothered any more.
◆ What kind of wages will I get if I go to work now?
◆ The whole community is violent anyway.
◆ My in-laws begged me to make it work.

However important the grain of truth in each answer, none of them addresses the central problem, which is that the woman is being beaten or abused.

Marital rape

Sexual intercourse against the woman's will may form part of the abuse. In the past, a husband could not be convicted of raping his wife. Since 1993, however, the Prevention of Family Violence Act has determined that rape and violence within a marriage are punishable offences. The 'marriage' may include a man and woman wedded to each other according to law or custom, or living together as husband and wife even if they are not married.

Responding to violence

Without knowing your exact situation and details of your man and your relationship with him, nobody can give you specific advice on how to handle his outbursts of violence. The most important concern is to avoid injury to yourself or to your children.

If your man has become enraged and seems likely to attack you, go outside, where your neighbours and passers-by can see you. He may be less likely to strike you when there are witnesses. If he doesn't calm down, go to a friend or relative where you will be safe, or contact the police.

By the time violence starts, it is probably too late to appeal to your man's reason or sense of justice. At another time, though, point out that you don't enjoy being beaten or abused, and that you don't deserve such treatment. Consider whether it might be useful to talk to his parents, other relatives or friends, but remember that he might consider this to be 'betrayal' or 'talking behind his back'. Try to persuade him to see a counsellor who will help him solve his problem, and assure him that you will go with him and support him.

Talking about it

It is very important that you talk to someone about your being battered, if this is happening to you. Talking to a counsellor will help you decide what to do about your situation, and you will be advised of your legal rights – the crime of your man beating you at home is as serious as a stranger beating you in the street. Counsellors will also tell you about people and organisations that will help you. You will need the support and reassurance of friends and neighbours, and organisations such as a battered women's support group, to give you strength and determination.

When you're ready to ask for help, try contacting one of these organisations: NICRO, POWA (People Opposing Women Abuse) or Life Line.

Profile of a wife-batterer

A man who beats up his wife usually has a 'macho' image of himself. This is probably a compensation for his feelings of inadequacy that come from his inferiority complex. A wife-batterer generally believes that men should be in charge and regards his wife and children as possessions rather than as people in their own right. Alcohol and drugs may make things worse, but will not, on their own, actually create a wife-batterer. He may seem at ease socially, but is unable to reason or argue logically with his wife, which brings his inadequacies to the fore and causes him to resort to violence. Women are a threat to such a man, particularly when they are seen as successful. He may belong to any social class, and probably had a strictly supervised childhood under a domineering father and a subservient mother. The violence may occur in cycles, interspersed with apologies, gifts, promises – and then more violence. He tries to break down his wife until she believes that she can't survive without him. He will also use the children in his manipulations.

Laying a charge

If you are badly injured – in great pain, bleeding heavily or with a broken limb, for instance – see a doctor as soon as possible, even before going to the police. If not, report the assault at a police station no more than a day or so after the assault, while bruises, scratches and other signs of attack are still visible. Take a trusted friend or relative with you to give you confidence.

Tell the police that you want to lay a charge of assault against your man and/or that you want to seek an interdict. The police may see it as a 'family affair' and be reluctant to take a statement, but you must insist on your right of access to the law. Make a note of the OB (Occurrence Book) and CAS (Criminal Administration System) numbers that the police assign to your case.

You will eventually have to appear in a criminal court and tell a magistrate your story, after which your man may be sentenced for assault. You may also seek an interdict in a civil court, prohibiting your man from assaulting or threatening you. If he disregards the terms of the interdict, he will have to appear before the magistrate for contempt of court. He may or may not be fined. If you intend to claim for damages, you will have to hire a private attorney.

Leaving home, going to court

Moving out of the shared home may seem to be the only solution. If you have nowhere to go, contact a welfare organisation such as NICRO to suggest the nearest place of safety. If you are married to the man who has been abusing you, he is obliged to support you for as long as you need support and for as long as he is able to provide it.

If you go to court, ask the clerk of the court whether there is a Victim Support Services Coordinator – a specialised social worker – you could talk to. He or she may help you to claim travel costs between home and court, wages lost through court appearances and the costs of accommodation during the trial.

HUSBAND ABUSE

On hearing of the phenomenon of husband abuse for the first time, many people are likely to react with amusement or disbelief. To them a battered husband belongs in a cartoon strip in which he is beaten by a large, aggressive wife with a rolling pin. But men are abused in relationships and, where physical abuse is unlikely to succeed, they are subjected to verbal or psychological abuse, including deliberate damage to their most cherished possessions.

A lethal kind of love

Statistics for interdicts served in South Africa against spouses for abuse, in 1994-1995, show that 98 per cent of interdicts were served against violent men, and 2 per cent against violent women. A study of violent households in the United States showed that the number of murders of women by men was very nearly the same as the number of murders of men by women. These findings suggest that women may be less likely to commit nonlethal assault, but are almost as likely to commit murder.

The abusive wife

She may belong to any social class and is likely to be insecure, possessive and jealous. She has never learned to control her anger and may feel frustrated – perhaps because of an inability to communicate satisfactorily with her spouse, or because of the demands of their joint lifestyle, including caring for children.

The nature of the abuse

It would not be abuse for a wife to say, for instance, 'I wish you'd stand up to your boss a bit more.' It would probably be abuse if she said, especially repeatedly, 'You're not a man because you don't stand up to your boss.' A smack on the shoulder or a light punch on the arm may be acceptable as signifying the wife's disapproval. Blows to tender areas such as the face, abdomen or genitals, or any assault with a weapon, would almost certainly be abuse. A feature of the abuse may be acts of aggravated spitefulness, such as deliberately damaging or destroying something that the man cherishes. Generally, abuse repeats itself, becomes habitual, and usually becomes more frequent and more severe.

Suffering in silence

A man who is being beaten, injured or otherwise abused by his wife is usually too embarrassed to report the matter. He is afraid of being seen as pitiful, unable to 'handle' a nagging wife, and as

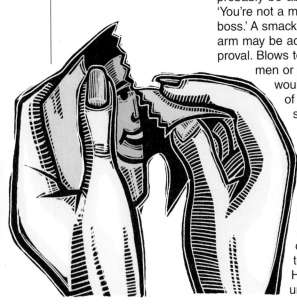

A passionate romance that went wrong

Apart from sexual attraction, friends saw little on which Abe and Emma could build a relationship. Playful but somewhat barbed teasing in public gradually became verbal abuse, usually started by Emma. In private, physical abuse began on the night that Abe said he had to travel on Emma's birthday and, in the course of an argument, threw Emma's birthday present at her feet. Emma kicked him, slapped his face repeatedly and kicked his video camera, which was badly damaged. The only physical contact that Abe initiated was in trying to restrain her. Outbursts of physical violence became increasingly frequent, with Abe finding it more and more difficult to refrain from hitting back. Emma said she thought it 'acceptable' for a woman to strike a man, adding that it was 'sort of romantic.' For Abe, however, romance died a few months later when Emma came at him with a pair of scissors. He obtained a court order that bound Emma to keep away from him.

Police comment: Violent assault is a crime at home just as it is on the street and you should report it to the police when it occurs. It is also advisable to seek professional help, since allowing the situation to drift could end in disaster.

a figure of fun. His wife may attack him repeatedly, without either of them attempting to resolve the situation in a reasonable manner. In some cases, the tragic end may be the murder by the husband of his spouse and children, followed by his suicide.

Self-defence

On average, men are stronger than women, but this does not mean that a man will always be able to restrain his wife from injuring him. This is particularly so where the assault is made from behind or while he is asleep, with a dangerous weapon such as a firearm, a knife, a bottle or a heavy piece of firewood.

If a husband defended himself and in so doing injured his wife, a court would consider whether the force he used was reasonable in relation to the threat she posed against him. If he shot her, say, when he could simply have held her off, or if he struck her repeatedly after she had fallen, it is likely he would be found guilty of a serious crime.

What to do

It's important to acknowledge the problem and to find help before anger and resentment build up to uncontrollable levels – perhaps on both sides. If your wife attacks you physically, try to defend yourself without striking back or using excessive force. Answering her abuse with violence will not solve the problem, and may make it very much worse.

If you have children, their wellbeing and safety demand that something be done. Before you look for help from outside the home, tell your wife that you are going to do so. Try speaking to your minister of religion, or to an older female relative whose opinions you respect. If their suggestions don't help, try counselling with one of the organisations that specialise in violent family difficulties (see pp266-71). You may also lay a charge at a police station and seek a court interdict against your wife.

WALKED INTO A DOOR

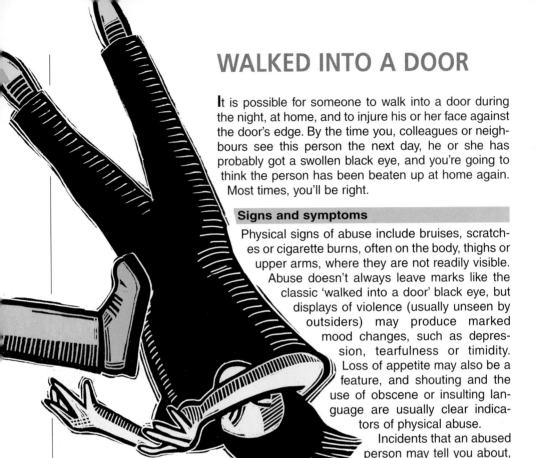

It is possible for someone to walk into a door during the night, at home, and to injure his or her face against the door's edge. By the time you, colleagues or neighbours see this person the next day, he or she has probably got a swollen black eye, and you're going to think the person has been beaten up at home again. Most times, you'll be right.

Signs and symptoms

Physical signs of abuse include bruises, scratches or cigarette burns, often on the body, thighs or upper arms, where they are not readily visible. Abuse doesn't always leave marks like the classic 'walked into a door' black eye, but displays of violence (usually unseen by outsiders) may produce marked mood changes, such as depression, tearfulness or timidity. Loss of appetite may also be a feature, and shouting and the use of obscene or insulting language are usually clear indicators of physical abuse.

Incidents that an abused person may tell you about, and which hold strong potential to develop into violence and injury, include:

◆ being deliberately denied sleep
◆ not being allowed outside the house
◆ being denied medical assistance when ill or injured
◆ being threatened with personal violence
◆ having valued possessions deliberately broken by the abuser
◆ having clothing torn or cut up
◆ being sexually assaulted
◆ being unjustly accused, often of sexual infidelity.

Interference . . .?

Many people accept violence as normal within their intimate affairs, so it may be difficult for you to know when to intervene, or whether to intervene at all. Your intervention may be resented by both the abuser and the abused, perhaps further complicating relations with your friend, neighbour or colleague.

Where sounds of violence are a regular occurrence, without apparent protest or injury, the situation may not be an emergency and calling the police might not be justified.

It would be unreasonable and unwarranted interference, and possibly grounds for legal action against you, if you:

◆ regularly called your neighbour's house or peered in at her windows, to make sure that she was all right

◆ discussed the rights and wrongs of her affairs with her at length
◆ encouraged her to take illegal or vengeful action against her abuser
◆ threatened the abuser – except perhaps in an emergency, to save someone from serious injury.

. . . or assistance?

If you believe that your neighbour is being injured and may be unable to call for help herself – you can hear the sounds of blows being struck, or of a man yelling and a woman crying and begging him to stop hitting her, for instance – you should consider calling the police. It is a crime for any person to assault another, even within a marriage or family. And it is your duty to do what you can to prevent the assault and ill-treatment of any person, especially those people, such as children and the disabled, who are not able to help themselves.

In an emergency, call the police Flying Squad at 10111. Tell them that a person is being seriously assaulted and give the address of the place at which the assault is taking place. It is advisable to give your own name and address as well, although this is not compulsory. You may ask the police not to say from whom they received their information when they call at your neighbour's address, but they cannot guarantee that they will not reveal your name.

You may consider that the situation requires immediate attention, and that the police are unlikely to arrive in time. Before you intervene personally, consider your own safety, especially with regard to your ability to end the abuse and to protect yourself if the abuser turns on you. Depending on what you know about the people involved, it might be helpful to call their doctor, their minister of religion or some other person with influence.

In non-urgent circumstances, try talking – or listening – to the abused partner and suggest that she or he contact an organisation such as Life Line or NICRO (see also Useful Phone Numbers and Addresses, pp266-71). It would be reasonable to provide the abused person with the telephone number or street address of an organisation that could offer help, and to allow her or him to use your telephone if she or he is unable to call from home. It might also be reasonable to provide emergency temporary shelter for the abused person and for any other person in that family whom you believe to be in danger of being injured by the abuser.

CHILD ABUSE

Parents and guardians have the right to discipline their children. But although there are no rules that prescribe in detail what degree of discipline is permitted, parents and guardians also have the obligation to protect their children from excessive or unnatural punishment and from any form of abuse.

What is child abuse?

Child abuse is the name given to a group of criminal acts or omissions that may have serious effects on the physical and mental health of a child. It is reckoned to be the saddest of all misdeeds, because it is so often inflicted by parents on their own children.

Physical abuse is the infliction of serious bodily harm, and may also include sexual abuse. Mental or psychological abuse covers 'unnatural punishments', such as abandoning a child, locking a child in a dark and confined space, or denying him or her food or water. The following are instances of child abuse.

◆ Gross neglect, where a child develops a skin disease from having to sleep in the same soiled bed linen for weeks.

◆ Burn marks, produced by a cigarette, on the child's skin.

◆ Malnutrition, although others in the household are well nourished.

◆ Marks produced by beating with a belt or stick.

◆ Evidence of sodomy committed on a child.

◆ Evidence of rape committed on a child.

The legal definition of a child in terms of age varies according to the crime. For example, with regard to sexual crimes, a child is any person under the age of 16 years if the offender is of the opposite sex, but any person under the age of 19 years if the offender is of the same sex.

The punishment of children

People in charge of children must act with restraint. When you punish a child, the punishment must be moderate and reasonable in relation to the child's offence as well as to the age, sex and size of the child. The motive for administering the punishment is also important – you or the person punishing the child should not be acting out of sadism, for instance.

The South African Schools Act of 1996 prohibits corporal punishment, such as caning or beating, as well as any form of physical or psychological abuse at all schools, public or independent.

Any staff member guilty of striking a child may be charged with assault, and, whether found guilty or not, may also be disciplined after an internal, departmental inquiry. The judgment may result in dismissal, suspension, a fine or the removal of the teacher's name from the roll of educators.

Cruelty to children

◆ The number of reported cases of cruelty and ill-treatment towards children under 18, excluding sexual offences, assault and murder, totalled 2 316 in 1996.

◆ The total number of crimes against children under 18 reported in 1996 amounted to 36 000, about double the figure for 1993.

◆ The reported incidence of child rape in 1996 came to 13 859 cases. However, this is estimated to be far fewer than the real number, many cases being unreported.

◆ Most victims of incest are girls.

◆ About 60 per cent of child abusers are the father or stepfather of the child, or the boyfriend of the child's mother.

◆ Almost 80 per cent of abused children know the person who abuses them.

One child's tragedy

A shocking story was told to Cape Town social workers by a 10-year-old girl who had been sexually exploited for several years. It had started when Shirleen was regularly abused by her mother's common-law husband and was later loaned, 'as a favour' to other members of the gang to which he belonged. When Shirleen eventually ran away from home she was picked up on the Cape Flats by a man who provided her with food, clothes and a place to sleep in exchange for prostituting herself in central Cape Town. Shirleen's case was brought to the attention of the police by an adult female prostitute, not because the woman felt sorry for the little girl, but to get rid of 'competition'. Shirleen was brought in for care, medical attention and a wholesome place to stay. However, she will need intensive psychotherapy to overcome the damage of her past, and it is highly likely that she will abscond, or be 'snatched' again.

Police comment: Shirleen's was a case of survival sex, tragically common in poor communities and among rural children newly arrived in towns. Where you suspect child prostitution or other abuse, report it to the Child Protection Unit or the nearest police station.

Warning signs

No warning signs in a child's behaviour can be taken as absolute proof that the child is being abused. Physical marks of injury on the child's body, however, or changes in the pattern of his or her behaviour, can indicate abuse. These are some of the signs to watch out for:

◆ bruises, scratches or welts on the skin
◆ broken bones
◆ perpetual neglect, such as unbrushed or unwashed hair and dirty clothes
◆ persistent discharge, especially vaginal
◆ burn marks on the skin, caused by cigarettes or any other hot object
◆ uncharacteristic wearing of torn or dirty clothes
◆ soiling underwear and, especially, apparently poor bladder control
◆ night-time bed-wetting
◆ changes in sleep pattern, often with nightmares
◆ decline in the quality of schoolwork
◆ appearance of speech difficulties, such as stammering
◆ changes in play patterns, or withdrawal from ordinary social contact with the family
◆ reluctance, especially if repeated, to visit any person or place
◆ fear of someone, or obvious uneasiness in their presence.

Defending your children

The law allows you the same rights to defend your children as you have to defend yourself. If you believe that your children are in danger from someone, you may use reasonable force to protect them. But the force must not be excessive in relation to the danger. You would not be justified in wounding your neighbour simply because he threatened to smack your child, for instance. Similarly, you would not be justified in using force in the absence of an immediate threat. You also may not hit someone because they have hurt your child in the past, or because you fear that they might do so at some time in the future. You would, though, probably be justified in using necessary force to prevent someone illegally taking away your child, even where there was no immediate threat of physical injury to the child.

Reporting child abuse

The Child Care Act of 1983 states that dentists, doctors and nurses who suspect that a child under their care has been abused or is suffering from malnutrition, must report the case immediately to the Director of Health Services.

If you suspect that any child is being abused, report the details at the nearest police station. The police will arrange for an appropriate inspection of the situation by a social worker, and your name will not be revealed to the parents or guardians of the child.

Children's courts

Children's courts have specific powers to deal with the protection of children. These courts may make orders concerning children under the age of 18 years. The orders are for periods of two years or less, and generally lapse on the child's eighteenth birthday.

The children's court may request a social worker to report on any aspect of the child's welfare, and may decide that the person in charge of the child is unfit to have custody because, while in that person's care, the child has suffered abuse. It may find that that person, who may even be the child's parent:
◆ is mentally ill and cannot care for the child properly
◆ has assaulted or ill-treated the child, or has allowed others to assault or ill-treat him or her
◆ has abandoned or neglected the child
◆ unlawfully keeps the child from his or her parents
◆ is unable to control the child – to ensure proper school attendance, for instance
◆ behaves in a way that may adversely affect the child.
The court may order that a child:
◆ be placed in the care of his or her parents, or of one particular parent
◆ be placed with a foster parent
◆ be sent to a children's home or a school of industries where he or she will be better cared for.

Pornography and paedophilia

Child pornography is any form of documentation in which children are the sexual object, and which is intended to stimulate sexual excitement. Pornography may be writings, pictures, films or video recordings of

Children's rights

◆ **The right to safety:** this means that children should not be placed in situations beyond their understanding or control.
◆ **The right to privacy:** this includes the right to call their bodies their own. Nobody may touch or fondle them anywhere at all if they don't like it, and kissing and hugging should not be forced on a child who is reluctant.
◆ **The right to say 'no':** this may entail walking away, even running away, if someone has made them afraid for any reason at all.
◆ **The right to refuse:** this includes refusing kisses, touches, sweets, ice cream, conversation or any form of contact at all that creates uneasiness or fear in the child, or is op - posed to the teaching of his or her parents.

sexual acts. All forms of child pornography are illegal under the Films and Publications Act.

Paedophilia is the sexual perversion in which children are the preferred sexual object. Paedophiles, who are people who engage in sexual activities with children, and people who exploit children in pornography, are child molesters and are guilty of abuse.

Finding their victims

Child molesters have well-developed methods of finding victims, who are often emotionally vulnerable children from broken homes, or victims of neglect and abuse at home.

Molesters identify easily with children. They know how to listen to them and talk to them, and may often have hobbies or activities that appeal to children, such as collecting dolls and toys, building models, or playing computer games. They get access to children by spending

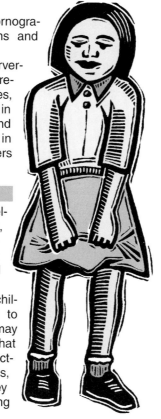

Profile of a child abuser

PROFILE

Many people who batter or sexually molest children are repeating the horrors of their own childhood.

The opportunist child molester doesn't necessarily prefer children as sexual partners, but may use them because he can obtain no other partner. The indiscriminate abuser is another opportunist, whose life is probably a pattern of abuse of friends and family, and who may want to experiment with sex, even victimising his own children. Some opportunists show disordered personalities, or may be mentally retarded or senile. Withdrawn and unconfident, they are unable to approach adult partners.

The preferential child molester prefers children to adults, and is likely to have far more victims than the opportunist. His characteristic behaviour may be seductive (showering attention, affection and gifts) or introverted, and he may molest strangers or very young children, including his own. He almost always has a long history of paedophile behaviour, was probably abused himself as a child and had restricted social contacts as a teenager, which is probably when his sexual interest in children began. He's likely to move or change jobs fairly frequently, to stay ahead of the law or to find

new victims. Attempts to obtain children may have involved high risks for this type of molester and have been carried out with extreme cunning. He is probably over 25 years old, may never have married, and may live alone or with his parents. If married, his sex life with his spouse is unsatisfactory. This type of molester has an intense interest in children, whom he often refers to in an idealistic way (as 'pure', 'clean', 'angelic', 'impish') or as objects ('That kid's barely out of the box').

Many child batterers similarly have suffered abuse in their own childhood. They have low self-esteem and do not cope well with the harsher realities of life, either at work or socially. They habitually see their own failures and shortcomings as someone else's fault. They are likely to abuse spouses and other family members, colleagues and friends, and will regularly lie, cheat and steal. They manipulate and use force on their own children because they are vulnerable and can't fight back, and sometimes as a way at getting back at their spouse, or sometimes with the spouse's connivance. A mother may permit the abuse of her child to retain some security in her relationship with her spouse or partner.

time at places where children congregate, such as shopping malls, or by finding positions of authority in youth clubs, Sunday schools or Scout organisations, or through chat lines on the Internet.

Child molesters manipulate children emotionally and win them over with attention, affection and gifts, important factors that often result in children not reporting molesters.

Many child molesters are guilty of incest in that they prey on their own children or young relatives – male or female – sometimes over a number of years.

No secrets

Talk to your children about what happens to them in their daily lives and, even more importantly, listen to them. Keep in close touch with their experiences.

Explain to your children that an incident is not a secret unless they want it to be – and, even then, you'd rather know about it. Explain that nobody can force them to keep a secret. It should not be a secret when an adult says, 'Let's make this our secret.' It should not be a secret if there's anything about it that makes them unhappy or uneasy. Kissing or touching, when it involves an adult, must never be a secret. Teach your children not to accept any form of touching or the kind of conversation that makes them feel uncomfortable.

Pay attention when children say they don't like someone, especially an adult, or if they don't like going to a particular place or attending a particular function. It's far more likely that information will come to you like this – indirectly – than in the form of a direct statement. Alternatively, children may simply tell you a story about what an adult does to them. The story is usually an appeal for help rather than an attempt to get someone else into trouble.

Children may see it as disloyal or disrespectful to accuse an adult, and may also fear that they will not be believed. So when they find the courage to tell you their story, they need to know that you will provide help.

If you don't help them, if you laugh or are angry, they may be intimidated and not come to you for help the next time. Lack of a sympathetic hearing may result in a child failing to report sexual assault, and the abuse continuing – perhaps for years – with its potentially devastating effect on the growing child.

A mother, too, should not keep silent when she knows her child is being abused. If she fears the abuser, or fears that he may lose his job if she reports his crime, she should seek help from a counsellor or welfare organisation (see Useful Phone Numbers and Addresses, pp266-71).

ELDER ABUSE

There are several factors that contribute to the vulnerability of the elderly, but the most significant is probably their relative inability to retaliate. Simply put, they can't fight back as a younger person might, so they are seen as an easy mark by criminals, swindlers, people offering inferior goods or services, and even by their own families.

Who are the elderly?

The life expectancy of South Africans as a whole is increasing – from 49 years for a person born in 1960 to 63 years for one born in 1995. And as people live longer, so our ideas of 'old' and 'elderly' are constantly revised upwards. But in general, the elderly most open to abuse are those who have either retired or are no longer in full-time employment. They depend to some extent – financially or in other ways – on the goodwill of others, especially relatives, for their maintenance. Even those who are able to maintain themselves financially become increasingly dependent on others as they become less mobile or mentally slower and confused, and this dependence is often ruthlessly exploited. For many people, old age is a period of deep insecurity.

States of mind

Apart from increasing frailty and dependence on others, the elderly may find themselves directly or indirectly responsible for circumstances that add to their vulnerability. These include:
◆ resenting and disregarding advice about their own health and security
◆ financial difficulties
◆ declining well-meant offers of assistance
◆ stubbornly clinging to an independent existence when this is no longer a viable option
◆ intolerance and rudeness
◆ an illogical belief in their own immunity to assault and other crimes.

Forms of abuse

Of many forms of abuse, the most obvious and unkind is likely to be physical. This is a problem that is greater than it seems, because few cases are reported and because records of assault do not always define the victim by age. Evidence includes bruises and abrasions, broken bones (although many elderly people do tend to incur minor injuries and even bone fractures in the ordinary course of events) or cigarette burns. Physical abuse may even include rape and indecent assault.

Psychological abuse primarily affects the mind but is frequently a product of forms of physical abuse, such as locking a person in a room, tying him or her to a bed, withholding food and medicine, obliging him or her to eat with dirty utensils from dirty crockery or failing to provide a proper place to sleep.

Verbal abuse, scolding and threats also have profound psychological effects that may lead to intimidation, fear and depression. Threats may be used to cover other forms of abuse – a threat to withhold food, for instance, if the victim reports having been beaten. A particularly spiteful form of psychological abuse involves telling a resident in a retirement home that relatives will not be coming to visit him or her, while knowing, in fact, that it is their intention to visit the resident. It can be taken further when the visitors arrive, by telling them that their relative has gone out, thereby distressing the elderly person, and causing resentment and anger on the part of the visitors.

Material abuse involves the fraudulent manipulation or taking away of someone's possessions, including money and investments. In an institution, it may include the theft of clothing, cash and jewellery by members of the staff.

Neglect, where it is deliberate, may also be a form of abuse, and includes failure to wash or clean the person, ignoring calls for attention or not changing the bed linen.

The abusers

Almost all of them start out with good intentions, such as an assistant nurse in a home for the aged, or a son intending to care for an ailing parent. However, proper care of the elderly is a difficult and specialised task that imposes a great deal of physical and psychological stress on the care-giver.

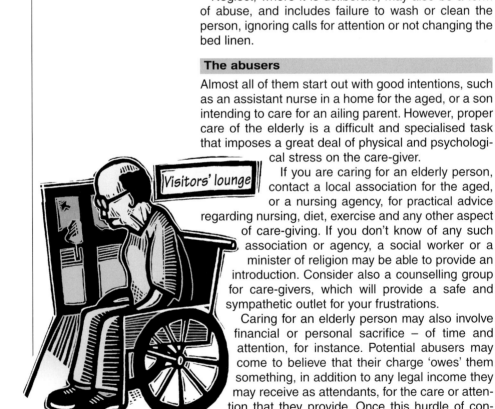

If you are caring for an elderly person, contact a local association for the aged, or a nursing agency, for practical advice regarding nursing, diet, exercise and any other aspect of care-giving. If you don't know of any such association or agency, a social worker or a minister of religion may be able to provide an introduction. Consider also a counselling group for care-givers, which will provide a safe and sympathetic outlet for your frustrations.

Caring for an elderly person may also involve financial or personal sacrifice – of time and attention, for instance. Potential abusers may come to believe that their charge 'owes' them something, in addition to any legal income they may receive as attendants, for the care or attention that they provide. Once this hurdle of conscience has been cleared, the vulnerability of the victim makes it easy to proceed with abuse. Care-givers who are addicted to drugs or alcohol, or who are mentally stressed or ill themselves, are most likely to become physically abusive. An adult who was ill-treated by his parents as a child may give in to the temptation to get his own back when the roles of responsibility are reversed in his parents' old age. Many abusers simply resent the fact that old people 'seem to have everything', which arises from a distorted view of the often pitifully few possessions that the elderly manage to retain, and an income that may or may not be adequate.

Positions of power

In many cases, the elderly themselves are reluctant or even afraid to report abuse. This is because those who abuse them may occupy positions of power, or have the potential to abuse them even more seriously, perhaps by withholding care or privileges. A domestic attendant in a residence for the elderly might refuse, for instance, to answer a summons from a particular resident. Another might repeatedly serve the most unpalatable portions of meals to a resident who has declined to lend her money. The 'power' wielded may seem trivial, but it can be a potent weapon against people who are dependent on others for their daily comforts and necessaries.

The effects of abuse

Although they may sometimes be mistaken for ordinary mood changes, especially when they first appear, the psychological effects of abuse tend to be longer lasting. Typically, victims may become withdrawn and extremely reluctant to talk about their own circumstances. Others may assume an unnatural, forced gaiety in assuring a visitor that nothing is wrong. Loss of appetite and of weight are other signs that something is wrong.

If you visit a resident in a home for the elderly, ask about his or her health and whether he or she is happy and satisfied with the conditions. Listen carefully to the reply – complaints may sometimes be indirect, or sound like ridiculous exaggerations. Speak to the fellow residents as well, and raise any misgivings with the staff and management.

When things go wrong

If you are an elderly person and the place in which you live has a set procedure for making complaints or for reporting irregularities – through a residents' committee, for instance – follow the guidelines. Ask for advice from nonresidents as well, such as a family member known for sound business practice, or one with nursing experience, depending on the situation. Speaking directly to the matron in charge or to the manager will probably resolve most problems, especially if you treat the matter as one in which you require help or advice, rather than as a complaint. If there is no improvement after a reasonable period, consider making a report to an association for the aged (see Useful Phone Numbers and Addresses, pp266-71), the Human Rights Commission or, in the case of theft and assault, to the police.

DRAMA IN REAL LIFE

Independence lost, insecurity gained

It was several months after Mrs Webb had moved to a home for the aged that her niece, Elaine, noticed that Mrs Webb never removed her long-sleeved cardigan, even on the hottest days. Her aunt's subdued manner also puzzled her. After a great deal of persuasion and patient questioning, the truth came out when Mrs Webb pulled up a sleeve to show that her arms were a mass of bruises. She didn't want to make trouble for anyone, Mrs Webb insisted, especially Nurse Vera. Vera frequently 'borrowed' small sums of money from Mrs Webb, and bullied her into 'lending' other articles, from an overcoat to items of food. When Mrs Webb protested, Vera would pinch her arm, pretending to make a joke of each incident. Elaine spoke to the matron of the home, and Vera, who was a domestic attendant rather than a nurse, was reprimanded and moved from Mrs Webb's section of the home.

Police comment: It may seem like a minor incident, but within the restricted round of Mrs Webb's daily life, Vera's conduct made her desperately unhappy and anxious. Mrs Webb revealed the source of her unhappiness only as a result of the observation and persistence of her niece. In this predicament, as in others, it is better to speak out sooner rather than later, by which time additional complications may have arisen.

Home alone

Elderly people living alone in the home they may have occupied for decades are frequently a source of anxiety to their friends and relatives. Not only are their security precautions likely to be inadequate (and too often neglected altogether), but their solitude and enfeeblement will probably attract criminals, from pilferers to murderers. All aspects of home security apply, but problems may arise through forgetfulness and obstinacy (in refusing to lock a door, for instance), and in being too trusting of callers who don't identify themselves properly. If you can't accommodate them yourself, try to persuade elderly relatives to exchange their old, inadequately protected homes for a more secure arrangement, such as a flat in a high-security block, a unit in a retirement village or a room in a well-run home for the aged.

Basic safety features

The lack of adequate safety features for the elderly may lead to loss, injury or death.

◆ Fit the door to the bedroom with a lock that can be opened from the outside.

◆ See that mats have a nonslip backing and do not curl up at the ends or along the edges.

◆ Site electric plugs 90 centimetres above the floor.

◆ Discourage the use of electrical appliances, such as irons, toasters, kettles and heaters, in the rooms.

◆ Prohibit the use of gas and paraffin heaters, and smoking, indoors.

◆ Fit built-in cupboards, firmly secured to the walls, so that they can't be pulled over accidentally.

◆ Install ramps, rather than stairs, where there are changes in floor level.

In homes for the aged, the law requires that every bedroom be fitted with a washbasin with hot and cold running water. There should be at least one bathroom and toilet per seven residents, and there should be handrails in all passages and for the full extent of stairs or ramps.

Security in your old age

Relatively few South Africans are able to make adequate financial provision for their independence in their later years. In many traditional communities, children care for parents within the extended family in which, for example, adult siblings may take it in turns to house and nurture their parents. Increasing urbanisation, however, is disrupting this traditional system.

Whoever you are, the better you are able to provide for yourself financially, the less dependent you will be on others, although there will always be a degree of physical and, probably, emotional dependence. If your terms of employment do not provide for a pension fund, ask your employer, employer's accountant or an insurance broker for their recommendation. (Insurance brokers do not charge clients directly for their services – their fee is deducted from contributions paid to the relevant fund.) If you can put some money aside every year into a retirement annuity fund, you will be establishing some form of independence when you stop working.

War veterans over the age of 60 years (or younger, if unfit for work), as well as civilian men over the age of 65 and civilian women over the age of 60 years, with low earnings, are eligible to receive social grants or pensions from the state. But the amount of money involved is not a great deal and should not be depended upon as the only means of survival.

For those who can afford to live in them, many retirement villages provide secure, independent housing as well as centrally prepared meals and a degree of nursing care for the frail. Before committing yourself to one, find out what the costs of frail care will be – they can be prohibitive. Some retirement villages sell housing to you that can be sold on your death, with the money passed on to your inheritors. Make sure that the contract stipulates this. Always get a family member to go over the contract for a home in a retirement village with you.

If a residence for the aged is a more likely option for you, plan on entering one long before you reach the age at which you will actually move in. You could offer to do volunteer work at a home of your choice, to find out if you like it. If you do, put your name on the waiting list of prospective residents. Most such institutions have very long waiting lists, so apply early.

Make sure your money is deposited with a reputable financial institution, and that it can be transferred or withdrawn on your signed instruction only. You can grant power of attorney to someone whom you trust, providing them with the legal authority to sign on your behalf if you should become disabled in any way, but it's best to insist that there should be two signatories.

DRUG ABUSE

A drug is any substance that produces a change in the human mind or body. It may be a tranquilliser prescribed by your doctor, a painkiller sold 'over the counter' at your supermarket, a tube of glue on the shelf in your hardware store, or a bag of dagga sold on the street corner. Dependence on and the influence of drugs can lead to crime.

Drugs and the law

Used medicinally and under strict control, many drugs may be helpful in curing or controlling disorders. It is legal to possess or use dependence-producing drugs in accordance with the prescription of a medical doctor or dentist. However, the Drugs and Drug Trafficking Act of 1992 makes it a crime for anyone to sell or use a dangerous dependence-producing drug or any substance from which such a drug can be made, without a prescription. The penalty may be imprisonment for up to 25 years, with or without a fine. The mere possession of such a drug could result in imprisonment for up to 15 years, with the possibility of a fine.

Despite this law, many substances that are abused as drugs are neither illegal nor restricted. These include glues, dry-cleaning fluids, aerosols, petrol and nail-polish remover, alcohol and tobacco, painkillers, laxatives and cough mixtures.

Abuse and dependence

Many young people use drugs experimentally – 'to find out for themselves' – without becoming addicted, but many do become addicted without intending to. Those who have unresolved problems with parents, peers or teachers may find that a drug-induced 'high' is a pleasant escape from their problems. Drug abuse may continue into adulthood or may even start only then, when drugs are used to cope with stress at work

DRAMA IN REAL LIFE

An inheritance no-one wants

A typical saga of multiple substance abuse unfolded when a schoolboy, aged 15, revealed at a drug-awareness meeting at a Free State school that he had begun using drugs to escape the horrors of alcoholism in his family. His mother and his father drank heavily every night, the boy said, and the loud verbal abuse to which they subjected each other and their son would continue until they fell into an alcoholic stupor. Remonstrating with his parents had not helped, and he had been too ashamed to seek outside help for them. At first, the 'high' he obtained from drugs, including dagga

and pharmaceutical products, seemed to help his domestic unhappiness, but his addiction soon created even more serious problems. Afraid of what the long-term effects of the drugs might do to him both physically and intellectually, he had turned to Alateen, a youth support group, for help.

Police comment: At least the boy had the courage and the will to break his own addiction. But, hard though it is, you should report a relative's or friend's drug abuse to the police so that at least they can apprehend the supplier.

or at home, or as a consolation for the disappointments and sorrows of advancing age. Identifying and dealing with these underlying problems is at the root of solving the problem of drug addiction.

As the body increasingly 'tolerates' a drug, it produces a craving to use it with increasing frequency and in greater amounts. The abuser will also increasingly take other drugs in conjunction with his or her primary habit. Eventually, the abuser is no longer able to function without drugs, and reaches the stage of physical dependence. Stopping the drugs at this point will probably produce the symptoms of withdrawal, such as anxiety, hallucinations, delirium and shaking.

Feeding the addiction – raising the money to pay for the drugs – is likely to result in antisocial or criminal activity, including theft (of cash or saleable objects), burglary, fraud, assault and prostitution. Every abuser spends, on average, between R20 000 and R100 000 on their habit every year.

The dangers of abuse

Drug abusers tend to neglect their health, spend more time in hospital and will probably die sooner than those who don't take drugs. The use of unsterilised needles may lead to contracting AIDS, blood poisoning or hepatitis. Sniffing heroin or cocaine destroys the mucous membranes in the nose. Apart from the drugs themselves, many impurities cause additional harm. Eventual failure of the heart, kidneys or liver is likely, while severe mental illness may also result.

Of the 'legal' drugs, alcohol causes liver and circulatory problems, while cigarette smoking causes lung cancer and disorders of the respiratory and circulatory systems, not just in the smokers but also in those nonsmokers who are constantly near them.

Many drugs seriously impair the user's judgment and may lead to accidental death through failure to recognise a hazard – falling from a roof, for instance, or stepping into traffic. Alcohol is involved in some 40 per cent of fatal traffic accidents.

Abuse eventually leads to the deterioration of the abuser's personality, with a loss of interest in healthy activities and the development of delinquent and antisocial behaviour.

Dagga

The most widely used illegal drug in South Africa is dagga, also known as dope, grass, hemp, marijuana and hash. It consists of the dried parts (leaves, stems, flowers and seeds) of the plant *Cannabis sativa* and is usually smoked as a cigarette, or in the broken-off neck of a bottle or in a short length of animal horn. Dagga is a physical relaxant but seriously affects perception and coordination in the short term, and may lead to disorders of the heart and lungs. It also reduces fertility in women and may damage unborn babies if smoked during pregnancy. Psychologically

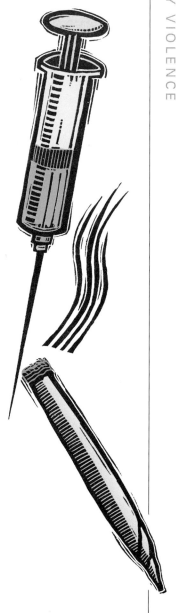

addictive, dagga may also produce the 'bad trip', fraught with panic and anxiety, that could be the start of lifelong mental illness. Commonly, dagga users lose interest in work and other activities, and have difficulty concentrating and remembering. Their eyes are likely to be red and glazed. Many users of 'heavier' drugs started on dagga, often in their teen years.

Mandrax

Mandrax is a hypnotic drug or sedative that is available as a tablet and is usually crushed, mixed with dagga and smoked in a pipe. Mandrax, also known as buttons or white pipes, is both psychologically and physically addictive, and severe withdrawal symptoms make it difficult for users to give it up. Signs of its use last several hours and include loss of appetite, dry mouth, slurred speech and stumbling. Abdominal pains, nausea and vomiting may also occur. When Mandrax has been smoked with dagga, there is likely to be redness and puffiness of the eyes, and, after sleeping, the Mandrax user may wake up with a hangover. Regular users have yellow or brown marks on their hands and, typically, lose weight.

Cocaine and crack

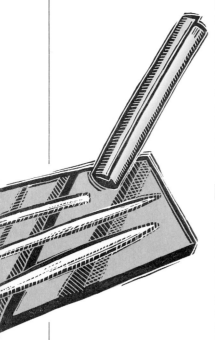

Sometimes inhaled through the nose, or 'snorted' in powder form, cocaine is most often smoked in its derivative form, crack, in a pipe or bottle, a method known as 'freebasing'. This produces an almost instant 'high' that includes increased alertness and energy. Cocaine and crack are powerful psychologically addictive drugs. Long-term effects include sleeplessness, loss of weight, impaired memory and concentration, anxiety and paranoia, convulsions, hallucinations, and heart and respiratory failure. In pregnancy, fetal damage and abortion may occur.

Solvents or inhalants

These are mostly used by street children between the ages of 10 and 16 years. A cloth is moistened with solvent and held over the nose and mouth, or it may be placed in a paper or plastic bag that is then held tightly to the face and breathed in. The effects take hold very quickly and include euphoria, hallucinations, drowsiness, slurred speech, unsteadiness and loss of consciousness. Other signs are nosebleeds, and sores and burns on the nose and mouth. 'Sniffing' leads to organ damage, and may result in death by suffocation or heart failure.

Ecstasy

The 'rave' drug of the nineties, Ecstasy is widely used by young people, especially at rave parties. Also known as E, doves, banana milk shake, yellow burger, pink champagne, snowballs or strawberry sundae, Ecstasy is typically swallowed, but is sometimes snorted or used as a suppository. It may contain other drugs or even strychnine (rat poison) as impurities. The effects include exhilaration or ecstasy, enhanced affection and sensuality, and increased stamina that, typically, helps users to dance for long periods without apparently becoming tired. However, dehydration, collapse and heatstroke may often occur, leading to death. Permanent psychiatric disorders also have been frequently recorded.

Ecstasy is psychologically addictive. Abuse may be associated with mood swings, loss of weight, exhaustion and sleeplessness, paranoia, depression and general debility. Many Ecstasy users chew gum to ease the jaw-clenching and tooth-grinding induced by the drug. Sweat-soaked clothing may also be an indication of the prolonged bursts of energy associated with the drug.

LSD

LSD (lysergic acid diethylamide) is available as a powder, a clear liquid, a capsule or a small, white pill. It is also soaked into sheets of absorbent paper that have pictures, often of cartoon characters, printed on them. It may produce ecstasy and euphoria or anxiety and desperation, and is known for producing hallucinations and sensory crossover, such as smelling colours and seeing sounds. Hallucinations or 'flashbacks' may occur suddenly and without warning at any time after taking LSD. A person who has taken LSD will have an increased heart rate, raised blood pressure, a flushed face with red eyes and may also tremble, vomit or have an unsteady gait.

How to help an addict

Many referrals to drug counselling centres come from the family, employer or friends of the addicts. But the only success in treating addiction comes when the addict decides that he or she wants to stop taking drugs and to get some help to do so.

Don't confront addicts with an emotional, aggressive or moralistic reaction. They need help, not criticism. Assure them of your continued love and support. Calmly, find out what you can about the situation. At this stage it may be more important to know why they are using drugs rather than what they are using, how long they've been using it or where they get it. Get help through a regional drug counselling centre, Life Line, and SANCA (the South African National Council on Alcoholism and Drug Dependence). Psychological support is offered through schools and through groups such as Tough Love (for the families of addicts) and Narcotics Anonymous (see Useful Phone Numbers and Addresses, pp266-71).

In an acutely toxic case, where the affected person may be unconscious or delirious, get medical attention as soon as possible. You may have to restrain the person to prevent self-injury or injury to others. Do this as gently as you can.

Advertising addiction

Especially among young people, watch out for:
◆ evasiveness about new friends
◆ their unexplained absence from home at unusual hours
◆ sudden mood swings
◆ inattention to appearance and hygiene
◆ increased spending without any readily apparent reason
◆ loss of concentration and decline in general performance
◆ long spells of solitude
◆ loss of weight or a decrease in appetite
◆ an increased need to sleep
◆ trembling, especially of the hands
◆ abnormal dilation or contraction of the pupils of the eyes
◆ a loss of physical coordination
◆ apparent drunkenness, including slurred speech, without the smell of alcohol
◆ sudden use of air freshener or incense
◆ presence of drug accessories, such as cigarette papers, syringes, pipes or bottlenecks
◆ brown or yellow stains on the hands and fingers
◆ use of unusually large quantities of solvents and glue
◆ the unexplained loss of money from your purse or wallet, or the loss of valuable objects from your home.

CONS AND CONSUMER FRAUD

As long as you have money, there will be someone willing to take it from you dishonestly, either by theft or by fraud. Fraud is a form of confidence trick. It is also a crime. The law regards fraud as a deliberate misrepresentation of the truth, resulting in someone suffering actual or potential loss, damage or injury. It is also referred to as a 'perversion' of the truth – that is, someone lies to you for their own ends.

Who are the victims?

Any person or organisation – including a government – may be taken in by a plausible fraud. The usual victims, however, are the elderly, strangers or newcomers to an area, and people living alone – especially women. Women are seen as being easier to defraud in 'technical' transactions, such as those involving motor vehicles and home repairs.

Some frauds prefer to operate outside ordinary business hours, so that you can't check on them during the short period they've given you in which to accept their offer.

Fraud or theft?

Suppose that Mr Jones, without your permission, starts your car one night, drives it away and has no intention of returning it. He would be guilty of theft. However, if Mr Lapi buys your car and pays you with a cheque that he knows will be dishonoured by the bank (see Paying Without Risk, pp176-9), he is guilty of fraud. Mr Lapi may have taken the car with your consent, but he deceived you into giving that consent, knowing that you would have no more than a worthless cheque in exchange.

Forms of misrepresentation

Misrepresentation is not telling the entire truth. Exaggeration is not the absolute truth, but it is not necessarily misrepresentation. This is especially true in advertising, where many extravagant claims are not meant to be taken literally – the image of a car flying, for instance, or travelling an impossibly long distance on a particular amount of fuel. However, if a man selling a farm to you claims that a borehole on it has delivered water consistently for three years, but fails to say that those three years ended 14 years previously, this is deliberate – or fraudulent – misrepresentation.

Misrepresentation does not always involve words. A person collecting money for charity while dressed in a stolen Salvation Army uniform might be guilty of obtaining money by fraudulent means (or false pretences), because his or her dress strongly suggests that the money is for the Salvation Army. Changing the odometer reading on a used car, to pretend that it has covered a shorter distance than it really has and thereby claim a higher resale value, is also fraud.

Fraud and promises

Suppose you bought a food mixer from Mrs Swart on the condition that she promised to replace a particular part and make the mixer workable by a certain date. On the date promised, however, the mixer still couldn't be used because the part wasn't available and Mrs Swart knew that it was no longer made. She would have committed fraud, because you had suffered a financial loss through her misrepresentation of an existing situation. If the part had been available, however, but Mrs Swart was still unable to keep her promise by the agreed date, because of circumstances unforeseen or beyond her control, she could not be found guilty of misrepresentation.

Fighting against fraud

Most people who practise fraud are accomplished and convincing con artists. In most cases, you probably won't suspect you're being conned – after all, if his victims suspected him of dishonesty, a con man wouldn't be able to make a living. Some con artists, though, may be simply too slick and too helpful, and this should raise your suspicions. Here are some suggestions to help you avoid becoming a victim of fraud.

◆ Before you sign any contract for a major purchase or service, ask friends and relatives what they know about the product or service, and the supplier. Ask the supplier to give you the full details in writing, including references. Insist on some time to consider the deal.

◆ Before offering credit or other easy terms when you sell or exchange anything costly, check the purchaser thoroughly. If the sum involved warrants it, let your attorney handle the transaction and do the checks on the purchaser's creditworthiness. But since the fact that someone has money in an account does not guarantee that you will be paid in the future, confirm a few other things before granting credit or other terms: the person's place of employment and how long they have worked there; their home address; their bank and account number; the names and addresses of previous or current creditors. If you don't know and trust the purchaser, ask for cash or a direct transfer to your bank account. As an option, you can insist on receiving the full price before handing over the goods.

◆ Keep any documentary evidence of the transactions, including receipts, guarantees, cancelled cheques, advertisements or contracts.

◆ It's very unlikely that any stranger will ever approach you with a genuine scheme to enrich yourself in exchange for a relatively small amount of cash. Don't be tempted.

◆ If you're told that you're going to lose an offer if you don't agree to it at once, let it go.

CONS AND CONSUMER FRAUD

Commercial crime

1994 – 53 441 cases
1995 – 51 117 cases
1996 – 54 846 cases

The figures above represent only the cases that were reported. The 1996 figures show a 7,3% increase over the figures for the previous year. The value of commercial crimes in 1996 was R3 834 294 788, an increase of 37% over the value of commercial crimes for the previous year. Most of these crimes (about 80%) were categorised as fraud.

REAL-ESTATE FRAUDS

Buying your own home or a piece of land may involve more money than you're likely to deal with in any other transaction in your life. For this reason it is very attractive to con men and you should take the strictest precautions in making sure that you are not swindled.

Owing and owning

Except where you have a bond on a property, you can't register that property in your name until you've paid for it in full. This might mean that, if the seller becomes insolvent before you've finished paying him, you could lose your investment. Where land is paid for in instalments and is intended to be used for residential purposes, the law does provide the purchaser with some protection. However, agricultural land is not covered by this law, and neither is land sold by the state or by local authorities. It is advisable, then, when property is not covered by a bond, to have it registered in your name as soon as possible – even if this means paying for it sooner than you had intended.

Voetstoots

It is common for sellers to include a paragraph stating that the property is sold voetstoots, or as it stands, that the seller gives no guarantee and that the seller will not be liable for defects, 'whether latent or patent'. It's true that the seller may not be responsible for fixing patent defects – that is, defects that should be revealed by a reasonably close scrutiny – which include broken windows and badly cracked walls. But the voetstoots clause removes his or her obligation in the case of latent defects – those that exist but are not readily apparent, such as a leaking roof, or wood borers in the floor joists. If the seller deliberately tried to conceal a latent defect (by plastering over cracks and saying nothing about them, for instance), you might be able to cancel the sale and demand damages.

Double-check documents

When you buy residential land you have the right to choose in which language the contract is drawn up. Because the contract involves such relatively large sums of money, it must be properly documented. There are many points of information that a document must contain to be lawful, and your bank, attorney or personal consultant should be able to tell you what these are. They include, for instance, the correct spelling of the company's name and address on the letterhead, which some crooks would expect you to overlook and therefore not notice that, in fact, the company does not exist.

Keep the following points in mind:
◆ The nonexistent development company – this recurs often in property frauds, and most of the intended

Three property protectors

◆ Never allow salespeople to hurry you into buying.
◆ Don't sign anything at all until it's been approved by your personal consultant. It has been known that a signature made 'just to confirm that you actually met the salesman and that he showed you the property' turned out to be an offer to purchase.
◆ Don't pay any money until your personal consultant tells you that it's safe to do so.

No small loss

It was such an exclusive property development that advertisement seemed to be only by word of mouth. Dan Nciya inspected the drawings, then the site, and approached the developer – Mr Small – who was also the seller. Mr Small presented the facts honestly, or so he said. The entire development had been approved but there was a slight delay at the Surveyor-General's office, so Mr Small would not ask for a full deposit at this stage, only a percentage to secure for Mr Nciya an option to purchase when the Surveyor-General released the plans. Mr Nciya paid, and heard no more until he read that Mr Small was being prosecuted for fraudulently accepting money to perform a transaction that he, Mr Small, knew to be impossible to fulfil. Mr Small did not own the land, nor did he have any authority to claim that it was, or would be, for sale. Mr Nciya lost his money.

Police comment: Even though he was simply paying for an option to purchase, Mr Nciya should have sought legal advice before handing over his money, or should have made sure that Mr Small in fact had the right to sell the property.

victims are taken in. If you've never dealt with the property company before, how do you know that it really exists? By law, the company registration number must appear on the company's official documents. To find out if it is genuine and the company solvent, have a search done (or get your bank or attorney to do it) at the Registrar of Companies, or the Registrar of Close Corporations in Pretoria.

◆ Check the company's references, such as those given for a previous building project. Ask some of the occupants, check with the building survey department of your local authority, and ask for the names and addresses of other projects with which the company has been involved. Ask occupants about the quality of the work as well. Don't confine your inquiries to the people and addresses provided by the company. They could be 'planted', so also ask people living in the vicinity, other people who have bought into the scheme, and anyone who might have some knowledge of the matter.

◆ Visit the address on the company's documents. Do the premises really look like the offices of a company of the status represented by their agent? Ask people in nearby offices how long the company has been operating from this address.

◆ Check that the company owns the property or has the owner's permission to sell it. The local authority or deeds office will be able to tell you who the legal owner is.

◆ If you're buying land to build a retirement cottage or factory on, check with your local authority that the land is appropriately zoned for that use. It is sometimes possible to change land use by applying to have it rezoned, but this may be costly in time and money.

◆ Having satisfied yourself that the seller's claims about zoning are correct, what about the neighbouring or nearby properties? Would it be lawful for someone to build a factory next to your proposed house, or to erect a block of flats that would destroy your view?

INVESTMENT FRAUDS

Investments are rarely entirely free of risk, but some may also be part of a scheme that is illegal. Never be tempted by a get-rich-quick scheme or moneymaking venture until you've first spoken to your bank's investment adviser or your attorney.

High returns, last chances

Beware of any investment that offers a rate of return or interest much higher than the rate generally obtainable on the market. And don't let yourself be hurried into parting with money by claims that an investment offer is a once-in-a-lifetime opportunity or by someone urging you to act 'before it is too late'.

Another approach, designed to flatter you, is to claim that you have been 'selected' as one of the few people to be asked to make an investment. You may even be advised that you have won a 'prize'. These approaches aren't criminal, but it's essential that you recognise them as part of the sales pitch, that you distance yourself from the seduction and consider carefully whether you want to participate in whatever is being offered.

Future factors

Don't be impressed by an offer to buy back your investment for a predetermined figure at some future date. A dealer in gold coins, for instance, may agree to buy back, in five years' time, all the gold coins that you buy from him. He may specify a minimum of the price you paid plus a percentage as interest or appreciation, as long as the coins are in the same condition as when you bought them. What is not guaranteed, however, is that he will still be in business in five years'

DRAMA IN REAL LIFE

Investment by invitation only

The caller, who said his name was Evan Watts, admitted he had obtained Ken's name from a friend in the local historical society. They wanted only people with a feeling for the past to participate in the project. 'They' were a syndicate that Ken was invited to join (on payment of R10 000 or multiples thereof), and the project was the recovery of the fabulous hoard of gold coins known as the Kruger millions. The fortune had been supposedly lost in 1900, but patient research, for which Evan produced impressive references, had revealed its whereabouts in a complicated system of tunnels near Lydenburg, in Mpumalanga. The recovery costs would be high, and included the purchase of the farm on which the tunnels were situated, and sophisticated mining equipment. There was no overt high-pressure salesmanship, but, as Ken admitted later, the prospect of wealth was so real that no pressure was required. Everything, even the share certificates, seemed so genuine. Ken, however, asked for a day to think it over. Evan collected up his papers and left. He never came back.

Police comment: Without investigation, it cannot be said that the scheme was fraudulent, but no genuine speculation should require its subscribers to hand over money without an opportunity to consider the investment. Time to think it over is also time to investigate the scheme.

time. After only five weeks he may be insolvent, and then there probably will be nobody to fulfil the terms of your guarantee.

Pyramid schemes

In these schemes the promoter advertises for investors and promises quick returns with a high rate of interest. Early investors find that they do receive the advertised return. However, the money does not come from a real return on their investment, but from new investors. And as new investment tails off (and it always does), the promoter is unable to pay out the returns, and the scheme collapses. Chain letters, in which you are promised a large sum of money if you send a small payment to certain addresses, operate in a similar way.

Pyramid schemes have been held in court to be a form of illegal lottery. They are sometimes misrepresented as stokvels, the pools of funds formed by groups of people, which, in contrast, are legal.

Be cautious

Highly attractive, but fake deals, such as the 'Nigerian 419 scam' (see p165), continue to entice new victims because the prospect of making a large profit is difficult to ignore. But even playing safe is not necessarily problem-free – where the staff of reputable financial institutions are dishonest, a single fraudulent transaction may involve huge sums of money.

Before you even consider investing, recall how you came to hear about the opportunity. If it was through a stranger or a casual acquaintance, it probably has nothing to recommend itself. But if you find it attractive, consult your banker, broker or attorney. They may be able to put a different light on the facts.

Don't be taken in by papers. Desktop printers have impressive capabilities in creating authentic-looking documents. Take any documents you are given to your bank or attorney to check their authenticity.

Getting your own back

If you have been the victim of fraud, find out whether others have been defrauded by the same person or organisation. If you are not alone, get together to decide on a course of action and how to share the costs of the action. You would need to show that the accused knowingly misrepresented the facts – verbally, in writing or by an act or omission. In a criminal case, where the accused is charged by the state, you would have to ask the court to make an order for compensation. In a civil case, in which you and the other victims would be the plaintiffs, you would have to pay legal costs in the hope of claiming them later.

DOORSTEP FRAUDS

Many con men and con women present themselves at your doorstep, with tricks that play on your sympathy or your trust in the basic honesty of your fellow humans, and relieve you of your money. Be suspicious of anyone who appears at your door with a story, and make sure you can verify it – with a superior, for example – before you take any further steps.

Who are they?

In terms of the amount of cash you stand to lose, the lower end of the scale is taken by small-time operators such as slightly disguised beggars, itinerant 'workers' claiming to be looking for odd jobs, and collectors for bogus (and usually obscure and untraceable) charities (see also A Stranger at the Door, pp80-1, and Street Cons, pp164-6). Children are sometimes used as accomplices, to add an appealing touch. The law requires collectors for charities to produce letters of authorisation on demand, and many of them will do so. Letters, however, are easily faked or photocopied, and there is seldom any way to connect the bearer with the letter.

At the other end of the fraud scale, you may be invited to lay out large sums of money to recover something that is allegedly 'yours', or that serves as a subscription which entitles you to free meals or goods. Or someone may be concocting a story that will persuade you to open your door and admit him to your home in order to burgle it or to assault you.

To give or not to give

Whether you give or not is a question for your conscience, your patience and your pocket. It's a sound principle, though, to discourage unsolicited callers at

---

D R A M A   I N   R E A L   L I F E

Forgotten money in search of an heir

The smartly dressed man with the briefcase said he was a tracing agent, and that he had good news for Mr Adrian West. Mr West, who had answered the door bell, identified himself. The agent quoted information from the will of Mr West's late aunt, Mrs Dobbs, who had died five years earlier, and Mr West confirmed that he had indeed inherited R14 000,00 from his late aunt. The agent stated other information from the will – which Mr West knew to be correct – and then said that a residual amount of R8 000,00 was 'waiting to be claimed'. If Mr West paid a 'processing fee' of R360,00, this would ensure that he received the R8 000,00 promptly. Impressed by the

agent's knowledge of his late aunt's will, Mr West nevertheless had doubts, and declined to hand over any money. He still wonders if he is legally entitled to that R8 000,00.

Police comment: There is almost certainly no R8 000,00 – or any other money waiting to be claimed. The information that the 'agent' produced can be found by anyone at the office of the Master of the Supreme Court. If Mr West was really concerned, he could have contacted his attorney or the executor of his aunt's estate, or he could have applied to the Master's Office himself for information.

your home. One group apparently doing business will soon attract another, and, very soon, there will be opportunist thieves and more serious housebreakers among the callers.

This is not to say that you shouldn't give to charities or to individuals whom you judge to be deserving. Every winter there are well-publicised appeals on behalf of the poor and homeless who require food, clothing and shelter. Choose a charity that you remember from last winter, or ask for a recommendation from a minister of religion. If you can, deliver the goods yourself at the collection depot, rather than have another set of strangers entering your home. Instead of constantly handing out small sums of money that may or may not buy taxi tickets or loaves of bread, make an annual cash donation to a central charity, such as a community chest.

Debts of the departed

Many frauds and con artists find their leads in the newspapers – in the classified columns, especially under Deaths. One that deserves to be better known (it was the plot of a Hollywood movie in the 1960s) concerns goods supposedly ordered by someone just before his or her death. The 'vendor', having obtained his information from the newspapers, calls on the next of kin and asks for payment for goods already delivered. In the midst of the confusion occasioned by bereavement, it is often easy to forget whether the goods were in fact received or indeed ordered, and to be taken in by this type of fraud.

Variations on this theme include unexpected windfalls from the loved one's will. Weeks or months after the death, when estate documents are available at the office of the Master of the Supreme Court, a con artist will write down enough details to be able to sound convincing. He presents himself to an inheritor, perhaps as a professional researcher, and says that he has discovered a document that will increase the inheritor's share of the inheritance. But, unfortunately, there are certain fees to be paid, which the inheritor gladly hands over to the researcher, who is never seen again.

When someone informs you that there is more money owing to you from an estate, tell the supposed creditor that his claim should be put in writing and submitted to the executor of the estate. Under no circumstances hand over money during the emotionally charged and confusing period that follows a death. If a 'researcher' claims to have found an additional inheritance for you, tell him you'll reward him when you receive the money. Don't, however, sign anything unless your attorney has approved it.

FRAUDULENT 'FRIENDS'

It's hurtful to think that someone may like you, not for your personality, conversation or even for your looks, but for your money and for what they can get out of you. In fact, they probably don't like you at all. They are simply pretending – they are fraudulent friends.

Frauds, not friends

If you think that frauds are shifty backstreet operators, think again. Those who prey exclusively on unsophisticated victims might not be able to deceive an alert, well-educated person, but all frauds owe some of their success to the fact that they fit so convincingly into their chosen setting. They are believable and are readily accepted as being the people they claim to be. Their reasons for wanting to help you, or to enrich you, seem so convincing. They just 'look right' and are so obviously honest and genuine. Remember, though, that there is no such thing as 'looking honest'. People may look respectable, they may seem to be helpful, they may be flattering and they may have excellent manners, but honesty is a quality that takes time to prove. Dishonesty shows up much more quickly, as many people discover to their cost. But by then their new 'friend' has probably moved on.

Frauds in friendly action

There are many tactics that are employed by unscrupulous 'friends', and all of them involve gaining the victim's trust and friendship. They can make more out of you by deceit than by merely robbing you. However, remembering and applying a few basic rules should keep you safe.

◆ Ask yourself why you have been singled out to receive this person's attentions.

◆ Don't be hurried into making investments or major purchases by someone who has only recently befriended you.

◆ Don't give money to any new 'friend' – especially one who claims to have a scheme to make you rich.

◆ Be suspicious if the 'friend' offers to share money with you – you're probably being set up.

◆ If something valuable needs to be repaired, entrust it to a reputable person or organisation recommended by a reliable friend.

◆ Be wary of strangers who offer to run errands for you – especially where money or valuable goods are concerned.

Winning ways

Perhaps the unkindest 'friends' are the ones who pretend to love you, but in reality are attracted only by the prospect of cheating you out of your cash or possessions. Their intention may become apparent when they 'accidentally' leave their cash at home and ask

Doting deceivers

◆ They are physically attractive and are usually very good dressers.
◆ They seldom offer verifiable information about themselves.
◆ Their interest in you is flatteringly but unrealistically intense.
◆ They steer the relationship quickly along emotional, physical and material channels.
◆ They tend to avoid commitments.

you for a small loan. This request progresses to bigger loans and to outright gifts, and perhaps to your providing free accommodation. If you are prepared to pay a dangerously high price for their company (don't make the mistake of believing that it's friendship), at least be aware that it may end with your suffering severe financial and other loss. This type of deceit is more commonly practised on women, and the victims are often too embarrassed or humiliated to prosecute the deceivers.

Would you?

When you're offered opportunities, service or attention out of proportion to your relationship with the person making the offer, pause and think. Ask yourself whether, under similar circumstances, you would do what your supposed benefactor is offering to do for you. If you would, ask yourself why you would do it. You'll probably find that it would be to gain an advantage of some sort, such as power or profit, whether honest, honourable or otherwise. The offer will probably begin to look much less attractive.

Genuine friends

Of course, no genuine friends will try to defraud you, but they may, unintentionally, give you bad advice. They may insist that with their help and expertise your investments will be able to earn a higher rate of interest, or that they'll get you a higher price for your house or your car. It may be embarrassing and difficult to disregard this advice without giving offence, but don't let the management of material assets become an issue or a condition in a relationship because deals between friends too often turn sour. By all means listen to advice and be grateful to have it, but don't be bullied into accepting it. You can love, trust or admire someone even if you do prefer to have your finances managed by your bank or your attorney.

DRAMA IN REAL LIFE

Should old acquaintance be forgot?

When Robert de Sousa met Fred Simons again, it had been 12 years since they had last met, playing rugby in their school's first team. Over drinks in a sports bar, Simons mentioned that he had had bad luck with an investment, and had come to Port Elizabeth 'to start again', as he put it. De Sousa offered Simons a week's free use of a room in the house he shared with several other people. Simons accepted gratefully but, after a week, was still in occupation. Others in the house noticed cash and small items missing and warned de Sousa who, with regret, asked Simons to leave. Simons, however, returned a few days later, and the daily domestic worker, thinking he still lived there, let him in. He was still there when she left at midday, but by the time de Sousa and his fellow residents came home from work, he had gone, together with jewellery, cash and firearms.

Police comment: Mr de Sousa may have known Simons at school, but 12 years later they were strangers. Mr de Sousa should have considered Simons as someone who needed to prove his trustworthiness before being admitted to the home. Always keep domestic workers informed about who and who is not to be admitted to your home.

THE ELDERLY AS VICTIMS

The elderly, living as most of them do on fixed and often inadequate incomes, are especially vulnerable to promises of discounts and large financial rewards. But many are also forgetful, fearful, easily manipulated and trusting. They are therefore easy targets for dishonest people – even members of their own families – who are happy to abuse them financially and defraud them out of their savings and other assets.

The approach

People living in a residence for the elderly may be protected from fraudulent operators to some extent by the screening of callers. However, not all dubious deals will be presented by smooth-talking salesmen; some illegal schemes may be advertised openly in the newspapers. Don't let anyone hurry you into buying anything. If they say something like, 'If you don't act this week, you're going to lose your chance', let it go. Let someone else have the good luck (or bad luck) that you've avoided by not acting in time.

No matter how attractive the scheme seems, always have it checked by your bank manager or a competent friend or family member before you sign any undertaking, and especially before you send any money. If you have no contact with a bank, ask your nearest branch of the Association of Retired Persons and Pensioners (ARP&P) to suggest a reliable authority.

A risk not worth taking

Many people, understandably, feel drawn to investments that promise a high rate of interest. But high rates also attract high risk, which is why these investments are better over the long rather than the short term. Since, as an elderly person, you're probably looking for relatively short-term returns, it is far wiser to place capital in safe but modest-earning investments. Don't, however, tie up all or most of your capital in a new or untried investment.

Even if you invest with a big, well-established organisation known for consistent profitability, your investment may suffer from dishonesty among the staff. For example, cheques or other payments to a particular fund may be diverted to another account and 'laundered' or illegally processed. However, such a firm is more likely to recover from employee dishonesty, with minimal loss to investors, than a smaller, more recently established company.

Never simply accept from a friend that an investment is good. If your money is administered by a bank or other financial institution, talk to the bank's broker or accountant about the scheme first.

DRAMA IN REAL LIFE

The good deal that never was

An elderly pensioner, Gladys Owen, was deeply attached to the little house in which she had raised her children. Burglarproofing was no better than basic, so Mrs Owen was relieved when a smartly uniformed young man called to tell her that his security company had a special offer for pensioners. He examined her house thoroughly and said that for only 50 per cent down and the remainder on easy terms, his company would replace her burglarproofing with modern equipment and monitor her house 24 hours daily. He offered to show her one of their recent installations, and Mrs Owen accompanied him in his car, two days later. She had been delighted, meanwhile, to find that his quote for her installation was unusually low. Mrs Owen handed over a cheque for half the quoted cost and never saw the young man again. Her cheque was cashed and her house was burgled soon after. It occurred to her some days later that she might get information from the occupants of the 'sample' house, but when she went there, it was deserted and the burglar bars had been removed.

Police comment: Mrs Owen made some serious mistakes. She admitted a stranger into her home who was able to note all her security precautions without arousing her suspicion. She did not ask him for trade or other references, such as the names and addresses of satisfied customers, but simply accepted his 'plant' in what was obviously a rented house. And she gave him a cheque merely on the strength of his word. It is likely that the young man, or an accomplice, was responsible for the burglary at Mrs Owen's house.

Better still, send the information in writing, giving full details of the agent, the nature and amount of the proposed investment, the name of the investment fund, and any other details you have. If you've been given any documents or a prospectus, send these as well.

Check the credentials

It's not enough that a caller should tell you he or she works for a well-known company. Check with the company that this really is so, and that the scheme being promoted is approved and underwritten by them. Then turn the matter over to your bank or to your own adviser to determine whether the purchase, deal or investment is worth making.

Beware signing

Never sign any document that you haven't read thoroughly beforehand. But because business documents and contracts may be wordy and complex, it's safer to get your bank or adviser to approve all such papers before you put your name to them.

Family frauds

If a member of your family asks you for financial help or invites you to invest in a business, don't be ruled by feelings of loyalty, sympathy or sentimentality. Ask for the facts and figures to be presented to you, and give them to your bank or attorney to examine. Be especially suspicious if you are asked not to reveal certain information to the bank or to other members of the family. If your money is lost you will probably not be able to replace it in your lifetime. It is not selfish for you to take sensible precautions to ensure your comfort and safety in your old age.

SELF-DEFENCE SKILLS

When you've tried everything to avoid becoming the target of a criminal, but find yourself face to face with an armed person who looks as though he may attack you, you need to resort to self-defence, and then for one prime purpose – to be able to get away.

Close bodily contact

There are times when it's worth resisting an attack:
◆ to try to prevent serious injury
◆ when you are confident that you can overpower your assailant
◆ when you can temporarily disable your assailant and reach safety quickly
◆ when any favourable opportunity presents itself – the nearness of help, for instance, or when your assailant's attention is distracted.

Get used to the idea that there's going to be close bodily contact, and that the person who attempts to rob or assault you is inviting retaliation. You will not be hitting out at an innocent party, but protecting yourself from an attacker, which you are legally entitled to do.

The intent to injure

Before you even think about arming yourself with a weapon, you need to realise that for it to be effective, it must be used with determination – with the intent to injure, or, if need be, to kill. If you are going to fight back, do it vigorously. Being polite or tentative about jabbing something into your attacker's eye won't help at all. Avoidance is still the best defence, but if you are forced to defend yourself actively, do it with all your strength. However, if you can overcome an assailant without causing major injury or death, the law expects you to do so, to use only 'necessary' force.

Others' experiences

It's almost certain you know someone who has had an encounter with crime or a criminal, and who is prepared to talk about it. Ask him or her to tell you about the experience, if it's not too painful to do so. Ask some questions of your own – to reconstruct the events and try to work out how the incident might have been avoided or, perhaps, influenced. For instance:
◆ Where and at what time did the incident take place?
◆ When did the victim first see the assailants?
◆ When did the victim realise she or he was going to be robbed or assaulted?
◆ If she or he thinks back, was there no way that she or he might have been alerted earlier?
◆ Was she or he alone at the time?
◆ How many assailants were there?
◆ Were the assailants armed?
◆ What does the victim think attracted the assailants to her or him?

◆ What was the assailants' first move – did they push, for instance, or hit? Or did they approach the victim under some pretence?

◆ Did the victim have a weapon, or any way of calling for help?

◆ If she or he didn't use the weapon, why?

◆ If it happened again, how would the victim react?

◆ What additional precautions is she or he taking now?

◆ Think about what you would have done under similar circumstances.

Putting this information together helps you create a vivid mental picture of a robbery or assault. Although an incident involving you is unlikely to be identical in every detail, the victim's experience at least introduces you to the reality of crime. Knowing about the victim's experience may make you less afraid, and enable you to react sooner and more positively than you would have done otherwise.

Keep fit

Keeping fit may be a part of your ordinary daily programme already. If it isn't, remember that any regular exercise, in moderation, is good for you and also speeds up your reflexes. Combine general exercise with practising unarmed combat. Practise with a friend, pulling back before striking any real blows.

For most people, self-defence will probably consist of no more than a few critical moves, and the muscles and joints used in these moves must work smoothly. For jabbing at an assailant's eyes, for instance, you'll use your shoulder, elbow and wrist, as well as the joints of your hand and fingers. Go to self-defence classes regularly to practise your protective moves.

Walking is probably the best general exercise you can do. Walk uphill, adjusting the distance and slope to your condition. Try to cover the same distance a little faster each day, even if it's by only a few seconds. Walking will also improve your lung power, which is useful if you need to shout for help.

Have a plan

Knowing in advance what you're going to do if you are attacked will at least remove some of the frightening element of uncertainty, and give you confidence. If you have a gun, keep it handy and practise using it at a range. Similarly, if you have a spray or other defensive weapon, make sure it's in working order and within easy reach. If you walk with a stick, make the stick a part of your defence, and practise jabbing with it, hard, in and out. And don't forget to practise your balance. If you carry keys when you go out, hold them so that they protrude beyond your knuckles.

Think about the other things you normally take with you – such as a handbag or a shopping trolley – that might attract a thief's attention and get in the way when you try to protect yourself. If you don't really need them, leave them at home.

PHYSICAL SELF-DEFENCE

In the end it may come down to having to defend yourself physically. Some people are stronger and have a more aggressive temperament than others, but anyone can learn a few basic techniques to protect themselves. The more you practise these techniques, the better you'll be able to use them, and the more confident you'll be. Remember though, physical self-defence is for use only when avoidance fails or where there is no other option.

Be prepared

Being prepared to offer resistance doesn't only mean being alert to your surroundings. It is certainly important to reduce the chances of being taken by surprise, but it's also important for you to keep as fit as you can. Your state of fitness determines how fast you can move and for how long you will be able to defend yourself. Speed of movement and the ability to recover balance decline with age, but even elderly people are capable of putting up enough resistance to discourage most attackers.

Before embarking on any course of unaccustomed exercise, have a medical examination – sudden strenuous exercise can be dangerous if you're accustomed to leading a leisurely lifestyle.

The martial arts

Karate and kung fu are just two of the Eastern martial arts systems that have become popular in the West. They, and other forms of unarmed combat, such as jujitsu and judo, are very effective but require a high level of dedication and practice, and involve a mental and spiritual discipline.

If you're 'frozen with fear', as some people are when suddenly confronted by an attacker, you probably won't be able to offer any resistance at all. Learning and practising defensive techniques will help you to control your fear and utilise that 'hot under the collar' feeling triggered by a stress-induced adrenaline rush. Adrenaline may give you greater strength than you thought you possessed.

Find out if martial arts or self-defence classes are held in your neighbourhood (see also Useful Phone Numbers and Addresses, pp266-71). If you do enrol, take them seriously and persist at training until you are competent. It's easy – and dangerous – to believe you know it all after only a few lessons.

Get fit, stay fit

The most important self-defence manoeuvre is running. The main reason for resisting an attack is to create an opportunity for you to escape – and run away. To run, you need to be fit. If you wish, go to a gym and take part in a general or specialised fitness programme, or see whether there's a local exercise group that meets regularly at someone's house or at a nearby church hall. Alternatively, join a running club.

How fit are you?

Before you start this simple exercise, read the exercise check list on this page. Sit, completely rested, for at least one minute and then count your pulse rate at the wrist. Now stand with your feet together in front of a step that is 200 millimetres high. For three minutes, step up and down at the rate of two complete movements every five seconds. This is one complete movement: one foot up, other foot up, first foot down, second foot down. Stop at once if you feel pain or discomfort. After stepping up and down for three minutes, sit and rest for exactly one minute and then take your pulse again. It should be close to the resting rate. A fit adult male should have a pulse rate below 90 beats per minute; a fit woman should have a pulse rate below 95.

Basic exercise

Every session of exercise should start with a few minutes of warming up to make your muscles supple and lessen the likelihood of injuring them. Warm-up exercises include slow and gentle stretching, turning and bending. Suppleness is an important part of fitness, especially for the elderly, whose muscles tend to be stiffer than those of younger people.

Another component of fitness is strength, which is developed by exercising your muscles against resistance – by weightlifting, for instance, or by press-ups, sit-ups or cycling.

The third part of fitness is stamina, or staying power, which is the ability to maintain a reasonably high level of physical activity without gasping for breath or collapsing. Jogging and aerobic exercises that involve large muscle groups, such as those of the legs, require stamina.

The key to fitness is taking regular, moderately strenuous exercise. It won't build you up into a fearsome fighting machine, but it will help you to feel well and to look stronger. It's worth remembering that cigarette smoking, apart from its other ill effects, reduces stamina and increases the heart (pulse) rate.

Take a walk

Even the way you walk may play a part in determining whether or not you become a victim. Statistics compiled in the United States indicate that a woman is less likely to be attacked by a rapist if she strides athletically and purposefully, as though she is fit and knows just where she's going. Her bearing suggests strength and fitness, and that she will put up more resistance than an assailant is prepared to overcome. Walking is a good exercise in itself, but choose the neighbourhood for your walk carefully. Go walking

EXERCISE
CHECK LIST

1. Consult your doctor before starting your exercise programme if you're very unfit, or if your medical history includes any of these conditions:
◆ heart disease
◆ high blood pressure
◆ diabetes
◆ persistent trouble with back or joints
◆ dizzy spells or blackouts.

2. Don't exert yourself until you've gradually built up your condition for at least six weeks.

3. Rest at once if you feel pain or discomfort.

4. Don't exercise if you're physically tired, or within two hours of a heavy meal.

5. Don't exercise if you feel ill or are feverish, or when you have a cold or flu.

Body targets

◆ **Eyes:** lunge at one eye with your fingertips, or at both with your index finger and second finger spread.
◆ **Nose:** butt it with your head or strike upwards at it with your fist or palm.
◆ **Throat:** hit the Adam's apple hard with the edge of your hand.
◆ **Ears:** slap your cupped hands hard over them.
◆ **Neck:** strike the back or sides of the neck hard, or squeeze the neck if you can.
◆ **Hair:** pull it very hard to force him to release his grip, and make him raise his head, exposing his throat.
◆ **Abdomen:** strike it with your elbow or foot – high enough to avoid belt buckles – as hard as you can.
◆ **Solar plexus:** this lies just below the arch of the ribs. Jab hard, with your fist, knee or improvised club.
◆ **Groin:** drive your knee or fist upwards hard into this area, or twist, pull or squeeze the testicles.
◆ **Knee joint:** kick it hard on the front or inside of the leg.
◆ **Shin:** kick or scrape the edge of a hard sole down its length.
◆ **Feet:** stamp your heel hard on the top of his foot and grind it in.
◆ **Kidneys:** strike them from behind, between the ribs and the hips.

only in daylight, and don't go alone (see Keep Fit, Stay Safe, pp130-3).

Set aside a regular time for walking – say, 30 minutes to an hour every day, and then gradually try to increase the distance that you cover in this time. Try to include an uphill section and remember to increase the pace only gradually over days or even weeks. Don't push yourself too fast – you will get badly out of breath or suffer painful muscle cramps, and you may injure yourself.

Walking doesn't have to hurt to do you good. The effort, though, should produce a slight increase in your heart rate. Check your pulse at the wrist, before setting out and again when you've just reached the top of the uphill section. You'll find, as you become fitter, that both your 'resting' and 'effort' pulse will slow down, and that the difference between them will become less. As you become fitter, begin jogging for a counted number of paces, and build this up into jogging for measured periods of time, until, eventually, you're able to jog comfortably all the way.

Your natural weapons

Even your natural weapons – the moving parts of your body – are more effective when you've taken the trouble to become skilled in their use. Practise your moves with a partner, especially responding to his or her moves so that you become able to predict what he or she will do and can block or deflect the blow. Don't actually hit one another, but try to get through your partner's guard to touch an agreed target – the forehead, perhaps, or the middle of the chest.

No fair play

It probably goes against your natural ideas of politeness and fair play to strike hard at another person. This other person, however, has no such inhibitions. He also has no right to assault or threaten you, your family and your property, and you are attacking him solely to protect these things. Concentrate your strength and attention on your attacker's most vulnerable spots (see box), whether you're fighting with your hands or with an improvised weapon, and strike as fast as you can. And don't give him time to recover between your blows – strike again, and again.

Head and teeth

Use your head in the early stages of an attack, and you may be able to end the assault right there. If your attacker is facing you and pulls you towards him, go forward and butt him hard with your head, trying to contact his nose with your upper forehead. If you're grabbed from behind, jerk your head backwards to hit him in the face – again, going for the nose, which is a very sensitive area. If your attacker is very tall, a quick head butt to the abdomen may be feasible. Bite any part of your attacker that you can get your teeth into, and bite hard. Don't let go. Not only will you be hurting him, you'll also be marking him so that he may be identified later.

Voice

In a populated or busy area, shout, don't scream, and do it as loudly as you can, using your abdominal muscles and diaphragm to force out your voice rather than squeezing it out of your throat. Your shouting may bring help, it may also distract and confuse your assailant and it will almost certainly give you courage. Don't shout, however, if you are in an isolated area – it may encourage your assailant to become more violent.

When grabbed from the front, bring your arms over your attacker's, pull down to pull him towards you, and butt him on his nose.

Fist

To make a fist, curl your fingers towards the palm, starting with the little finger. Now place your thumb over the fingers. Don't curl the fingers over your thumb, or you may injure yourself, and be careful that neither your thumb nor your little finger sticks out beyond the ball formed by your fist.

Lock your wrist so as to form a straight line from your forearm through to your knuckles. When you punch, use your body to get as much weight as possible behind the blow. Plant your feet solidly, and turn slightly at the waist to add power. Don't draw back your hand before you punch – it tells your assailant what you're going to do and gives him a chance to deflect the blow.

A convenient way for you to use your fist is as a hammer – it's effective and you're less likely to injure your hand than when you connect with your knuckles. Imagine that your forearm is the shaft or handle of a hammer and that your hand, when you make a fist, is the head of that hammer. Make a fist and lock your wrist as before. Strike your assailant with the fleshy surface of the edge of your closed hand.

Holding your fingers straight and tightly together, jab them hard into one of your attacker's eyes.

Your hands, although the fastest and most readily used of your natural weapons, are easily damaged, so be careful of throwing a punch to the head – use them for striking soft targets instead.

Fingers

Vulnerable themselves, fingers are best used to attack the face and eyes. If your fingernails are long enough to do damage, swipe at your assailant's face or drag your nails slowly across his skin, pressing down firmly. To strike at the throat or at the eyes, lunge with fingers held tightly together, like a chisel edge or duck's bill. To strike at both eyes, form a V with the first and second fingers.

Pull your assailant's hair downwards to force his chin up; hit his chin upwards with the palm of your hand.

Palm

The edge of your palm is useful for striking at the throat, neck and, in a sweeping, upward blow, at the nose. The heel of the palm can strike the jaw harder

Feign a surrender by putting your hand up, then quickly drive your elbow up under your assailant's chin.

As an attacker lunges towards you, bend your knees slightly, move your weight onto your outer leg, then raise the foot of the inner leg and kick out and downwards hard onto his knee joint.

than a fist and put your fingers close to an assailant's eyes. Draw your hand back slightly at the wrist, curl fingers and thumb out of the way without covering the palm, and aim to strike with the fleshy part nearest the wrist.

Elbow

Versatile and hard-hitting, your elbows can deliver blows upwards to the chin and nose, or you can sweep them back or sideways into an assailant's abdomen, solar plexus, collarbone and the back of the neck.

Forearm

Especially when you're partly turned away from an assailant, a back swing with the forearm can deliver a very heavy blow to a sensitive point such as the nose or throat.

Knee

Your knee can deliver disabling blows to the abdomen, solar plexus, groin, thigh and head. A two-stage knee attack involves striking him in the groin or abdomen with the first blow, and then, as he doubles up, bringing your knee up hard into his face.

Feet

A leg can keep your attacker at a distance, especially when you're on the ground and aiming for his groin. You need to deliver your kicks quickly, if possible without giving away your intention. Your foot must go in and out fast – any hesitation, and your attacker may grab your raised leg and easily twist you off balance. With shoes on, your foot can do a lot of damage to a knee joint, shin and your assailant's foot.

Summing him up

Always try to avoid violence. Calm words may be able to defuse the situation: tell your assailant that he can have your money if he'll just let you go. Tell him where you were going, what you were doing. This 'humanises' you, and lets him see you as more than just someone to rob – but look for an opportunity to get away all the while. If he's armed or has accomplices, think carefully before you strike. However, if it becomes clear that he's going to assault you anyway, the decision to fight back is easier to make.

Once you've struck the first blow, there's usually no turning back until it's all over – which means that adequate help has arrived or you've got away. Taking note of his appearance may warn you what to expect.

◆ A flushed face and bloodshot eyes may indicate recent drinking or drug-taking. He probably won't be amenable to reason, but he may be clumsy and relatively easily made to lose his balance.

◆ A tense facial expression and voice, and jerky, aggressive hand movements often come before violence. He's tense and anxious, but you may be able to talk him out of assault.

◆ His heavy boots may cause you serious injury. Be prepared for him to use them as weapons – if you can't get away, you may have to get in close to limit his ability to kick effectively.

◆ Weapons worn on his person suggest that he may be no stranger to violence. He may just be hoping to intimidate you, but at least you have an idea of the course that a struggle might take.

Keep your balance

If you're seated when trouble threatens, make sure that both your feet are flat on the floor, so that you can keep your balance in the event of an attack. There's little enough you can do while sitting down, but having your legs crossed will make your situation even worse.

Stand up if it looks as though the trouble is not going to pass you by. Put your feet apart – about the width of your shoulders – and keep yourself slightly sideways on to your assailant, with your knees slightly bent. Keep your arms bent, with hands raised to protect your throat and chin and with elbows tucked in to your sides. Drop your head slightly to give extra protection to your face and throat. Keep your movements smooth or you may lose your balance and be pushed over, and keep your arms up.

If you're tall, you may be able to outreach an assailant. Shorter people are often less easy to push over and may be able to get in under an assailant's guard to deliver a head butt.

Breaking a neck hold

If your attacker is standing behind you, there are several things you can do. First, grab one of his fingers – the little finger is the easiest to get your fingers around – and bend it back as hard and suddenly as you can. Jerk your head backwards and upwards to try to butt him in the face and, preferably, on the nose. If his arm comes within reach, bite it, and stamp hard on the top of his foot with your heel. Swing your elbow back hard to hit him in the solar plexus.

Breaking a head lock

This is a version of the neck hold in which your assailant holds your head tightly against his side, bending you down and forward. Bite anything you can reach – his hand, arm or side – and try to bend back one of his fingers. While you're bent forward, try hitting upwards at his groin or grabbing his testicles.

Breaking a frontal grab

If someone in front of you grabs you on your chest or around your neck, put your arms over his and press down hard. As this movement pulls his head forward, butt his nose with your head. If necessary, follow up this action with a knee to the groin, and kick him hard in this sensitive area.

Blocking a frontal lunge

As an attacker lunges towards you, kick upward into his groin with your knee – kicking with your foot may land you in trouble since, if he grabs your leg, he'll then be able to knock you off balance and make you fall down. Alternatively, kick his shins, and stamp on his feet with your heels.

Get your arms up so that he can't pin them to your sides, and attack his face – jab at his eyes with outstretched fingers, or hit him hard under the nose with the heel of your palm. Grab his hair and pull his head down. At the same time, jerk your head up to butt him on the nose.

Multiple attackers

It's practically impossible for anyone but the most experienced exponent of unarmed combat to cope with more than one assailant at a time. This is generally true whether you're armed or not. A determined gang of children, for instance, can bring down an adult by clinging to his limbs and body while, at the same time, rapidly going through his pockets.

If you can single out and hurt a ringleader – the one who seems to be giving commands, perhaps – the others may give up and break off. Keep moving towards a busier area – don't let them hold you back. Use your natural weapons and anything else within reach. Shout at your assailants, shout for help.

If all they want is to rob you and if you can't struggle free, think about 'collapsing' or falling to the ground and lying limp, as though you've suffered a heart attack. This is most likely to work if you're middle-aged or older, and will allow them to take your goods and leave, while you may be able to escape injury.

The elderly

The senior citizen is seen as a pushover – often literally – so your assailant is not necessarily going to be a muscular young man. It could be a woman, a child or a group of children, and the fitter you are, the better you'll be able to resist. Carry a stout walking stick or umbrella, even if you don't need one for support. And remember that it's much more difficult for an assailant to block a jab than it is for him to deflect a swinging motion.

If you're carrying an umbrella when you're attacked from the front, grab the umbrella halfway down its length and jab it hard into your assailant's face or abdomen.

Helping others

If someone else is being attacked, robbed or threatened, try to do something, even if it is simply to raise the alarm or to fetch help. This is especially important where the person actually appeals for help. Your failure to respond is likely to be a long-standing source of guilt, regret and recrimination.

FEMALE TACTICS

Most people believe that the average woman is unable to defend herself successfully against an attack by a man. This is generally not true, but a woman has to know when and how to fight back.

Your choice

Would-be rapists believe that a woman cannot defend herself against them. And there are other people who argue that a woman who resists is merely going to provoke greater violence. But, if she resists vigorously and effectively, preferably from the moment of confrontation, she can succeed in escaping harm. Where there is a real and immediate threat of serious injury or death from a lethal weapon, however, submission may be the wisest course. Many rape victims feel that they had no option but to submit. Only they are in a position to judge, but it's worth remembering that most rapists are not out looking for a fight. If they meet with determined resistance, they're likely to give up.

Passive resistance

You may be able to talk an attacker out of sexual assault, especially if he's someone you know. Crying or begging may also work on acquaintances, but are unlikely to move a stranger. He'll see crying and begging as signs of weakness that merely emphasise his power over you, which is what rape and assault help him to express. If you are unable to bring yourself to fight with all your strength and determination, try reasoning with him. But it's almost never too late to fight.

Fighting back

If you're assaulted, you're bound to be frightened, but try to be angry, too. It's a more useful emotion under dangerous circumstances. Your objective must be to hurt your assailant so much that he will let you go, giving you a chance to get away. Don't think of fighting back as standing toe to toe with an assailant and trading blows with him. Memorise his body targets (see Physical Self-Defence, pp242-8) and practise the use of your natural weapons. Remember that what you lack in brute strength you make up for in having a better sense of balance and probably greater agility than most men.

If he releases his grip, even for just a moment, take advantage of it and run. Or, watch for your chance to hurt him and run. Don't look back. Don't wait to get in that extra kick he so richly deserves. Get away.

For as long as he's holding onto you, keep striking at him. If you're carrying anything when you're attacked, let it go if it's going to restrict your movements, and concentrate on getting away. Use these tactics on an assailant who isn't armed with a knife or firearm. If your attacker is armed, try to get him to put the weapon down, by complying with his demands, and then look for your chance to get away from him.

Talk him out of it

In an indoor confrontation, tell your assailant to take what he wants and to go, and that your husband or boyfriend and his friend will be arriving soon. If your attacker's intention is rape, there are several things you can tell him that might put him off. For instance, say that you're having your period, and that you're not clean. Or say you've got an infection, that you've only just started treatment and that the treatment won't work if you have intercourse. Also, make it clear that he will catch the disease, and you can choose AIDS, gonorrhoea or syphilis. The reason for the story about the treatment is that he probably won't believe that you'd want to stop him getting AIDS or some other unpleasant disease.

If he produces a condom, pretend to be relieved and offer to put it on for him. This will give you the opportunity to get at his most vulnerable part – his testicles.

Relax

If you're being held, relax – suddenly. This will catch your attacker off guard and, depending on how he's holding you, may also put him off balance. Relax for no more than about a second or two, and then go straight into a counterattack. Here's an example: you're on your back and your assailant is astride you, with a hand clamped on each wrist on either side of your head. Relax. As he shifts, or as he starts to relax too, shoot your arms out as straight as you can. His weight, already forward, will be pushed further forward, making him concentrate on his balance rather than on holding onto you. Twist your body so as to raise one of your hips, and try to follow with a half-roll.

DRAMA IN REAL LIFE

The memory that saves you

Martie Viljoen had attended martial arts classes as a child but, like so many beginners, soon found her enthusiasm waning when this disciplined pursuit failed to provide the glamour she had expected. But she remembered a few basic positions and principles, although she never considered herself capable of repelling a serious attack. Several years later, she was walking home one evening, and had just reached her front gate when she felt a tug at her shoulder bag. She spun round, raised her forearms in what she imagined was the correct defensive position, and yelled as loudly as she could. Her assailant fled, and Ms Viljoen was realistic enough to be grateful that her shaky memory of unarmed combat had not been put to the test.

Police comment: Ms Viljoen was probably up against a timid and inexperienced mugger. It is most likely that what saved her here was the fact that she yelled loudly, that she was already at her front gate and close to potential assistance, and that her attacker was not armed. This tactic does not always work and depends on the state of mind of the attacker.

If you're right-handed, raise your left hip and half-roll to the right. This movement should bring your mouth within biting range of his arm. Bite hard. Bring a knee up – left and right alternately – as hard as you can against the base of his spine. Twist to bite his other arm. As soon as he releases one of your hands, switch it to an attack on his face: scratch or go for his eyes, or strike at his nose with the heel of your palm.

Where it hurts most

The groin area and, particularly, the testicles, form a man's most sensitive spot. As with other body targets, you need to be really close to get at this area. It's usually possible to manage only a fairly short swing if you're attacking with your fist or the edge of your hand. There may be an opportunity to put a knee in, hard. Grabbing hold and squeezing really hard for as long as you can will cause excruciating, debilitating pain and perhaps even brief unconsciousness. It should certainly disable him long enough for you to get away – he won't be able to follow you for several minutes at the very least.

Knee clutch

You're seated and the stranger sitting next to you puts his left hand on your right knee. This is a fairly mild offence, but you don't have to tolerate it. Put your right hand over the molester's hand, find his little finger (nearest the inside of your knee), pull it sharply backwards and hold on. Don't try to lift his hand, just pull the finger back and he'll raise his hand himself, to try to relieve the pain. Raise your left arm to ward off any attempt to strike at you with his right hand, stand up and, still holding his little finger, draw attention to your situation – by shouting, for instance, something like 'How dare you put your hands on me?'. Then release his finger and move quickly out of his range.

Bottom grab

While you're standing or walking, someone behind you attempts to fondle your bottom. Like the knee clutch, this may be a relatively mild attack, but you should put a quick stop to it. Half-turn and, as you do so, chop at the back of his wrist with the outside edge of your hand, so as to knock his hand clear of your body. If he's standing next to you, try to swing your elbow into his solar plexus.

Talking with his hands

He's probably a friend or acquaintance, and when he's with you or talking to you, he touches you in a way you don't like. Simply remove his hand and drop it. If he does it again, tell him firmly to take his hands off you. If necessary, slap his hand away and create a confrontation by warning him loudly, but make sure there are people present who will hear and sympathise with you.

EVERYDAY ITEMS AS WEAPONS

Empty your pockets or handbag, and you may be surprised at the things they contain that you could defend yourself with. You'll also find your kitchen, workroom, garage and even bedroom to be an armoury of implements, even though they weren't intended for violent use. Remember, though, that any weapon you produce may be turned against you.

Lightweights

◆ A ballpoint pen or a nailfile makes a good jabbing implement, especially at such soft targets as faces, eyes, ears and nostrils.

◆ A comb scraped across an assailant's cheek – or, even more effectively, just below his nose – can produce severe pain. It will also leave a mark by which he can be identified for several days.

◆ Coins, lipstick, anything scooped up from the bottom of your bag, thrown hard into an assailant's face may distract him long enough for you to get away.

◆ Keys, protruding between your fingers when you make a fist, can be used to rake an assailant's face. Or jab or grind them into the back of his hand to make him release his grip.

◆ Shoes, especially ladies' shoes with pointed heels, are useful weapons whether worn on the foot, when you can stamp on your assailant's foot or scrape his shin, or held in the hand and used as a hammer.

◆ Any garment you're carrying, such as a coat or a jersey, can be used to help cushion blows aimed at you, and a sleeve can be used as a blindfold or to strangle your assailant.

◆ An umbrella is a good stand-in for a sword, but you must hold it about halfway down its length and jab with it – hard. It's too light to be used as a club, although the curled handle is useful for slipping around necks and ankles, to pull someone off balance.

◆ Any aerosol sprayed at an assailant's eyes – whether it's furniture polish, hair lacquer, shaving cream or insecticide – will alarm and distract him, perhaps long enough for you to break away. Oven-cleaning aerosols, which contain a corrosive substance, are likely to cause blindness. A pepper or chilli extract spray aimed at the eyes is also effective (see Non-ballistic Weapons, pp254-7). While he's reeling from a burst of spray, hit him hard on the bridge of his nose with a downwards movement of the spray can.

◆ If he's within range, your assailant is a target for anything hot from the stove. Be sure, though, that you can pick it up and throw it at him – preferably into his face – without spilling it over yourself.

◆ Anything that's hinged or pivoted – such as a door, window or shutter – can be used to slam against an assailant who's in range of it, and has the advantage that it's readily available to be used again if necessary.

◆ Anything you may be carrying, such as a bag or a briefcase, can also be used. Swing it as hard as you can at his groin, or at his throat. A newspaper, folded in half and then tightly rolled, is also an effective weapon when thrust at an assailant's groin, abdomen or face.

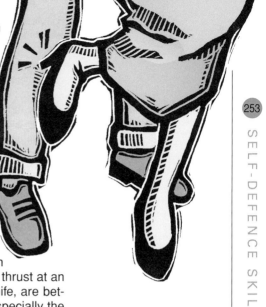

Heavier weapons

There are two basic classes of impromptu weapon – cutters and bludgeons – although some, like the garden spade, are adaptable. Some cutting implements, such as a dining fork or even a garden fork, serve better when they are thrust at an attacker, while others, such as a steak knife, are better for slashing with. Sports equipment, especially the bludgeon sort, such as hockey sticks, baseball bats and cricket bats, needs space if you're going to swing and deliver a really hard blow. If you're short of space, try thrusting with this type of weapon, using both hands and going for the face, abdomen or kneecaps.

Familiarise yourself with whatever club or bat is in your home, and practise swinging or thrusting it, so that when you need to use it the action won't be completely strange. A heavy frying pan, swung edge-on against an assailant's neck, could be fatal. Lighter pots and pans make good missiles.

The dark

If you're confronted by an intruder in your home at night, consider plunging the place into darkness. Obviously, you'll need to be able to reach the main switch without trapping yourself in a corner, but you'll be placing him at an instant disadvantage. It might just allow you time to get out and get away. Briefly flashing a bright light into someone's eyes will also disorient him for a moment or two. But remember to move quickly from the position from which you shone the light – an assailant or intruder will almost certainly make a lunge in that direction.

Unlikely obstacles

If you are being attacked or pursued on familiar territory, you probably have an advantage. You know the layout, whereas your attacker does not. Someone who is chasing you will be concentrating on you as hard as he can – especially visually. He probably won't see the potential traps that you know about and are leading him into. These could be a low branch that will catch him squarely across the face, a birdcage hanging in a doorway, a mat on a slippery floor – anything that will give you the advantage of a few extra seconds or metres, and allow you to escape.

NON-BALLISTIC WEAPONS

To many people, it's a relief not to carry a firearm and bear the responsibilities that go with this form of weapon. If they have to carry a weapon at all, these people would rather carry another kind with which to defend themselves in case of attack and to give them a chance to escape.

'Cultural' weapons

It is traditional for the men of various indigenous ethnic groups in southern Africa to carry particular weapons, especially round-headed clubs or knobkerries, when walking. Although these traditional, or cultural, weapons may be reasonably classified as dangerous, you would be likely to be prosecuted for carrying one only if the state could show that you were carrying such a weapon with the intent to commit an unlawful act.

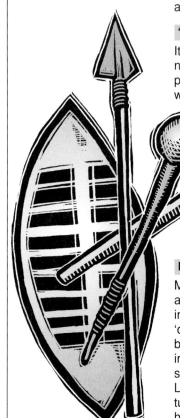

Carrying a particular cultural weapon in a defined area may be prohibited by a proclamation issued by the government, for a specified time or until the proclamation is rescinded.

Replica firearms

Many replica firearms are so realistic in appearance and feel, that they will deceive firearms experts standing only a few metres away. Do not consider using a 'dummy gun' as a defensive weapon, however, because there is a strong probability that it will increase the potential for violence. You may just be successful in rounding up a burglar with your plastic Luger, but if he discovers the deception he's likely to turn very angry in reaction to the fear and shock of having – supposedly – had his life threatened, and will probably vent his anger on you.

The police do not recommend that people carry dummy guns. In the confusion of a violent incident, people with guns are likely to be 'taken out' as a priority, and nobody will know until too late that the weapon you were carrying was only a toy.

Noise alarms

Most of these alarms are not, in fact, weapons, but are designed to alert other people to your plight when things go wrong, and so deter an attacker or rapist. Noise alarms are powered by air blown out of your mouth (as is a whistle), by battery or by compressed air (as is an aerosol). Some will emit a continuous blare of between 110 and 130 decibels – the pain threshold for sound is 90 decibels. Blown loudly close to an assailant's ear or head, they have a disorienting effect and may actually damage the hearing.

If you buy the aerosol type of noise alarm, make sure it has a switch that will lock into position, so that, even if you drop it, the alarm will continue to sound. When you buy an aerosol alarm, check its expiry date – it should have a shelf life of at least two years.

Some noise alarms can be attached to your clothes or to a chain around your neck, so that they are within easy reach all the time. A tubular whistle, of the type carried by police, is an efficient and economical noise alarm. Wear one on a string around your wrist, so that it falls naturally into your hand – never wear it around your neck. Some battery-operated models can also be worn on your wrist.

Electric shock sticks

Superficially, many shock sticks resemble a torch or rolled umbrella. They are powered by alkaline batteries. When the stick is switched on and its small metal contacts are pressed against an assailant, a low-amperage current of up to 150 000 volts enters the assailant's body. This produces severe pain and temporary paralysis, allowing you to escape. The effect is greatest if the contacts are applied to the assailant's neck or shoulder region. Some versions of the shock stick are spring-loaded and propel the contacts over a distance of a few metres.

A disadvantage of those shock sticks that you press against your attacker is that you, like many people, may find it difficult to make direct contact with your assailant's body when under stress. If you carry one, you must be prepared to use it as it is intended.

Knives and knuckles

Knives and knuckle-dusters, while not illegal, are generally regarded as offensive rather than defensive weapons. The use of such a weapon – depending on

DRAMA IN REAL LIFE

A fright in the night

Sally and her friend, a fellow student, had just moved into a house together, and hadn't had time to put up burglar bars or install an alarm system. Sally came home at midnight one night and went to the kitchen for a glass of water. As she stood there, a man came crashing through the sash window, with a large knife in his hand. She just had time to run down to her bedroom and shut the door. But before she turned the key he forced the door open. Her assailant pushed her down onto the bed and yelled at her to stop screaming, or he would stab her. She managed to collect her thoughts and asked him what he wanted. When he said he wanted money, she told him that her purse was on her desk. She then remembered that her gas pistol was also on the desk, and offered to get the money for him. He allowed her to get up and get the purse, and while she held it out to him with one hand, she reached for the gas pistol and sprayed it straight into his face. Shocked, he ran out of the bedroom, allowing her to lock the door after him. He escaped, even though a neighbour tried to apprehend him.

Police comment: Sally showed great presence of mind and was lucky that she was able to get to the desk. Most burglars would not have let her get the money herself. She was lucky too that the intruder didn't get angry at her counterattack and become more violent towards her. In the end, although it was the spray that saved her, if he was only after her money she should probably have let him have it and avoided provoking a more serious attack.

the circumstances – might lead to a charge of assault with a dangerous weapon being laid against you, and a fine or imprisonment.

Aerosols

Defensive aerosol sprays can be bought from a variety of shops, including those that sell firearms and other types of weapon, hardware stores, discount retailers and convenience stores. These sprays may also be available through organisations such as sports clubs. They are useful during recreational activities because they are light and easy to carry.

Aerosol sprays are made in several container sizes and configurations. Some double as a key-ring attachment and are easy to carry in your hand or attach to your clothes – although a spray probably won't help you if it's attached to your clothes when you need to use it. Others are shaped like a small tube with grip indentations, so that your fingers fit round it easily.

Some containers discharge their contents in measured 'bursts', usually of two seconds, every time you press the discharge button. The number of discharges varies among brands, and ranges from four to about 18 two-second sprays. Other protective sprays discharge for as long as the button is held down. Ask the retailer to show you how the one you are choosing works, before you buy it.

Gas pistols are usually made of matt black plastic, to deliberately resemble a firearm. Although they may look more threatening than an ordinary aerosol spray, their action and effects are similar. Some have a translucent plastic cartridge that reveals the level of the contents. Their resemblance to a real firearm is only superficial, and is unlikely to intimidate a mugger once he's got over his surprise. Police do not recommend the use of spray containers that resemble firearms, or of any other dummy firearm, because of their potential to spark off violence.

The effects

The most widely used active ingredient in defensive sprays is an extract of chilli pepper (capsicum) in a vegetable-based oleoresin. When sprayed under pressure at a person's face, it causes temporary blindness, disorientation, nausea and shortness of breath. The effects usually last from 10 to 15 minutes, but may be more severe in people suffering from asthma or allergies. Some sprays also contain an indelible dye that will mark an assailant for several days before the colour fades.

Check the expiry date

Before you buy a defensive spray, check the expiry date on the label or on the pressurised container. It should have a shelf life of at least two years – that is, after two years it should still spray out its contents at the designed pressure and over the advertised range.

The shelf life of the chemical reagent should also be at least two years, and is usually longer.

Store all pressurised containers in a cool place, out of direct sunlight. Replace the can or cartridge after two years, whether you've used the spray or not, and ask your security dealer to dispose of the old one.

Using the spray

Familiarise yourself with the spray so that, working by feel alone, you are able to pick it up and discharge aimed bursts away from you without looking at it. (It is best to practise this outdoors, on a windless day.) Discharging too early is a common (and understandable) fault, and may result in the user being more affected than the assailant. This may occur if the gas is discharged before your arm is extended, and while the spray container is still too close to your face.

Whatever its chemical composition, a defensive spray should still be fully effective at three metres from the point of discharge. In practice, however, you would be more likely to discharge it at a closer range. In confined spaces, such as a lift, the spray may be hazardous to you as well as your assailant. Similarly, at ranges of 60 centimetres or less, the spray may affect you, too, by being deflected back from the target. As a rough guide, if you discharge the spray at arm's length outdoors you should escape its effects. Once you've used a defensive spray, wait at least 20 minutes before you touch your face or eyes with the hand that held the can.

While you're walking outside, carry the spray in your hand ready to use but with your finger off the discharge button until the last moment when you decide you are going to have to use it. Some containers have a form of safety catch – usually a hinged or sliding cover over the discharge button. Whether you carry it with the safety engaged or not depends on how easy it is to operate.

Things to remember about sprays

◆ Sprays are not effective immediately – they take a few seconds to react on the assailant.
◆ The effects of a spray may be less marked on someone who is enraged, or who is under the influence of drugs or alcohol.
◆ If you're too close – less than 60 centimetres – you're likely to be affected by the spray yourself.
◆ Check the expiry date of your spray, and replace it if necessary.
◆ Periodically check the container for leaks, especially around the spray opening.
◆ Shake the container periodically to check how much spray is left.
◆ Learn to handle and use the protective spray entirely by feel.
◆ Keep the spray out of reach of children and pets.
◆ Keep it ready for use – not in your handbag.

FIREARMS

There's something to be said for having a firearm with which to defend your home and family, once you've applied all the other measures, such as bars and alarms. Faced with a criminal who, at the very least, is likely to do you serious injury if you don't stop him, your firearm represents your stopping power.

Disadvantages

The problem with carrying a firearm in the street is that if you're attacked you'll almost certainly be taken by surprise and you may even be outnumbered. You probably won't even reach it, let alone have it out and ready to use. There is no doubt that your assailants will take it away from you if they can, and if you're lucky, they won't use it on you.

Firearms in the home are too often involved in family violence or in the tragic loss of life through simple negligence in failing to store the weapon safely. It is therefore very important that you teach the members of your family safe practices with firearms, to prevent a tragic accident.

However, when a gun is locked away it is out of reach and you may as well not have it at all. If it is locked away when you are attacked at home, your attackers will probably force you to show them where it is, and take it from you.

Taking it with you

When it's not securely locked away, your firearm should be worn on your person at all times in a suitable holster, except when you're sleeping or taking a bath or shower. If you feel that it's necessary to have a handgun nearby while you're bathing, put it where it can't fall accidentally, such as on a mat on the floor, or on a folded cloth in the washbasin. Covering the gun with a towel or garment (to prevent excessive wetting) creates the possibility that someone may come in, pick up the cover and drop the gun, which may go off. Locking the bathroom door will prevent this, and will also delay an intruder expecting to catch you unawares. Dry your hands before you handle the gun, and wipe it clear of moisture.

When travelling, you may find a firearm reassuring. In most attacks while you're in a car, you usually have time to draw your weapon if you are wearing it. Remember, however, that when you're carrying a firearm, it must be properly concealed from view.

Never sleep with a gun under your pillow. If you want the gun close to you while you're in bed, the safest place to keep it is in a night holster that attaches to the side of the bed base, or on the floor. Keeping a gun on the floor means that an accidental nudge before you're fully awake won't cause it to fall. However, it does expose the weapon to attention from children, so if you are a heavy sleeper it may be safer to place the gun on a high shelf in a locked cupboard during the night. Remember, without fail, to return a gun to its permanent daily storage place when you wake up. To make sure that you don't forget, put something under the gun that you'll need almost as soon as you get up in the morning. It could be your toothbrush, car keys, spectacles or wallet.

Holsters

Carry the gun in a comfortable holster into which the weapon fits snugly and from which it can be withdrawn smoothly and with a minimum of effort. A weapon that slips from a holster – when you bend to retrieve a dropped key, for instance – is likely to go off when it hits the ground, even if the safety catch is engaged or 'on'. This is especially the case with automatic weapons.

When travelling by car, don't wear a firearm in a waist holster under the seat belt. In the event of a collision or sudden stop, the weapon will be forced violently into your abdomen and may cause serious injury, such as a ruptured kidney. Remember that it's easier for a right-handed person, when driving, to draw from a holster worn on the left side.

But the most important criterion of any holster is accessibility – how quickly you can reach it and withdraw the firearm. Ask a shooting instructor or dealer to recommend a suitable holster. Leather is a comfortable and durable material, and, with continued wear, soon becomes soft and pliable. Many holsters made of synthetic material are also quite satisfactory.

Most holsters are worn over the shoulder (by special straps) or on an ordinary waist belt. Some allow the gun to be worn out of sight under your shirt, although this naturally makes it difficult to draw in a hurry. Smaller weapons may be worn well concealed in an ankle holster or, under skirts, in a thigh or suspender holster. Choose the type that suits your lifestyle best – depending on your occupation, you may need more than one type.

Choosing a gun

Ask friends whose judgment, technical expertise and balanced opinions you respect, whether they have a firearm for personal protection. If they've elected not to own a gun, consider whether their reasoning applies to you too. If they do have a gun, ask why they chose that particular type. Read local shooting magazines, most of which are happy to publish and answer queries from their readers. Make use of their expertise. This accumulated information may help you to make up your own mind.

The usual choice is a handgun, which can be held and operated (most of the time) in one hand. The two types of handgun usually used are the revolver and the automatic pistol (really a semiautomatic or self-

Your gun and the law

◆ Keep weapons and ammunition in a safe place. If your firearm is lost or stolen through your negligence, you may be prosecuted and also prohibited from owning another one.
◆ Except in a desperate emergency, you may not discharge a firearm in or near a built-up area.
◆ It is an offence to point a firearm, without lawful cause, at anybody, whether it is loaded or not.
◆ You must warn the person you're aiming at that you're going to shoot.
◆ You may shoot someone in self-defence only as a last resort, and a court may require you to convince them that your action was justified and reasonable in the circumstances.
◆ You may be justified in shooting and killing any person who has committed or attempted to commit a serious Schedule 1 offence (see p161), if there is no other way to detain him or to prevent him from fleeing. In shooting after a fleeing person, however, you would have to take account of innocent people who might be hurt by your action and whose relatives might subsequently sue you.

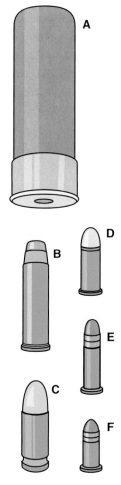

A shotshell (A), this one made for a 12-bore shotgun, is highly destructive at close range. The most popular calibres, and the most suitable for defence, are the .38 Special (B) for a revolver, and the 9mm Parabellum (C), for an automatic pistol. The .25 Automatic (D) is designed for use in a pistol only. The .22 Long Rifle (E), originally developed for such a weapon, is now also used in handguns, as is the smaller .22 Rimfire (F).

loading weapon). Both types are made in ultra-compact models of suitable calibres for personal defence.

Tell the firearms dealer what you think you require. Tell him whether you need to carry the weapon and/or use it for home defence. Your purchase must be dictated solely by your needs and you should buy the best-quality firearm, preferably new, that you can readily afford. It's irrelevant that the pistol is lightweight if it fires underpowered ammunition. But don't be steered into buying a weapon that's too bulky to carry with the sort of clothes you normally wear, or a powerful weapon with a heavy recoil that you find difficult to control. If it's uncomfortable or intimidating, the chances are that you'll neither carry it nor use it.

What calibre to choose

Almost all firearms are designed around existing ammunition, so it follows that the larger the calibre of the ammunition, the larger the finished firearm will be. Calibre is really the inside diameter of the barrel or bore of the weapon, given in inches or in millimetres, and is also applied to the ammunition. Combined with muzzle velocity, or the speed at which the bullet leaves the barrel, calibre determines what is known as the 'stopping power' of a bullet.

Small-calibre weapons are cheaper to buy and easier to carry, but lack the all-important stopping power of the larger calibres. However, a hit with an easily wielded, small-calibre firearm is preferable to a miss with a powerful Magnum. Suitable calibres for a revolver are a 0.357 Magnum and a 0.38 Special. The most popular calibre for an automatic pistol is a 9 mm Parabellum (not 9 mm Short) and, for a shotgun, 12 bore (about 18,5 mm).

Ask the dealer to suggest a suitable calibre. Ask him, too, for brochures on different makes of guns and make notes of what he says and recommends, but don't buy anything at this stage.

The revolver

The bullets (usually five or six in all) are contained in a bulky cylinder. Most revolvers have an external hammer that must be pulled back, by pressure on the trigger or by a separate thumb movement, before firing each shot. Most revolvers do not have a safety catch, but this is not a serious omission because a quick examination shows whether a revolver is loaded (that is, it has ammunition in it) and cocked, or ready to fire.

Ask an experienced person to show you how to open a revolver to check whether it is loaded, and to show you the positions of the hammer when cocked or safe. To fire a revolver, point it at the target and press the trigger. Cocking the hammer first – all the while keeping the muzzle of the weapon pointed away from yourself and from others – improves your aim because it means that only slight pressure is required on the trigger. You then pull the trigger (cocking the hammer first, if you prefer), until the five or six bullets in the cylinder have been fired, remove the fired cartridge cases, and reload.

The greatest advantage of the revolver is that it is simple to use and requires no particular strength to operate. Its disadvantages are that it is bulky and difficult to conceal, and slow to reload without a 'speed loader', which is also bulky.

Automatic pistols

These handguns, which are strictly speaking semi-automatics, are generally flatter and more compact than revolvers. Although much more complex in design, they are usually thoroughly reliable if used with ammunition loads recommended by the manufacturer. The bullets – up to 15 or more – are contained in a removable boxlike magazine that fits into the handle.

Some automatic pistols, but not all, require that a hammer be drawn back before firing the first shot. To cock the pistol – that is, to place a round or bullet into the chamber ready for firing – point the muzzle away from yourself and from others, keep your fingers clear of the trigger, pull back the hammer fully (it will 'click' into the cocked position), then draw back the slide that surrounds the barrel, and release it. The pistol is now ready to fire and the safety catch may be applied.

You can carry a pistol in this condition – 'cocked and locked' – or, instead of engaging the safety catch, you can gently lower the hammer and, as an extra precaution, engage the safety catch again. A shooting instructor or firearms dealer will show you how to do this with the particular model you're using.

Most pistols do not show whether or not there is a round in the chamber, and the only way to find out is to pull back the hammer fully, and partly pull back the slide until the chamber (where the bullet fits before firing) comes into view. If there is no bullet in the chamber, you feed one from the magazine, by pulling the slide back fully and releasing it.

To fire the pistol, aim at the target and pull the trigger. Self-loading is virtually instantaneous and the pistol will fire every time you press the trigger until the magazine is empty. Most pistols indicate an empty magazine by having the slide come to rest in the rearward position after the

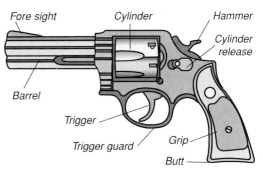

Revolver

Automatic or self-loading pistol

last shot. Remove the empty magazine and replace it with a full one, or refill and replace the original magazine. If you have a spare magazine, and spares are readily available from firearms dealers, reloading is much quicker than with a revolver.

Some automatics operate on a system known as 'double action' which means that it is not necessary to draw back the hammer before firing the first of a sequence of shots. There is usually an appreciable heaviness to the trigger pull when firing the first or double-action shot.

The advantages of an automatic pistol over a revolver are its rapid fire, speed of reloading and its large ammunition capacity (although most situations in which you would be justified in shooting should not require firing more than a few shots). An automatic is usually more comfortable to carry than a revolver, and is more easily concealed. A disadvantage of most models is that they need to be cocked before firing the first shot. If there is no bullet in the chamber, this almost always requires using both hands, and slightly built people, in particular, may find the slide difficult to draw back against the recoil spring.

Rifle

This is a long weapon designed to be fired from the shoulder, and, in a variety of calibres, is widely used for hunting and long-range target shooting. Although people in many households possess rifles, these weapons are not suitable for self-defence. It is virtually impossible to carry a rifle concealed and ready for use, and rifles are difficult to manipulate in the confined spaces of an ordinary house. The very long lethal range of most rifles (well in excess of two kilometres) means that a bullet might not only kill the targeted person, but, passing through him, kill or injure several other people as well. There is also a danger, especially when using high-powered ammunition in a confined space, of injuries caused by ricochets, where the bullet is deflected by a wall, for instance. In general, rifles are better suited to hunting and military applications than to ordinary civilian use.

Shotgun

This too is a long weapon, designed to be fired from the shoulder and primarily used for hunting, although the 'riot gun' is a development specifically intended for

The riot gun, like an ordinary shotgun, is a highly effective short-range defence weapon. Its pistol grip makes it easy to wield, and it can carry from 7 to 9 rounds.

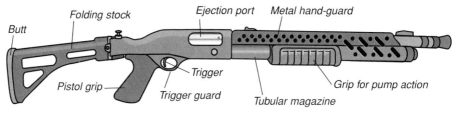

Butt · Folding stock · Ejection port · Metal hand-guard · Trigger · Pistol grip · Trigger guard · Tubular magazine · Grip for pump action

Riot gun

The guard who was too efficient

Matthys Fisher had an impressive record as a private security guard who, when it came to preventing burglaries, always got his man – dead. Whenever he went to investigate a suspected break-in, Fisher did so with his weapon, a large-calibre revolver, at the ready. There were many encounters in dark alleys and warehouses from which Fisher, a deadly shot, emerged as the sole survivor – and the only witness. As the toll of would-be burglars mounted, it was noted that none had been armed with anything more lethal than a stick or a length of metal. Then an autopsy revealed that the latest burglar had been shot while crouching in an extremely confined space, from which he could scarcely have mounted a serious threat to anyone. Further investigation showed that he had been hiding in an oil drum. The remains of Fisher's earlier victims were disinterred and submitted to further examination. It was found that all had been shot under circumstances that suggested the possibility of murder.

Police comment: The law is very strict about the discharge of firearms – especially where this results in injury or death. The court ruled that Fisher could have overpowered or arrested the intruders without using his firearm, and he was found guilty of several murders.

personal defence. A riot gun is a short-barrelled shotgun with a tubular or drum-shaped magazine (usually holding up to seven rounds) beneath the barrel. A slide or 'pump' under the barrel is moved briskly backwards and forwards to feed another round into the chamber after each shot.

Some riot guns have a folding stock (the portion behind the barrel) but even these are not easy to conceal when carrying. Pointed rather than aimed, and often fired from the waist, a riot gun is devastating at short range and is suitable for use in the home.

Semiautomatic shotguns (in which reloading is automatic and the operator has only to depress the trigger for each shot) are legally available but licences to possess them are not readily granted.

Target practice

Before buying a gun, contact a shooting club or the management of a shooting range and tell them that you are interested in shooting, that you would like to attend a meeting but don't have a weapon of your own. At the meeting, try to find out how many people are using the type of weapon that the dealer recommended, and whether the general opinion of it is favourable. If you are given the opportunity to shoot with it – or with any other weapon – accept it. When you're shooting at a range, wear earmuffs or plugs to protect your hearing.

Once you've selected a weapon, pay a deposit to ensure that the dealer will keep it for you, and enrol for a course of instruction leading to a certificate of competence in the use and handling of firearms. Most dealers can enrol you. Take the certificate, together with your identity document and details of the firearm to your nearest police station and apply for a firearms licence. Once the licence has been granted, persevere with target practice at an indoor range until you

Escape from a gunman – is it possible?

It is always safest to do as a gunman tells you rather than try to escape. But there are a few cases in which you might be able to get away, if you are familiar with firearms:

◆ If your attacker's revolver is not loaded. You can usually tell by looking into the chambers in the cylinder – if the chamber in line with the hammer shows the gleam of a metal jacket, it contains a live bullet; an empty case shows as dark and matt.

◆ If the safety catch is still engaged.

◆ If your assailant has misfired – he's pulled the trigger, you heard the click but nothing happened. You may have time to act quickly if he's using an automatic pistol. He'll almost certainly need both hands to clear the faulty round, but with a revolver he need only pull the trigger a second time to line up a different round.

◆ If he's out of ammunition – the slide of an automatic pistol will stay in the backward or full recoil position, and he will have to remove the empty magazine and insert a fresh one. It won't take long, but he will definitely need both hands and may also have to take his eyes off you for a few seconds.

enjoy shooting and until you can produce a respectable score. Make sure that the first time you fire a gun is not the time you need it to save your life.

In joining a shooting club you'll learn more than you'll ever derive from any authority or book on the subject. It will also help you to sort out the shooting facts from fiction.

◆ Does the law insist that you fire a warning shot? No, it doesn't, but it does expect that, where possible, you will shout a warning to your target of your intention to shoot.

◆ Can you dodge a bullet? Yes, but only if you're unusually nimble and at least several hundred metres away. The muzzle velocity, or speed at which the bullet leaves the gun, of a typical 9mm Parabellum automatic pistol is 340 metres per second, slightly faster than the speed of sound. The muzzle velocity of an AK47 is 710 metres per second – more than twice the speed of sound. In both cases, the bullet will reach you before you even hear the bang.

◆ Do some guns recoil so violently that they can break their operator's bones? It's possible for this to happen with very powerful weapons, but only if they aren't held properly.

To prevent freezing up in the event that you have to point your gun at someone and pull the trigger, psych yourself up by reminding yourself of what a gunman intends to do to you if you don't stop him.

Get over 'gun-shyness' by routinely wearing ear-plugs to block out the worst of the noise when practising at a shooting range. With only a little practice, you'll get to know what the gun is going to do and how you can control it.

Pulling the trigger

Don't pull the trigger, 'squeeze' it as though you're gently squeezing an orange. Any rough or violent movement with your gun is likely to deflect your aim from the target.

Where you need to fire off a quick shot to save a life, keep the firing motion as smooth as you can, even though it's likely to be a compromise between a pull and a squeeze.

You're on target when your eye, the notch or V of the rear sight, the blade or bead of the front sight, and target itself, are all in one line.

Taming the recoil

The more powerful the cartridge and the lighter the weapon, the more severe will be the recoil. The best way to reduce the effect of recoil is to hold your weapon firmly.

With a rifle or shotgun, rest your cheek on the stock and press the butt firmly against your shoulder, using both hands. Controlling the recoil of a revolver or pistol is part of the all-important stance adopted when firing, and should be practised regularly – preferably with an unloaded weapon. Some handguns have a pistol grip for the trigger hand (or gun hand) and a grooved rest for the forward hand.

Using your gun

The Weaver stance is the standard position for using a handgun, whether for long- to medium-range shooting practice or for close-up self-defence. Firing from the hip with one hand is unlikely to produce results.

◆ Check that the weapon is unloaded – 'break' a revolver to examine the cylinder; remove the magazine of an automatic pistol and draw back and release the slide smartly several times. Gently release the hammer and apply the safety catch.

◆ Hold the pistol in your gun hand so that the back of the grip rests in the angle between your thumb and forefinger. Extend your forefinger across the trigger guard and wrap the other three fingers firmly round the grip of the pistol. Place the other hand so that the fingers cover the three fingers of the gun hand on the grip, and the thumb crosses the thumb of the gun hand. Place the first joint of the trigger finger – the forefinger of your gun hand – lightly on the trigger. Don't push the whole finger through the trigger guard.

◆ If you are right-handed, place your left foot forward and point in the direction in which you intend to shoot.

◆ Raise the gun, maintaining the grip as above, and extend your arms. Brace your arms against the recoil by pushing forward with your gun hand and pulling back with the other. Only gentle effort is required, and too much will cause unsteadiness.

◆ Your gun arm should be straight, and most of your weight on your forward foot. Line up the sights on your target and gently squeeze the trigger, remembering that when you do this with live ammunition, the force of the recoil will tend to throw your hands upwards.

◆ When it's not practical to hold the weapon with your arms extended, draw your hands towards your body, maintaining the grip with both hands. You can keep the sights at eye level, or, if the target is very close indeed, hold the pistol at waist height.

Keep it clean

Misfires are rarely caused by faulty modern ammunition produced by a reputable manufacturer. A dirty or poorly maintained firearm, however, may fail just at the moment you need it most. Clean your firearm every month, even if you haven't used it, and after every occasion on which you fire it. A cleaning kit, including a rod with the correct size of bronze brush and jag (an attachment used when wiping the inside of the barrel), can be bought for almost all calibres. You will require a box of soft flannel patches and a tin of combined solvent and lubricating oil. Pipe cleaners and an old toothbrush are also useful. Before you start cleaning your gun, make sure that it is unloaded and that the ammunition has been put in a safe place.

CLEANING CHECK LIST

1. With an automatic pistol, remove the slide, barrel and attached parts such as the recoil spring. Place a few drops of oil on the bronze brush and pass it back and forth through the barrel about 10 times, allowing it to protrude at both ends. With a revolver, also pass the brush through the chambers of the cylinder.

2. Using an oil-moistened flannel patch, wipe the frame or body of the weapon.

3. Use a pipe cleaner or toothbrush to reach the awkward parts inside the grip or around the trigger.

4. Attach a clean flannel patch to the jag and pass it through the barrel several times. Repeat with another clean patch until visible oil has been removed from the barrel. (An oil build-up in the barrel will produce violent recoil and may be dangerous.)

5. Wipe the weapon all over with a clean patch, and polish lightly with a soft cloth, removing visible fingerprints from the metalwork. (Fingerprints eventually cause corrosion.)

6. Reassemble, reload and store safely.

GENERAL EMERGENCY NUMBERS

Crime Stop
For toll-free anonymous reporting of crime. Tel. 0800111213

Emergency numbers
Consult the first few pages of your local telephone directory for numbers for the fire brigade, ambulance services and hospitals in your area. If you experience difficulties with emergency numbers, dial toll-free 1022.

Flying Squad 10111

SAPS (South African Police Services)
The numbers of local police stations are listed at the back of telephone directories under the Government Departments, Police Service (SA) section.
The different departments within the SAPS are also listed in this section of the telephone directory, eg the Murder and Robbery Unit, Housebreaking Unit etc.

SECURITY IN THE HOME

Security Officers' Board
Head office
Private Bag X817
Pretoria
0001
tel. (012) 3243850
fax. (012) 3243337

South African Neighbourhood Watch
Head office
PO Box 4024
Randburg
2125
tel. (011) 8864555
fax. (011) 8861320

ON THE STREET

Tourist Assistance Unit (SAPS)
Cape Town only: tel. (021) 4182852

IN THE WORKPLACE

Business Against Crime
Gauteng office:
PO Box 784061
Sandton
2146
tel. (011) 8830717
fax. (011) 8831679

Resource station:
tel. (011) 7263380
fax. (011) 7263932

KwaZulu-Natal office:
tel. (031) 3077784

Coswa (Centre for Occupation Social Work Services)
Part of the FAMSA organisation, offering employee assistance programmes.
Johannesburg: tel. (011) 8345672

Offices:
Soweto: tel. (011) 9389095
Lenasia: tel. (011) 8522146
Riverlea: tel. (011) 8332057/8

SAPS Business Watch
Usually situated in the CBD area – contact your local police station to establish if there is a Business Watch in the area. They will also have the relevant contact numbers.

TRAUMA AND VIOLENT CRIME

KwaZulu-Natal Programme for Survivors of Violence
Offers counselling for victims of violence.
1211 Sangro House
417 Smith Street
Durban
4000
tel./fax. (031) 3053497

Trauma Centre for Victims of Violence and Torture
Offers counselling and group therapy.
PO Box 13124
Sir Lowry Road
Cape Town
7900
tel. (021) 457373
fax. (021) 4623143

Trauma Clinic, Centre for the Study of Violence and Reconciliation
Focuses on counselling victims of violent crime.
PO Box 30778
Braamfontein
2017
tel. (011) 4035102
fax. (011) 4037532

FAMILY AND DOMESTIC VIOLENCE

FAMSA (Family and Marriage Society of South Africa)
FAMSA National Council
The National Director
PO Box 2800
Kempton Park
1620

tel. (011) 9757106/7
fax. (011) 9757108

Offices and branch offices:
Benoni: tel. (011) 8451840/1
  (services also Boksburg, Springs,
  Kempton Park, Bedfordview, Kwa-
  Thema, Tsakane, Duduza, Wattville,
  Vosloorus, Katlehong, Tokoza)
Bloemfontein: tel. (051) 438277
Border: tel. (0431) 438277
Cape Town: tel. (021) 4617360/1/2
Durban: tel. (031) 3048991
George: tel. (0441) 745811
Goodwood: tel. (021) 5922063
Grahamstown: tel. (0461) 22580; 22545
  (services also Port Alfred)
Guguletu: tel. (021) 6376706
Ibhayi: tel. (041) 660444
Khayelitsha: tel. (021) 3619098
Kimberley: tel. (0531) 812368
Knysna: tel. (0445) 825129
Mossel Bay: tel. (0444) 911411
Oudtshoorn: tel. (0443) 227020
Parkwood: tel. (011) 7884781
Pietermaritzburg: tel. (0331) 424945
  (services also Imabli)
Plettenberg Bay: tel. (04457) 31236
Port Elizabeth: tel. (041) 559393
Potchefstroom: tel. (0148) 2932272;
  2932344
Pretoria: tel. (012) 3227136/7
  (services also Stanza Bopape and
  Boikutsong)
Roodepoort: tel. (011) 7663283
  (services also Dobsonville, Randfontein,
  Mohlakeng, Westonaria, Bekkersdal,
  Krugersdorp, Kagiso)
Soweto: tel. (011) 9331301
Uitenhage: tel. (041) 433245
  (services also Kwa Nobuhle, Jarman
  Hall, Highfield Road, Schauderville)
Vanderbijlpark: tel. (016) 338128
  (services also Sebokeng)
Welkom: tel. (057) 3525191
  (services also Kroonstad, Virginia,
  Hennenman, Ventersburg, Allanridge)

Family Life Centre
Johannesburg: tel. (011) 8332057/8

Life Line
Phone-in counselling service with drop-in
centres nationwide.
National Director
PO Box 2259
Bedfordview
2008
tel. (011) 8809676
fax. (011) 4474048

National Secretary
PO Box 78440
Sandton
2146
tel./fax (011) 7842478

National PRO
PO Box 2259
Bedfordview
2008
tel./fax. (011) 6226880

Crisis lines with drop-in centres:
this listing is for centres that offer a
phone-in counselling service (sometimes
limited to office hours) and face-to-face
counselling. Centres offering only face-to-
face counselling are listed separately.
Actonville: tel. (011) 4218614
Alexandra: tel. (011) 4435026
Benoni: tel. (011) 4224242
Cape Town: tel. (021) 4611111
Durban: tel. (031) 232323
East London: tel. (0431) 220000
Empangeni: tel. (0351) 922222
Grahamstown: tel. (0461) 318180
Johannesburg: tel. (011) 7281347
Kagiso: tel. (011) 4103895
Khayelitsha: tel. (021) 3615855
Klerksdorp: tel. (018) 4621234
Krugersdorp: tel. (011) 9534111
Margate: tel. (03931) 75447
Mmabatho: tel. (0140) 814263
Nelspruit: tel. (013) 7553606
Pietermaritzburg: tel. (0331) 944444
Port Elizabeth: tel. (041) 555581
Pretoria: tel. (012) 460666
Rustenburg: tel. (0142) 972000
Sun City: tel. (01465) 73777/8
Vanderbijlpark: tel. (016) 337333
Welkom: tel. (057) 3522212

Life Line drop-in centres:
Bishop Lavis Day Hospital
Rehabilitation Centre
864 Lavis Drive
Bishop Lavis
Cape Town
7490
tel. (021) 9344822

Boitekong
Tsholofela Clinic
Unit 4
Boitekong

Ga-Rankuwa
Marula Shop CU10B (Unit M)
Mabapane
District of Odi
Ga-Rankuwa

**Nicro (National Institute for Crime
Prevention and Rehabilitation of
Offenders)**
National office:
PO Box 10005
Caledon Square
Cape Town
8000
tel. (021) 4617253
fax. (021) 4615093

Services also at:
Aliwal North: tel. (0551) 2217
Bloemfontein: tel. (051) 4476678
Botshabelo: tel. (051) 5344084
Cape Town: tel. (021) 474000
Durban: tel. (031) 3042761/2/3
East London: tel. (0431) 24123
East Rand: tel. (011) 8122475
Johannesburg: tel. (011) 3365236/7
Kimberley: tel. (0531) 811715
Kroonstad: tel. (0562) 51861
Mitchell's Plain: tel. (021) 3976060/1
Namaqualand: tel. (0251) 41496
Nelspruit: tel. (013) 553540
Outeniqua: tel. (0441) 742531
Pietermaritzburg: tel. (0331) 454425
Port Elizabeth: tel. (041) 542611/2/3
Pretoria: tel. (012) 32653312
Queenstown: tel. (0451) 81602
Soweto: tel. (011) 9861021
Standerton: tel. (01771) 21092
Tembisa: tel. (011) 9262708
Tygerberg: tel. (021) 9492110
Umtata: tel. (0471) 310598
Vaal: tel. (016) 225019
Zululand: tel. (0351) 21574

People against Human Abuse
Mamelodi: tel. (012) 8057416

South African National Council for Child and Family Welfare
Umbrella organisation for all child and family welfare organisations.
Head office:
PO Box 30990
Braamfontein
2017
tel. (011) 3395741
fax. (011) 3398123

Regional offices:
Eastern Cape
PO Box 12686
Centrahil
6006
tel. (041) 560468
fax. (041) 563393

Free State and North-West
PO Box 6203
Bloemfontein
9300
tel. (051) 4307507/24
fax. (051) 4305848

Gauteng
PO Box 131000
Northmead
Benoni
1511
tel. (011) 4252142
fax. (011) 4252142
or
5th Floor
Heerengracht Building

87 De Kort Street
Braamfontein
2017
tel. (011) 3391924/72
fax. (011) 3394087

KwaZulu-Natal
210 Scotts Building
3/9 Brickhill Road
Durban
4001
tel. (031) 3685455
fax. (031) 3685458

Mpumalanga
PO Box 1190
Witbank
1035
tel. (0135) 6562794
fax. (0135) 903598

Western Cape
PO Box 144
Goodwood
7460
tel. (021) 5924191/2
fax. (021) 5924120

Consultants:
Benoni: tel. (011) 4222604
Bethlehem: tel. (058) 3034432
Braamfontein: tel. (011) 3391924/72
Cradock: tel. (0481) 711279
Embalenhle: tel. (017) 6854612
Empangeni: tel. (0351) 21569
George: tel. (0441) 744612
Heilbron: tel. (0588) 930065
Kimberley: tel. (0531) 816400;
   cell. 0832120903
Mdantsane: tel. (0403) 614777
Nelspruit: tel. (013) 7501779
Port Shepstone: tel. (039) 6824173
Potchefstroom: tel. (0148) 29483333
Queenstown: tel. (0451) 8383876;
   cell. 0832120905
Stellenbosch: tel. (021) 8338454;
   cell. 0832611613
Steytlerville: tel. (04952) ask for 158
Summerstrand: tel. (041) 531338
Vereeniging: tel. (016) 4212792
Vryheid: tel. (0381) 809403
Welkom: tel. (057) 3531891
Worcester: tel. (0231) 25003

VIOLENCE AGAINST WOMEN
Advice Desk for Abused Women
Durban: tel. (031) 8202862

Agisanang
Soweto: tel. (011) 4401231

Ilitha la Bantu
Counselling for abused women and rape and child abuse survivors.
Cape Town: tel. (021) 6332383

Lungelo
Soweto: tel. (011) 9862283

Masimanyane Women's Support Centre
East London: tel. (0431) 439169

Mitchell's Plain Crisis Centre
Counselling for abused women and rape survivors.
tel. (021) 327128

The National Network on Violence against Women
Referral service to national organisations.
Pretoria: tel. (012) 3481231/2/3/4

Nicro Women's Support Centre
Counselling, support.
Cape Town: tel. (021) 221690

Nisaa
Lenasia: tel. (011) 8545804

POWA (People Opposed to Women Abuse)
Johannesburg: tel. (011) 6424345
Katlehong: cell. 0824510280
Krugersdorp: tel. (011) 9535163;
  page 8301179 code 6128

Rape Crisis
Bloemfontein: tel. (051) 4476678
Cape Town: tel. (021) 479762
Grahamstown: tel. (0461) 28442
Khayelitsha: tel. (021) 3619085
Oudtshoorn: tel. (0443) 291377/82
Pietermaritzburg: tel. (0331) 456279
Port Elizabeth: tel. (041) 543804
Somerset West: tel. (021) 8524868

Women Against Women Abuse
National office:
PO Box 1478
Johannesburg
2000
tel. (011) 8365656
fax. (011) 8365620

Branch office:
Eldorado Park: tel. (011) 9455531

Women's Bureau
National office:
PO Box 75749
Lynnwood Ridge
0040
tel. (012) 3481231/2/3/4
fax. (012) 3481235

VIOLENCE AGAINST CHILDREN

Child Abuse Action Group
Lobbying group.
Carletonville: tel. (0149) 7875006
Johannesburg: tel. (011) 7935033

cell. 0832506821
Pretoria: tel. (012) 3292103

Child emergency service
(toll-free) 0800123321

Child in Crisis
Child abuse investigative and referral service.
PO Box 1056
Muldersdrift
1747
cell. 0824444000

Childline
(toll-free) 0800055555

Child Protection Unit, SAPS
Benoni: tel. (011) 4219390;
  cell. 0832516897
Bloemfontein: tel. (051) 4479808/19;
  cell. 0832556536
Cape Town: tel. (021) 5922641/4;
  cell. 0832556323
Carletonville: tel. (0149) 7884080;
  cell. 0832556535
Durban: tel. (031) 3077000;
  cell. 0832556540
East London: tel. (0431) 27646;
  cell. 0832556523
Germiston: tel. (011) 8243750
Johannesburg: tel. (011) 4033413;
  cell. 0832512612 or 0832512613
Kathorus: tel. (011) 8242184
Kimberley: tel. (0531) 811818;
  cell. 0832556538
Klerksdorp: tel. (018) 4645111;
  cell. 0832556539
Krugersdorp: tel. (011) 9511719;
  cell. 0832516898
Ladysmith: tel. (0361) 22365;
  cell. 0832556522
Mabopane: tel. (01461) 28680/4;
  cell. 0832821976
Mafikeng and Mmabatho:
  cell. 0836269139
Mdantsane: tel. (0403) 612012
Middelburg: tel. (0132) 491644
Mothibistad: tel. (01404) 31848
Nelspruit: tel. (013) 591227
Phuthaditjhaba: tel. (058) 7134489
Pietermaritzburg: tel. (0331) 453668;
  cell. 0832556524
Pietersburg: tel. (0152) 2911731;
  cell. 0836252487
Port Elizabeth: tel. (041) 431989;
  cell. 0832556541
Port Shepstone: tel. (0396) 824805;
  cell. 0832556537
Potchefstroom: tel. (0148) 2997315;
  cell. 0832556521
Pretoria: tel. (012) 3296872/7;
  cell. 0832516895
Richard's Bay: tel. (0351) 44445/6;
  cell. 0832556324
Rustenburg: tel. (0142) 944410/9

Secunda: tel. (017) 6242000
Soweto: tel. (011) 9320040;
  cell. 0832516896
Taung: tel. (01405) 51153
Temba: tel. (01464) 2839
Umtata: tel. (0471) 312112
Upington: tel. (054) 311006;
  cell. 0832556520
Vanderbijlpark: tel. (016) 331196/7/9;
  cell. 0832516899

RAPCAN (Resources Aimed at the Prevention of Child Abuse and Neglect)
Cape Town: tel. (021) 6860061

Safeline
For victims of child sexual abuse.
Cape Town: tel. (021) 261100
Somerset West: tel. (021) 85261100

William Slater Hospital
Therapy for abused adolescents.
Cape Town: tel. (021) 6855116

ALCOHOL AND DRUG ABUSE
Al-Anon
For families of alcoholics.
Head office:
PO Box 32883
Braamfontein
2017
tel. (011) 3394301

Regional offices:
Cape Town: tel. (021) 4180021
Durban: tel. (031) 3041826
Johannesburg: tel. (011) 4359792
Port Elizabeth: tel. (041) 307122
Pretoria: tel. (012) 3226067

Alcoholics Anonymous (AA)
General Service office:
PO Box 46339
Orange Grove
2119
tel. (011) 6407146
fax. (011) 6401413

Information offices:
Cape Town: tel. (021) 4180020;
  fax. (021) 4180022

Intergroup offices:
Benoni: tel. (011) 4211534
Durban: tel. (031) 3014959
Johannesburg/West Rand:
  tel. (011) 4832470/1
Pretoria: tel. (012) 3226047

Other centres:
Eastern Cape Area Services Committee,
  Port Elizabeth: tel. (041) 554019
Western Cape Area Assembly,
  Cape Town: tel. (021) 247559

Alcoholism Information Centre
Cape Town: tel. 4194159

Cape Town Drug Counselling Centre
tel. (021) 478026 or 478035

HAD (Helderberg against Dependence)
tel. (021) 8524820

Nar-Anon
Cape Town: tel. (021) 7822622
Johannesburg: tel. (011) 7820636 (after hours)

Narcotics Anonymous
Cape Town: tel. (021) 4194159
Durban: tel. (031) 255289;
  cell. 8027778077
Johannesburg: tel. (011) 4407073

SANCA (South African National Council on Alcoholism and Drug Dependence)
National office:
PO Box 30622
Braamfontein
2017
tel. (011) 7255810
fax. (011) 7252722
e-mail sanca@sn.apc.org

Clinics and regional offices:
Bloemfontein: tel. (051) 477271/5
Boksburg: tel. (011) 9175015
Cape Town: tel. (021) 4194159
Dirkiesdorp: tel. (017730) 0096
Durban: tel. (031) 3032202
East London: tel. (0431) 21257
Eersterust: tel. (012) 8067535
Empangeni: tel. (0351) 23290 or 23201
Fordsburg: tel. (011) 8343228
Giyani: tel. (0158) 2436
Heidelberg: tel. (0151) 97050
Johannesburg: tel. (011) 4501546
  (Institute for Health Training and
  Development)
Johannesburg: tel. (011) 8362460
Khutsong: tel. (01497) 832491
Kimberley: tel. (0531) 811699
Klerksdorp: tel. (018) 4623072
Laudium: tel. (012) 3742100
Lenasia: tel. (011) 8545986
Nelspruit: tel. (013) 7524376
Newcastle: tel. (03431) 23641
Nongoma: tel. (0358) 310314
Pietermaritzburg: tel. (0331) 454173 or
  4544537
Pietersburg: tel. (0152) 2953700
Port Elizabeth: tel. (041) 436021
Pretoria: tel. (012) 5421121/2
Reiger Park: tel. (011) 910 4922
Roodepoort: tel. (011) 7601052/3/4
Umtata: tel. (0471) 25850
Vanderbijlpark: tel. (016) 332055
Vereeniging: tel. (016) 222470
Vosloorus: tel. (011) 8994519

Welkom: tel. (057) 352544
Witbank: tel. (0135) 6562370/1

Tough Love
Provides counselling for the families of
substance abusers.
Central Information:
tel. (011) 8863344
fax. (011) 8895775
pager (011) 4871202, code 1079 (24hrs)

FRAUD
Public Protector
Investigates complaints against government agencies or officials, companies
and corporations in which the state is a
shareholder and statutory councils.
National Office:
Private Bag X677
Pretoria
0001
tel. (012) 3222916
fax. (012) 3225093

ADVICE FOR THE ELDERLY
**CPOA (Cape Provincial Organisation
for the Aged)**
Head office:
231 Main Road
Rondebosch
7700
tel. (021) 6867830
fax. (021) 6856689

Friends of the Frail and Aged
Cape Town: tel. (021) 725754
  fax. (021) 753760

Human Rights Commission
Head office:
PO Box 2700
Houghton
2041
tel. (011) 4848300
fax. (011) 4848403

Branch office:
Cape Town: tel. (021) 262277

South African Council for the Aged
Head office:
PO Box 2335
Cape Town
8000
tel. (021) 246270
fax. (021) 232168

Regional offices:
Eastern Cape
PO Box 23349
Port Elizabeth
6000
tel. (041) 471466
fax. (041) 472304

Free State
PO Box 7805
Bloemfontein
9300
tel. (051) 4325927
fax. (051) 4324458

Gauteng
PO Box 7603
Johannesburg
2000
tel. (011) 3318509
fax. (011) 3318510

KwaZulu-Natal
PO Box 70319
Overport
Durban
4067
tel. (031) 2074540
fax. (031) 2074544

Mpumalanga
PO Box 2089
Middelburg
1050
tel. (013) 2434775
fax. (013) 2434775

Northern Transvaal
PO Box 4199
Pietersburg
0700
tel. (0152) 2915709
fax. (0152) 2953531

North-Western Transvaal
91 President Street
Potchefstroom
2531
tel. (0148) 2981116
fax. (0148) 2981116

Western and Northern Cape
PO Box 13673
N1 City
7463
tel. (021) 5921095
fax. (021) 5911125

SELF-DEFENCE
Self-defence Workshops
Karate, self-defence and rape-prevention.
Sanette Smit, Cape Town
  cell. 0824153960

Sigma Risk Management
Basic security and self-defence courses
for women.
Nic Snyckers
PO Box 11381
Erasmuskloof
0048
cell. 0832524856
fax. (012) 3486817

ACKNOWLEDGMENTS

Consultants:
Ann Bramhill, First National Bank
Sub-Inspector Lloyd Castle, Cape Town Traffic Department
Superintendent Gerald Davis, Vehicle Crime Investigation, SAPS
Marilyn Lilley, Concerned Friends of the Frail and Aged
Duncan Marshall, Futek Systems
Heidi Johnson-Barker, Attorney
Jane Keene, NICRO Women's Support Centre
Scott Lindsay, Cape Town Drug Counselling Centre
Dr Micky Pistorius, SAPS
Senior Superintendent Sharon Schütte, Communication Service, National Detective Service, SAPS
Sanette Smit, Self-Defence Workshops
Senior Superintendent John Sterrenberg, Media Liaison, SAPS
Superintendent Carl Thiart, Tourist Assistance Unit, SAPS

Thanks also to:
A-Bar Security CC
Advanced School of Motoring, Killarney
Association of Retired Persons & Pensioners
Automobile Association of SA
Bembridge Hall & Co (Pty) Ltd
Blue Hills Plot Watch
Brian's Glass Centre
Business Against Crime
Cape Gate Fence and Wire Works (Pty) Ltd
Cape of Good Hope SPCA
Child Protection Unit, SAPS
Childline
Crime Information Monitoring Centre (CIMC)
Intercom & Time Control (North) CC
René Johnson, Vaughan Higson & Co (Pty) Ltd
Municipality of Cape Town, Building Control
NICRO
RAPCAN
Security Officer's Board
South African Neighbourhood Watch
Spoornet
Telkom Information Service
The Protection Shop
Captain André Traut, Business Watch, Cape Town
Zone Armed Response CC